We the People

THE CITIZEN AND THE CONSTITUTION

Teacher's Guide

Center for Civic Education 5146 Douglas Fir Road ■ Calabasas, CA 91302-1467 ■ (818) 591-9321

Directed by the
Center for Civic Education
and
Funded by the
U.S. Department of Education by act of Congress
Established 1987 under the
Commission on the Bicentennial of the United States Constitution

Copyright © **Center for Civic Education** 1995

Second Printing 1996

The development of this text was originally funded and cosponsored by the Commission on the Bicentennial of the United States Constitution.

The U.S. Department of Education disclaims the responsibility for any opinion or conclusions contained herein. The Federal Government reserves a nonexclusive license to use and reproduce for government purposes, without payment, this material where the government deems it in its interest to do so.

ISBN 0-89818-178-X

Acknowledgments

General Editor
Duane E. Smith

Contributing Writers
Herbert M. Atherton
J. Jackson Barlow
Charles N. Quigley
Duane E. Smith

Editors
Michael J. Conroy
Theresa M. Richard

Photo Research
Lisa Hartjens/Imagefinders

Editorial Assistants
David W. Hargrove
Esther G. Libman

Staff Associates
Charles F. Bahmueller
Margaret S. Branson
Michael Fischer
Jack N. Hoar
Joseph S. Jackson
Richard P. Longaker

Principal Writer
Teacher's Guide
Kenneth Rodriguez

Research Assistant
Andrea Kochan

Production Director
Pat Mathwig

Art Director and Illustrator
Richard Stein

Desktop Publishing
Valerie Milianni

Unit Resource Papers and Reviews
Jack Coogan, Consultant

Michelle Dye, Honors Research Associate, Dept. of Political
Science, University of Colorado

Howard Gillman, Assistant Professor, Dept. of Political
Science, University of Southern California

Calvin Jillson, Professor, Dept. of Political Science,
University of Colorado

Donald Nieman, Professor, Dept. of History,
Clemson University

Thomas Pangle, Professor, Dept. of
Political Science, University of Toronto

Melvin Urofsky, Professor, Dept. of
History, Virginia Commonwealth University

Tinsley Yarbrough, Professor, Dept. of
Political Science, East Carolina University

Outline Preparation
Howard Gillman, Assistant Professor
Dept. of Political Science,
University of Southern California

The Center wishes to express special appreciation to Chairman Warren E. Burger and the staff of the Commission on the Bicentennial of the United States Constitution for their support of the development of the **We the People...** program. We are also grateful to Anne Fickling of the Department of Education who has provided support to the Center in all aspects of this project.

The Center is also grateful for the many helpful comments and suggestions that have been received from the following persons who reviewed the original manuscript. The Center has attempted to be responsive to all the many valuable suggestions for improvement in the text. The final product, however, is the responsibility of the Center and does not necessarily reflect the views of those who have contributed their thoughts and ideas.

Field Review and Critique

William Baker, Governor's Task
Force on Citizenship Education, Indiana

Alvin Bell, Teacher,
Findlay High School,
Findlay, Ohio

R. Freeman Butts, William F. Russell
Professor Emeritus in the Foundation
of Education, Teachers College,
Columbia University,
New York

John Calimano, Teacher,
East Brunswick High School,
East Brunswick, New Jersey

Jim Creighton, Teacher,
Alden Central High School,
Alden, New York

Carter Hart, Jr., Consultant,
New Hampshire Department
of Education,
Concord, New Hampshire

Martha de la Houssaye, Teacher,
Academy of the Sacred Heart,
New Orleans, Louisiana

Pat Hussein, Teacher,
Fremont High School,
Los Angeles, California

Leon Letwin, Professor,
School of Law,
University of California
at Los Angeles

Preface

The years 1987 to 1991 marked the 200th anniversary of the writing, ratification, and implementation of the basic documents of American democracy, the Constitution and the Bill of Rights. Our Constitution has stood the tests and stresses of time, wars and change. Although it was not perfect, as Benjamin Franklin and many others recognized, it has lasted because it was carefully crafted by men who understood the importance of a system of government sufficiently strong to meet the challenges of the day, yet sufficiently flexible to accommodate and adapt to new political, economic, and social conditions. Many Americans have but a slight understanding of the Constitution, the Bill of Rights, and the later amendments to which we pledge our allegiance. The lessons in this book are designed to give the next generation of American citizens an understanding of the background, creation, and subsequent history of the unique system of government brought into being by our Constitution. At the same time, it will help them understand the principles and ideals that underlie and give meaning to the Constitution, a system of government by those governed.

Warren E. Burger
Chief Justice of the United States, 1969–1986

A constitutional democracy, more than any other type of government, depends upon an informed, responsible citizenry. While James Madison and Alexander Hamilton hoped that creating the right institutions would solve the problems of self-government, thinkers like Thomas Jefferson and John Adams recognized that these institutions require the support of an enlightened people.

The experience of the past confirms their beliefs. The operation of even the most carefully designed political institutions is ultimately dependent upon the character of its citizens. As Montesquieu argued, if tyranny rests on fear, a free government must rest on civic virtue.

From the inception of the public school system in America, educational institutions have played a major role in preparing young people for the responsibilities of citizenship. Schools today, as in the infancy of our republic, must serve and sustain civic competence, civic responsibility, and a reasoned commitment to our fundamental principles and values.

To assist schools in fulfilling this critical role and to help educate students about our most essential founding documents, the Center for Civic Education has developed **We the People...The Citizen and the Constitution**. Its goal is to promote an increased understanding of the principles and values upon which our political institutions are based.

In the process, students will develop skills helpful in becoming effective and responsible citizens. It is hoped that by increasing student understanding of the rights and responsibilities of citizenship, they will be more likely to promote and protect liberty and justice for all.

Charles N. Quigley
Executive Director, Center for Civic Education

Contents

Goals of the Instructional Program

We the People...The Citizen and the Constitution introduces students to the study of constitutional government in the United States. It is not a text in constitutional law. Rather, its intent is to provide students with an understanding of how the Constitution came into existence, why it took the form it did, and how it has functioned for the past two hundred years.

The aim of this text, then, is to provide students with an understanding of the American past and to equip them intellectually to be active participants in the American present and future. It is a text that enables students to learn something about political philosophy, history, and political science. It other words, it attempts to provide students with the foundation of a civic education.

This text is based on a conceptually oriented approach that blends expository and inquiry methods, both of which call for active participation by students throughout. The approach stresses the development of analytic and evaluative skills, which will enable students to apply basic substantive knowledge to a wide variety of political questions and controversies. Students are actively involved in their own learning process, acquiring the necessary knowledge for developing an understanding of the American past. They also learn the relevance of the past for an understanding of the American constitutional system in the present.

ASSESSMENT AND CULMINATING ACTIVITIES OF THE PROGRAM

After students complete the lessons in the text, they take a 60-question multiple choice test. If they achieve a score of 70% or above, they receive a Certificate of Achievement signed by their member of Congress or another prominent public official.

As a culminating activity of the program, teachers are encouraged to involve their classes in a simulated congressional hearing. The hearing provides an opportunity for students to demonstrate their knowledge and understanding of constitutional principles. The entire class, working in cooperative teams, prepares and presents statements and answers questions before a panel of community representatives who act as congressional committee members. Teachers and their students may select either the noncompetitive simulated congressional hearing option or the annual competition.

Both of the program's major assessment components may be modified as needed to fit the chosen instructional plan. For more information about all aspects of participating in the We the People... program, please see the Program Participation Handbook included with the instructional material set.

Teacher's Guide Format

Unit format. The teacher's guide, like the student book, is organized into units. Each begins with a **Unit Overview**, parallel to the **Purpose of Unit** section of the student text. These overviews provide a brief introduction to the forthcoming group of lessons.

Lesson format. The teacher's guide is designed to complement and extend the student text. Each lesson begins with a **Lesson Overview** to describe the overall purpose of the lesson. Next is a list of **Lesson Objectives**, written in behavioral terms. These parallel the list of behaviors found in the **Purpose of Lesson** in the student text. Students can be expected to be able to perform these tasks upon completing each lesson. The material is conceptually cumulative, however, so mastery is not expected or required at each step along the way.

The lesson objectives are followed by a section titled **Preparation/Teaching Materials**. This section identifies the applicable pages in the student text and suggests additional preparation or materials needed to teach the lesson. The next section is **Teaching Procedures**. These are suggested instructional strategies which you can adapt to your particular learning environment. They include ideas for introducing the lesson, additional information about lesson topics, discussion questions, and answers to specific student exercises. This section also offers activities and strategies for concluding the lesson.

A section titled **Optional Activities** completes each lesson in this guide. This section includes individual, small, and whole group activities designed to reinforce or extend what students have learned in the lesson. The suggestions in this section offer a variety of techniques and develop a number of skills helpful in studying conceptually oriented material. These activities also can easily be adapted as part of the lesson presentation. Where appropriate, **Teacher References** providing additional information or specific court decisions related to the lesson have been included.

Teaching Strategies

The following are instructional methods recommended for use with the *We the People... The Citizen and the Constitution* student text.

CONDUCTING CLASS DISCUSSIONS

Study of the history of ideas includes controversy, debate, evaluation, and reevaluation. So, too, does the study of *We the People... The Citizen and the Constitution*. Effective civic education presents and discusses controversial subject matter which is what makes this curriculum exciting for both students and teachers. Through the discussion process, students develop knowledge, decision-making skills, conflict management experience, and a commitment to citizenship participation.

To ensure that the experience with this curriculum is stimulating and rewarding for both you and your students, you may wish to consider the suggestions on the next page for successful classroom discussion of controversial issues and contemporary topics.

- Emphasize the legitimacy of controversy, compromise, and consensus. They are the lifeblood of a democratic society.

- Try to present the central issues of controversy in tangible form. Make allusions to similar problems and dilemmas students face in their own lives.

- Stress historical antecedents so students can see how similar conflicts have been managed in the past. Acknowledge those times when we have not lived up to the ideals and principles upon which our nation was founded. Examining the interpretation and application of these concepts over time will help students appreciate the fluidity of our constitutional system and the role individual citizens play in helping our nation better realize its goals.

- Emphasize the legitimacy of various viewpoints by encouraging students to examine and present conflicting views in an unbiased fashion. It is incumbent on the teacher to raise any opposing views students may have missed.

- Keep students focused on discussing or dealing with ideas or positions, rather than people. Stress that in controversial issues, reasonable people might very well differ. Encourage students to offer dissenting opinions when they do not agree with the majority—even if they are the only one to dissent.

- Help students identify specific points of agreement or disagreement, places where compromise might be possible, and places where it is unlikely to occur. Emphasize that the outcomes or the decisions which they reach on an issue may not be as important as improving their ability to develop a reasoned decision and to express it in a civil manner, respecting the views of others.

- Conclude, or debrief, lesson or discussion by evaluating the arguments presented and exploring the likely consequences of the various alternatives suggested. An effective debriefing also involves both the teacher and the students in evaluating the process used for conducting a discussion, preparing group work, or presenting a class activity.

Before beginning this program, in which class discussion and sharing of opinions are critical components, you may wish to establish a few basic ground rules. For example:

- When expressing an opinion, always be prepared to justify it.

- Politely and respectfully listen to the opinions of others. You may be called on to tell which one (other than your own) you liked best.

- Everyone will get a chance to talk, but only one person will talk at a time.

- Do not argue against people; argue with reasons and ideas.

- You may change your opinion at any time. Be prepared to share your reasons for doing so.

EFFECTIVE QUESTIONING STRATEGIES

Question and response sequences are an important feature of the curriculum. The effective use of questions is critical to the learning process and requires careful planning. While some questions may be useful to establish how much knowledge students have gained, the primary goal of your questioning strategies should be to help students increase their ability to reach effective, responsible decisions. Therefore, you will want to choose questioning strategies that lead students into analysis of situations and into synthesis and evaluation of concepts, thus enabling them to use skills acquired in this program on a lifelong basis.

There are generally six categories of questions you should consider when planning class discussions. Following is a brief description and example of each:

- **Knowledge.** These questions involve recall of specific facts or information.
  Example: What were the objections of the Federalists to a bill of rights?

- **Comprehension.** This involves the ability to understand the meaning of the material. This may be shown by translating material from one form to another, and by interpreting material.
  Example: Create a drawing illustrating a person fulfilling a responsibility of citizenship. What is the central idea of this lesson?

- **Application.** This involves the ability to use learned material in new situations.
  Example: What examples can you cite from your own experience where these ideas apply? How might you use this process to resolve a conflict in the future?

- **Analysis.** This involves the ability to break down material into its component parts. This includes identifying the parts and establishing the relationship among the parts.
  Example: What are the consequences of government's invasion of privacy in this situation? Which consequences are advantages and which are disadvantages?

- **Synthesis.** This is the ability to put parts together to form a new whole. The emphasis is on creating new patterns of thought.
  Example: What argument can you make that we should increase the authority of the United States Supreme Court?

- **Evaluation.** This is the ability to judge the value of the material for a given purpose. This may be a process for choosing among competing values or deciding whether a principle still meets the criteria of effectiveness for the common good.
  Example: How useful were the critical thinking strategies in helping you decide who should be held responsible for a particular event? What are the likely consequences of alternatives you have suggested?

It is possible to structure questions so that students listen to and respond to each other and not just to their teacher. Encourage students' active participation in the following ways:

- Pose a question and ask students to discuss the answer with a partner.

- Ask students to clarify their responses. This will benefit themselves as well as others.

- Ask students to extend their own or other students' responses by providing additional facts, information, viewpoints, etc.

- Ask students to generate questions of their own on material just presented in class.

- Pause at least seven seconds after asking a question to allow students time to think.

- Ask students to expand on their responses if they provide short or fragmentary answers.

- Call on more than one student per question.

- Encourage students to react to other students' responses.

- Call on nonvolunteers as well as volunteers.

ENCOURAGING SMALL GROUP LEARNING

The critical thinking exercises in the student text are generally designed as cooperative learning activities with a study partner or in small group environments. Each individual's participation is essential for the successful completion of an exercise. Students are encouraged not only to contribute academically, but to develop and use appropriate interpersonal skills.

Important issues arise for the teacher in planning and implementing cooperative group learning. One such issue concerns the size of groups. Consideration of the research can help you determine the optimum number of students per group within your classroom.

David A. Welton and John T. Mallan in their book *Children and Their World: Teaching Elementary Social Studies*, Fourth Edition, Houghton-Mifflin, 1991, have identified some general behavioral characteristics of differently sized groups:

- **Groups of two**. High exchange of information and a tendency to avoid disagreement are two features of pairs. In case of disagreement, however, deadlock occurs because there is no support within the group for either participant.

- **Groups of three**. Triads tend to be characterized by the power of the majority over the minority of one. However, triads are the most stable group structure with some occasional shifting of coalitions.

- **Groups of even numbers**. More disagreement is prevalent in groups with even numbers of members. This is due to the formation of subgroups of equal size resulting in deadlock.

- **Groups of five**. The most satisfying learning group size seems to be five. There is ease of movement within the group. The 2:3 division provides minority members with support. The group is large enough for stimulation, yet small enough for participation and personal recognition.

- **Groups larger than five**. As group size increases, so does the range of ability, expertise, and skill. However, so do the difficulties in keeping all members on task, ensuring everyone the opportunity to speak, and coordinating group actions.

Another issue teachers face in planning and implementing cooperative group learning is whether to allow groups to self-select or to establish the groups by assignment. David W. Johnson, et al. in *Circles of Learning: Cooperation in the Classroom,* published by the Association for Supervision and Curriculum Development, 1984, describes the following characteristics of groups:

- Student-selected groups are frequently homogeneous with high-achieving students selecting other high achievers, males selecting males, and members of different cultural groups selecting those from similar backgrounds.

- There is often less on-task behavior in student-selected than in teacher-selected groups.

- More creative thinking, more frequent giving and receiving of explanations, and greater perspective-taking in discussion seems to occur in heterogeneous groups.

A useful modification of the select-your-own-groups method is to have students list three peers with whom they would like to work. Place the students with one person they chose and other students selected by the teacher. Careful consideration should be given to building a supportive environment for students no one selects.

You also may want to consider randomly assigning students to groups by having them count off. For example, to establish six groups of five students each in a class of thirty, have the students count off from one to six, repeating the sequence at the end of six. Then, place the "ones" together, the "twos" together and so forth. Once groups have been assembled, you may want to have them work together over a period of time rather than forming new groups for each activity in the student text.

Below are some general recommendations you may want to consider in implementing small group work in your classroom:

- Make sure the students have the skills necessary to do the work. If they do not, you will quickly know because they will not remain long on task.

- Give clear instructions for completing work and check for understanding of the process or procedures to be followed during an activity.

- Allow adequate time to complete the assigned task. Think creatively about ways to constructively occupy groups that finish ahead of the others.

- Be explicit in dealing with management issues. If someone must report to the class on the group's work, be sure there is a process for selecting a reporter.

- Think about how your evaluation strategies are affected by the use of small groups. Develop methods to reward group efforts.

- Monitor group work and act as a resource to guide your students' development.

COMMUNITY RESOURCE PEOPLE

Involvement of people from the community who possess appropriate experiences or expertise can greatly enhance and extend student understanding of the concepts presented in *We the People... The Citizen and the Constitution*. Community resource people can contribute in the following ways:

- make the lessons come alive by sharing real-life experiences and applications of the ideas under consideration

- help implement activities in the classroom such as role plays, moot courts, and simulated legislative hearings and debates

- enrich field experiences by serving as a guide and by responding to questions during visits to places such as court rooms and legislative chambers

- establish an on-going relationship with a class in which the resource person is available regularly by phone to respond to questions or issues that may arise during a particular lesson

The range of individuals who can serve as resource people is as varied as the community itself. Commonly this includes police officers, lawyers, judges, legislators, state and local government agents, and professors of political science or law. Specific types of occupations and individuals who can enliven and enrich your study of the concepts in *We the People... The Citizen and the Constitution* are suggested in the teacher's guide.

Making the involvement of a community resource person as meaningful as possible requires careful planning. Attention should be given to the following considerations:

■ A resource person's involvement should be relevant to the lesson or concept under consideration.

■ The principal mode of involvement should be interaction and participation with students. A resource person should be asked to assist students in preparing a role-play or moot court arguments. The resource person can act as a judge, serve on a panel with students, or respond to questions about specific details of a lesson. Also, a resource person should participate in the concluding discussion of a lesson or activity.

■ A resource person should offer a balanced picture of the topic, including a variety of perspectives. When objectivity is not possible, you might consider inviting a second resource person to ensure a balanced experience. The guest also should avoid professional jargon and speak as simply as possible.

■ Before a visit by a resource person, students should be prepared well to maximize their thoughtful participation when the visitor is present.

■ Most resource persons are not trained teachers and should not be responsible for classroom management. The teacher should be in attendance during the entire visit. Sometimes it might be necessary for the teacher to give direction to the guest by asking appropriate questions or offering clues that can help the resource person communicate effectively with students.

■ For a successful visit, the resource person should receive a copy of the lesson in advance. Usually, a pre-visit meeting or phone call is useful to help clarify what is expected of the guest.

Owing to busy schedules and the limited length of this program, it is advisable to extend invitations as soon as possible. A committee of students should be responsible for hosting the guests on the day of their visit and for the follow-up thank you letter.

INTERACTIVE TEACHING STRATEGIES

An essential feature of *We the People... The Citizen and the Constitution* is the use of instructional methods which actively involve students in developing and presenting positions on related issues. Students learn to apply their knowledge to contemporary issues as well as to a variety of socio-political questions. In addition, these learning strategies promote certain dispositions and participatory skills that increase students' capacity to act effectively as citizens in a constitutional democracy. For example, students learn to work cooperatively to reach common goals, to evaluate, take, and defend positions on controversial issues, and to deal with conflicting opinions and positions in a constructive manner. These learning strategies also teach students how government works.

The key learning strategies in this curriculum include, among others, legislative hearings, moot courts, and town meetings. The following material describes these instructional methods and offers specific suggestions for implementation in the classroom.

Legislative Hearing Legislative hearings are held by committees of the United States Congress and other legislative bodies to gather information upon which to base recommendations regarding subjects regulated by law or for which laws are being considered. These hearings are a basic function of legislative branches of government.

Role-playing a legislative hearing provides participants with an opportunity to gain increased understanding of the purpose and procedures of such hearings as well as the roles and responsibilities of committee members. Participants also gain experience in identifying and clarifying the ideas, interests, and values associated with the subject being discussed.

How to Proceed

1. **Clarify topics.** Help students understand the topic of the legislative hearing. The topics are clearly identified in the lessons in the student text and in this guide. You also will want to ensure that students understand the role of committees in the legislative process.

2. **Contact resource persons.** Invite a local legislator, local groups, or local chapters of national organizations to serve as resource people on the topic of the hearing.

3. **Assign roles**. Explain to participants the purpose of a legislative hearing and assign the appropriate roles:

   a. **Legislators.** Six legislators is a practical number for a committee, but the number may vary according to class needs. Designate one legislator as the chairperson to preside over the hearing.

   b. **Witnesses.** The number and nature of the witnesses depend on the topic being discussed. The specific roles described in the lessons and in this guide are designed to present differing points of view on the topic.

   c. **Recorder.** This role is optional. This person will keep a record of the proceedings and present a review or summary of any recommendations that may emerge during the discussions.

   d. **Newspaper reporters.** This role is optional, but is useful in helping students gain insights on the function of the press in the democratic process. Select students to represent newspapers with varying perspectives. Ask them to interview legislators and witnesses, to observe the proceedings, and to write brief articles or editorials about the topic. They should share and discuss their work with the class.

4. **Prepare presentations**. Allow time for participants to prepare for the legislative hearing in accordance with their assigned roles.

   a. Legislators should identify the key issue(s) and prepare questions to ask each witness.

   b. Witnesses should define their position on the issue(s), prepare an opening statement, anticipate questions from the legislators, and formulate possible responses.

   c. Witnesses may wish to discuss similarities in positions with other witnesses.

   d. When appropriate, have a resource person work with the students or allow students to contact outside resources for assistance in preparing their position on an issue.

5. **Arrange the classroom**. Set up the classroom to resemble a legislative chamber. Include a table for the legislators, a desk for the recorder, and a desk or table for the witnesses. Provide a gavel and nameplates with the students' names and their roles. You may want to arrange the use of a hearing or committee room of a local legislative body.

6. **Conduct the hearing**. The following procedures should be used to conduct this activity:

   a. The committee chairperson calls the hearing to order, announces the purpose of the hearing and the order in which the witnesses will be called to testify.

   b. The chairperson calls each witness. The witness makes an opening statement, followed by questions from members of the committee. You may want to establish time limits, usually three to four minutes for openings and five to six minutes for questions from the legislators. Appoint a timekeeper to enforce time limitations.

   c. The chairperson is the first to question the witness, followed by the other members of the committee. A committee member may interrupt to ask a question or make a comment any time during the proceedings.

   d. After the witnesses have been heard, the legislators review the testimony, discuss the issue(s) and make recommendations on what their next step(s) will be.

7. **Debrief the activity**. Debriefing questions vary according to the topic. Begin by having the legislators announce their decision. Discuss the facts and arguments presented on the topic and evaluate the strengths and weaknesses of the positions taken. Also ask students to evaluate their experience with the hearing process itself. Conclude the debriefing by having students discuss the effectiveness of this activity as a tool for learning, including how well they performed their role in it. If a resource person assisted with the activity, that person should be included in the concluding discussion.

Legislative Debate

Legislative debate is often used productively in the formulation and development of laws. Role-playing a legislative debate provides participants with an opportunity to increase their understanding of the purpose and value of the power of legislatures to make laws and to debate matters of public policy.

How to Proceed

1. **Clarify topics.** Help students understand the topic of the legislative debate. The topics are clearly identified in the lessons in the student text and in this guide. You also will want to ensure that students understand the process whereby bills are enacted into law.

2. **Contact resource persons.** Contact state and national legislators or their staff assistants to help serve as resource persons.

3. **Assign roles.** Consider the entire class as the legislative body with a student or the teacher assuming the role of the presiding officer. Legislators may then be assigned to groups representing various positions in regard to the issue. Groups are clearly identified in the student text and in this guide. You also may want to assign a recorder responsible for tracking key points of discussion during the debate.

4. **Prepare presentations.** Allow time for participants to prepare for the legislative hearing in accordance with their assigned roles.

   Each group should select a spokesperson and a recorder and then proceed to follow the directions given in the lesson. Students should analyze and evaluate the issue before developing their positions. In some cases they will be asked to offer amendments to the bills already given in the lesson. In others they may write a proposed bill designed to alleviate problems raised by the issue.

As each group completes its amendment or proposed bill, the spokesperson reports to the presiding officer asking that the bill be placed on the agenda. Bills should be placed on the agenda in the order in which they are received. Students may wish to discuss any similarities in their proposed amendments or bills with other groups to predetermine whether they can unite behind a common proposal.

5. **Arrange the classroom**. Set up the classroom to resemble a legislative chamber. Include a table for the presiding officer, a desk for the recorder, and a podium if you want to have presentations made more formally. Provide a gavel and nameplates with the students' names and their roles. You may want to arrange the use of a legislative chamber in your community.

6. **Conduct the legislative debate**. Time limits for the various steps in legislative debates should be decided ahead of time. The presiding officer should be empowered to cut off speakers when the time limit has been reached. Conduct the legislative debate using the following procedures:

   a. The presiding officer calls the legislature to order, indicates that all votes will be decided by a simple majority, announces the issue, and opens the debate.

   b. The first bill on the agenda is introduced by the group's spokesperson. The spokesperson stands, addresses the presiding officer, and describes the bill the group has written. After the presenting the bill, the spokesperson may recognize two other members of the group who may make additional comments on the bill.

   c. The bill is discussed and debated by the legislature. Representatives from other groups may ask questions, offer criticisms, or suggest modifications.

   d. The steps above are repeated for any additional bills that might be introduced during the session.

   e. When the discussion and debate on all proposed bills is completed, legislators may move: (1) that one of the bills be voted on, (2) that the session be recessed to enable the groups to consider the bills that have been presented. If the session is recessed, each group meets to decide upon a course of action. A group may decide to support one of the bills as presented, suggest amendments to one of the bills presented, or develop a compromise bill.

   f. When the session is reconvened, the presiding officer asks for a motion to vote on one of the bills as presented, for a motion to amend one of the bills, or for the introduction of a compromise bill. If amendments or compromise bills are proposed, they are individually debated and voted upon.

   g. This process is repeated until a bill is passed or the time allotted for the session is up and the legislature is adjourned.

7. **Debrief the activity**. Debriefing questions vary according to the topic. Discuss the facts and arguments presented on the topic and evaluate the strengths and weaknesses of the positions taken. Also ask students to evaluate their experience with the legislative process itself. Conclude the debriefing by having students discuss the effectiveness of this activity as a tool for learning, including how well they performed their role in it. If a resource person assisted with the activity, that person should be included in the concluding discussion.

Pro Se Court   A *pro se* (or do it yourself) court allows students to role-play a court case with a minimum of participants and simple rules of evidence. The court is organized as a triad consisting of a judge, who will hear the two sides and make the final decision; a plaintiff, who is the person bringing the action before the judge; and the defendant, who is accused of wrongdoing or causing injury.

Pro se courts provide students with a simplified look at judicial decision making. *Pro se* courts provide an opportunity for all students in a class to be actively involved in the activity.

How to Proceed

1. **Clarify topic.** Help students understand the facts and issues in the case. The cases are clearly identified in the lessons in the student text and in the teacher's guide.

2. **Contact resource person.** Invite an attorney or judge to act as a resource person.

3. **Assign roles.** Divide the class into three equal groups—judges, plaintiffs, and defendants.

4. **Prepare presentations.** Have the students meet in their respective groups to help each other prepare their presentations. Each student will be actively involved in the role play, so preparation at this stage is vital to effective participation in the activity.

    Instruct the judges to review the case and the issues raised. Ask them to prepare questions that they would like to ask of the plaintiffs and defendants during the presentation phase of the activity. The questions should be designed to clarify positions on the issues which the judges will be called upon to decide. Do take some time to review with the judge's group some simple rules of procedure, like the following:

    a. The plaintiff should present first, without interruptions from the defense. The defense presents their case second.

    b. Allow brief rebuttals from each side in the case.

    c. The judge may interrupt the presentations at any time to pose questions designed to clarify the arguments being made.

    Instruct the plaintiff and defendant groups to prepare an opening statement and arguments supporting their positions on the issues raised in the case.

5. **Arrange the classroom.** You will have multiple courts in session simultaneously; therefore, arrange the desks in the classroom into groups of three, one for each of the roles in the activity.

6. **Conduct the court hearing.** Before beginning the activity, match one student from the judge's group with one student from the plaintiff and one from the defendant groups. You may want to have the judges first take a desk in each of the groupings arranged around the room. Then ask one plaintiff and one defendant to join the group. Matching role-players may be more easily accomplished by providing role "tags" so students can quickly identify who is a judge, plaintiff, and defendant.

    Conduct the activity using the following procedures:

    a. Instruct the judges that when each has a plaintiff and a defendant, he or she may begin the court session.

b. The judge should first hear opening statements by the participants—first the plaintiff and then the defendant. An appropriate time limit should be imposed on these statements.

c. The plaintiff makes arguments and is questioned by the judge.

d. The defendant presents his or her defense and is questioned by the judge.

e. The judge asks each side for brief rebuttal statements.

f. The judge makes his or her decision and explains the reasoning which supports it.

7. **Debrief the activity**. Debriefing questions vary according to the topic. Begin by asking individual judges to share with the class their decision and the reasoning supporting it. Discuss the facts and arguments presented in the case and evaluate the strengths and weaknesses of the positions taken. Also ask students to evaluate the court process itself. Conclude the debriefing by having students discuss the effectiveness of this activity as a tool for learning, including how well they performed their role in it. If a resource person assisted with the activity, that person should be included in the concluding discussion.

Moot Court

A moot court is patterned on an appeals court or Supreme Court hearing. The court, composed of a panel of judges or justices, is asked to rule on a lower court's decision. No witnesses are called, nor are the basic facts in a case disputed. Arguments are prepared and presented on the application of a law, the constitutionality of a law, or the fairness of previous court procedures. In many ways the moot court is like a debate, for each side presents arguments for the consideration of the justices.

Since moot courts are not concerned with the credibility of witness testimony, they are an effective strategy for focusing student attention on the underlying principles and concepts of due process.

How to Proceed

1. **Clarify topic.** Help students understand the facts and the legal or constitutional issues in the case. The cases are clearly identified in the lessons in the student text and in this guide. You may also want to ensure that students understand the purpose and procedures observed in appellate court proceedings.

2. **Contact resource persons.** Invite an attorney or judge to act as a resource person.

3. **Assign roles.** Assign students to play the roles of justices of the court (in intermediate appellate courts members of the panel are called judges. In the federal or state supreme courts they are called justices). You may establish a court of five, seven, or nine justices. Divide the remaining students into two groups representing the litigants in the case. One group will represent the person or group bringing the challenge before the court, or the plaintiff. The other group will represent the person or group defending against the challenge, or the defendant. Sometimes terms like petitioner or respondent, or appellant and appellee, are used to identify the litigants in an appellate case. For pedagogical purposes, it is best to keep it simple by using the terms plaintiff and defendant.

4. **Prepare presentations**. Each group should meet to prepare arguments for its side of the case. The group should select one or two students to present the arguments.

The justices should meet to discuss the issues involved and any questions they feel need to be addressed in order for them to reach a decision. The justices should select one student to serve as chief justice. The chief justice will preside over the hearing. He or she will call on each side to present its case or (more realistically) justices (judges) should ask questions without needing to be recognized (i.e., judges should feel free to interrupt lawyers' presentations whenever they want).

Participants should take it as given that the factual details presented in the summary of the case were established by a trial and are not subject to further dispute.

Arguments should not concentrate on legal technicalities. Any argument that is persuasive from a philosophical, theoretical, conceptual, or practical standpoint can be made. Groups should rely on principles found or implied in the United States Constitution.

5. **Arrange the classroom**. Set up the classroom to resemble an appellate court. The justices should be seated at a table at the front of the room. The attorneys for each side should sit on opposite sides of the room facing the justices. Other group members should sit behind their respective attorneys. You may want to take the class to an appellate courtroom or to a mock trial room at a law school.

6. **Conduct the moot court**. The chief justice should preside over the proceedings and begin by calling the court to order. The chief justice should observe the following procedures:

   a. Each side should be allotted five to ten minutes for the initial presentation and five minutes for rebuttal. The chief justice should call for presentations in the following order:

Plaintiff	Initial presentation
Defendant	Initial presentation
Plaintiff	Rebuttal presentation
Defendant	Rebuttal presentation

   b. During and/or after each presentation, the justices can and should actively question the attorneys in an effort to clarify the arguments. Attorneys may request time to consult with other group members before answering questions. For clarity and continuity, it is suggested that during the initial presentations lawyers be given three minutes to present their cases before being interrupted with questions.

   c. After arguments have been presented, the justices should organize themselves in a circle. They should consider the arguments and make a decision by a majority vote. Each justice should give reasons for his or her position. The rest of the class may sit outside of the circle and listen, but they may not talk or interrupt the deliberations.

7. **Debrief the activity**. Debriefing questions vary according to the case. Begin by asking the justices to share with the class their decision and the reasoning supporting it. Justices should present dissenting opinions. Discuss the arguments presented in the case and evaluate the strengths and weaknesses of the positions taken. Also ask students to evaluate their experience with the appellate process itself. Conclude the debriefing by having

students discuss the effectiveness of this activity as a tool for learning, including how well they performed their role in it. If a resource person assisted with the activity, that person should be included in the concluding discussion.

In an actual case, you should share the Court's decision with the class during the debriefing. In order to dispel the notion that there is one "right" answer, also share relevant parts of the dissenting opinion. Help students understand the reasoning which supports both the majority and dissenting opinions.

A town meeting provides members of a community with an opportunity to participate in the decision-making process. A community forum usually considers matters of public policy. A town meeting can serve as a local governing and decision-making body by performing functions similar to those of a representative town or city council. It also can be advisory in nature, providing elected representatives with the views of citizens.

How to Proceed

1. **Clarify topic.** Help students understand the topic of the town meeting. The topics are clearly identified in the lessons in the student text and in this guide. You also will want to ensure that students understand the nature and purpose of a town meeting.

2. **Contact resource person.** Invite a member of the city council or a local interest group to serve as a resource person on the topic of the meeting.

3. **Assign roles.** Organize the town meeting by assigning individuals the following roles:

   a. chairperson

   b. elected officials who represent the entire community in the town or city council

   c. representative groups in favor of the proposition

   d. representative groups in opposition to the proposition

   e. community members at large

   f. recorder

4. **Prepare presentations.** Allow time for students to prepare for the town meeting in accordance with their assigned roles.

5. **Arrange the classroom.** Include a table for the chairperson and for the elected officials, a desk for the recorder, and a podium from which members of interest groups and the community can speak. Provide a gavel and nameplates with the students' names and their roles. You may want to arrange the use of a hearing or committee room of a local legislative body.

6. **Conduct the town meeting.** The following procedures should be used to conduct this activity:

   a. The chairperson calls the meeting to order, announces the purpose of the meeting, and introduces the elected officials in attendance. Elected officials may make a brief opening statement about the importance of the issue being considered (not his or her personal views on the topic). The chairperson also establishes any rules that are to be followed during the meeting, such as time limits for presentations.

b. The chairperson has the authority to cut off debate when time limits have been reached. A person may not speak unless recognized by the chair, and no one may interrupt while another person is speaking. If a speaker wanders from the point, abuses other people, or in any way defeats the purpose of the meeting, the chairperson may declare him or her out of order.

c. The chairperson calls upon a representative of the group favoring the proposition to describe that group's position. After the representative has finished speaking, he or she may ask people brought as witnesses to stand and speak. The chairperson announces that any person in favor of the proposition may stand and speak. They will be recognized in the order in which they stand. Alternatively, you may want to have students sign in and ask the chairperson to recognize speakers by the order in which they signed in.

d. The chairperson calls upon a representative of the group opposed to the proposition to speak. After the representative has finished speaking, he or she may ask people brought as witnesses to stand and speak. The chairperson announces that those people opposed to the proposition will be recognized in the order in which they stand.

e. After all people on both sides of the proposition have had an opportunity to speak, the chairperson opens the question for additional discussion or debate. During this time any person may stand, be recognized, and present his or her point of view or argue against the point of view of someone else.

f. At the end of the discussion or debate the chairperson calls for class vote on the proposition. The vote is decided by a majority.

7. **Debrief the activity.** Debriefing questions vary according to the topic. Begin by discussing the results of the vote taken on the proposition. Discuss the facts and argument presented on the topic. Ask students to evaluate the strength of the positions taken and of the procedures used to develop and support a position. Also ask students to evaluate their experience with the town meeting itself. Conclude the debriefing by having students discuss the effectiveness of this activity as a tool for learning, including how well they performed their role in it. If a resource person assisted with the activity, that person should be included in the concluding discussion.

Debates

Debate begins with the assumption that the debater has already found a solution or approach to a specific issue. The intent of the debater is to persuade others that his or her solution or approach is the proper one.

Debate can be an effective device for encouraging students to clearly and logically formulate arguments based upon evidence. Debate teaches a means to adequately support a position on an issue. It also develops a sense of efficacy and confidence in a person's ability to sway public opinion or to change public policy.

How to Proceed

1. **Clarify topic.** Help students understand the topic of the debate. The topics are clearly identified in the lessons in the student text and in this guide. Formulate the topic into a resolution (resolutions always ask for a change from the status quo, e.g., Resolved: that capital punishment should be found unconstitutional by the United States Supreme Court).

2. **Contact resource person.** Invite someone from the community or a local interest group to serve as a resource person on the topic of the debate.

3. **Assign roles.** Select students to take part in the debate. Divide them into two teams, one in support of the resolution, the other opposing it. Make certain that those participating in the debate are familiar with the procedures to be followed during the debate. Select a moderator and a timekeeper.

4. **Prepare presentations.** Allow sufficient time for students to prepare their "constructive arguments" (argument based upon three to five major points logically developed and substantiated by factual evidence in support of a particular position). Help students see the dimensions of the problem and develop clear, logical arguments supported by evidence on the position they defend in the debate. Also, ask them to anticipate the views of the other side in preparation for their "rebuttal arguments."

   Help students gain an understanding of some of the implicit values in debate such as learning to make convincing arguments from another frame of reference, as might be the case if one is debating a position that does not correspond with one's own beliefs. This furthers development of students' abilities to understand and respect the right of individuals to hold opinions and beliefs that are different from their own.

5. **Arrange the classroom.** The moderator and debaters are seated at the front of the audience, usually with the team in opposition to the resolution to the left of the moderator.

6. **Conduct the debate.** The form of debate described here is widely used, but is rather formalized. You may wish to make the procedures less formal or use some other form of debate.

   a. The moderator briefly introduces the subject and the resolution to be debated and establishes the time limits to be observed by the speakers.

   b. The moderator introduces the first speaker from the affirmative team and asks the speaker to present his or her constructive argument. The order in which constructive arguments will be given by each member of the team should be determined in advance of the debate. The timekeeper will inform the speaker when the time limit has been reached.

   c. The moderator introduces the first speaker from the team in opposition to the resolution and asks the speaker to present his or her constructive argument.

   d. The moderator next introduces the second speaker from the affirmative team. This procedure is alternated until each debater on both affirmative and opposition teams have given a constructive argument.

   e. Rebuttal arguments follow the constructive arguments. At this time each debater is given the opportunity to weaken the position of the opponents by attacking their position and by answering attacks that have been made upon his or her position. No new issues may be introduced during rebuttal arguments. Rebuttal arguments always begin with the team in opposition to the resolution. Again, follow the same alternating procedures used during constructive arguments.

   f. At the conclusion of the debate, the moderator makes a few concluding remarks and the debate is ended.

7. **Debrief the activity**. You may wish to evaluate the success of the debating teams by informally polling the class to determine how many people agree with the team in support of the resolution and how many agree with the team in opposition to the resolution. You may then ask class members to explain whether their own positions were strengthened or changed as a result of hearing the debate and why. Also ask students to evaluate their experience with the debate process itself. Conclude the debriefing by having students discuss the effectiveness of this activity as a tool for learning, including how well they performed their role in it. If a resource person assisted with the activity, that person should be included in the concluding discussion.

Continuum

The continuum is an exercise in which participants are presented with a range of possible attitudes or approaches on a controversial issue. Participants are asked to determine which element of the continuum (e.g., strongly agree or strongly disagree) most approximates their own attitude. Issues that are clearly controversial and characterized by polar position are suitable for using this method. The issues should have legitimate opposing view points, such as whether equal rights can best be achieved by an amendment or whether gun control is an effective way to stop crime. Issues that are above debate such as the morality of a holocaust or sexual abuse of children are obviously not legitimate topics for a continuum.

The continuum is a useful tool for introducing controversial issues. It can help students see the ranges of values or opinions which exist on a given topic and understand the reasoning which supports those positions. The continuum provides an orderly method for discussing controversy, especially at the early stages of a lesson when students may be expressing "gut-level" reactions rather than informed opinions.

How to Proceed

1. Identify an issue to be discussed. The issue should be one in which one can identify polar positions, such as the death penalty.

2. Before initiating the activity it is important to cultivate a classroom atmosphere of trust where opinions can be expressed freely. Being receptive and nonjudgmental is critical to open discussion.

3. The teacher should initiate the activity by describing the issue(s) in enough detail so that the polar positions are clearly understood. These should be written on the board.

4. Students should be asked to write their position on the issue (e.g., strongly agree, agree, can't decide, disagree, strongly disagree) and to list the two most compelling reasons why they believe as they do.

5. While the students are writing their statements, the teacher can draw a continuum line across the chalkboard. When the students are finished writing, the teacher can print along the continuum brief versions of some possible polar position on the issue. Ask a limited number of students to stand at the position on the continuum where they believe their position on the issue falls.

6. At this point, students should be asked to explain or clarify, but not to defend their positions. They should be encouraged to move their position along the continuum as they listen to others clarify their positions.

7. Students now can be asked to state their reasons for positioning themselves as they have. The teacher may wish to post on the board the different reasons expressed by the students. At this point, students can respond to questions concerning their reasoning, but argumentation should be discouraged.

8. In order to assure that students listen to and consider opposing points of view, all students should be asked to present the arguments that, although contrary to their positions, give them pause, make them think twice, or are the most persuasive.

9. Finally, students should be asked to consider the consequences of alternative policy choices. This involves identifying the existing law or policy on the issue being considered, if one exists. The class can then discuss what impact the polar positions presented on the continuum would have on society as a whole and on individuals.

Keeping Journals

Journal writing provides a systematic way for students to maintain a personal record of summary statements, reflections, or questions about what is being learned in a particular instance. Journal writing encourages students to reflect on the "what," "why," and "how" of their own learning. Taking time to reflect is a good study habit to develop. Journals have the additional benefit of improving writing skills.

Because the content introduced in *We the People... The Citizen and the Constitution* contains many new concepts and experiences, opportunities for students to reflect on what they are learning are especially important. Some opportunities for journal writing are identified in the teacher's guide, but many more exist in this curriculum. You may want to allow a few minutes at the conclusion of a lesson or at the close of an activity for students to complete a journal entry. Encourage students to discuss some aspect of the content studied, to record a personal reaction to the lesson or the outcome of an activity, or to record questions the lesson or activity raised about an issue. Sometimes you may want to assign journal notations as homework.

Whether or not to grade journals is a personal choice. However, you should periodically collect journals to offer students some feedback on the content. Writing comments and personal observations in the journals can be an effective tool in establishing a personal dialogue with students. Do encourage students to share their journals with other students and with their parents if they wish. By so doing, students demonstrate to themselves and others what they have learned.

Evaluating Student Achievement

The methods used to evaluate student achievement of the concepts, knowledge, and skills offered in the *We the People... The Citizen and the Constitution* curriculum need to be both comprehensive and varied. The methods selected for measuring progress may range from the more traditional paper and pencil tests to performance-based assessments.

Traditional paper and pencil tests are valuable for checking knowledge and understanding of specific concepts, ideas, or procedures. For this purpose, the *We the People... The Citizen and the Constitution* program provides a multiple choice test in the Program Participation Handbook that accompanies the text. When teachers ask students to apply their complex knowledge and skills in various contexts, teachers need to measure students' achievement in similar contexts. For example, students who participate in a simulated legislative hearing during instruction should be asked to demonstrate their knowledge and skills in a similar context during testing. Thus, the *We the People... The Citizen and the Constitution* program includes performance assessment activities to measure achievement of the curriculum's higher level goals and objectives. The culminating performance assessment activity for the curriculum is the simulated congressional hearing which is fully explained in the accompanying Program Participation Handbook.

Performance assessment differs from traditional testing in that students are not asked to recognize and select correct answers to questions focused on discreet, isolated facts. During performance assessment, students demonstrate their knowledge and skills by addressing complex questions within a meaningful context (e.g., a legislative hearing) for which there is usually not just one correct answer. Students, therefore, construct or create appropriate answers, or a product, as a means of demonstrating what they know and what they can do.

Performance assessment is particularly well suited to the content, skills, and learning experiences emphasized in the program. Classroom activities such as group discussions, debates, and other creative projects provide prime opportunities for integrating performance assessment as part of the learning. Other opportunities for integrating performance assessment may be found in this guide at the end of each lesson in the section titled "Optional Activities: Reinforcement, Extended Learning, and Enrichment."

Below are some general guidelines for performance assessment you may want to consider in designing your evaluation of student achievement in this program:

- Assess desired behavior in the context in which the behavior is used. To assess students' ability to do **X**, have them do **X**.

- Assess how well students can apply what they learned in one situation by asking them to apply similar knowledge and skills in other, similar situations. Structure situations in which students can construct or create appropriate answers, rather than select from a menu of choices.

- Assess the process and the quality of a performance or product, not the ability to identify correct answers. Stress the thinking and reasoning that supports a quality performance or product.

- Assess how well students see the connections among a variety of related ideas and skills. For example, in preparing for a debate students should combine reading, research, writing, speaking, and critical thinking skills. Students also should see how knowledge and skills from other disciplines can help them deal with challenging topics.

- Provide the criteria for successful performance in advance and make sure that they are clearly understood. When possible provide models of exemplary performance.

- Provide criteria for effective and successful group work. Teamwork and group interaction are important skills that are given legitimacy when students know they are being assessed.

- Structure opportunities for students to assess their own progress, to judge for themselves when they have or have not done well. This will help them internalize high standards and learn to judge for themselves when they measure up. Because most learning strategies in this text are used more than once, students will have successive opportunities to reflect on their progress.

- Offer plenty of opportunities for students to receive feedback from the teacher, their peers, and community resource people who participate in activities with the class.

Reflecting on the Learning Experience

At the conclusion of each lesson and each unit of study in *We the People... The Citizen and the Constitution* it is recommended that students evaluate the extent to which they achieved the objectives of that particular lesson or unit. This includes thinking about the content as well as the instructional methods used to learn about that content.

At the conclusion of each unit or the entire curriculum, distribute a copy of the "Reflecting on Your Experience" handout on the next page to each student. Ask students to respond to the questions. Remind them that they should not only reflect on and evaluate their own learning experiences, but also those of the entire class. Conduct a class discussion in which students have an opportunity to share their reflections on the learning experiences offered in *We the People... The Citizen and the Constitution*.

Reflecting on Your Experience

It is always a good idea to think about, or reflect upon, experiences you have had or projects you have completed. That is one way to learn, to avoid mistakes in the future, and to improve your performance.

Now that your class has completed this study, you have an opportunity to reflect upon or evaluate what and how you and your classmates learned. You also have an opportunity to think about what you might do differently if you were to study other topics similar to this.

Use the following questions to help you reflect upon and evaluate your experience:

1. What did **I** personally learn about issues we studied from working with my classmates? _____
   _____
   _____

2. What did **we** as a class learn about the issues from the reading, the class discussions, and critical thinking exercises?_____
   _____
   _____

3. What skills did **I** learn or improve upon as a result of this experience? _____
   _____
   _____

4. What skills did the **class** learn or improve upon as a result of this experience? _____
   _____
   _____

5. What are the **disadvantages** of working with study partners and in small groups? _____
   _____
   _____

6. What are the **advantages** of working with study partners and in small groups?_____
   _____
   _____

7. What did **I** do well? _____
   _____
   _____

8. What would **I** want to do differently the next time I study a topic similar to this? _____
   _____
   _____

9. What did **we**, as a class, do well?_____
   _____
   _____

10. What would **we** want to do differently the next time we study a topic similar to this? _____
    _____
    _____

Unit One: What Are the Philosophical and Historical Foundations of the American Political System?

UNIT OVERVIEW. This unit introduces the study of the United States Constitution and Bill of Rights. The lessons in the unit present the principle ideas that shaped the Founders' views about the purpose of government and the need to protect individual rights. Students learn that the Founders were influenced by their belief in certain political philosophies, their understanding of history, and their own experience with government during the colonial period.

The first lesson raises some of the basic questions about government asked by political philosophers: Why do we need government? What should it do? What makes it legitimate? Students learn the answers provided by John Locke and other natural rights philosophers. In addition, they examine how the ideas of the natural rights philosophers apply to the Declaration of Independence and to the Constitution.

The next two lessons describe the ideas about government and rights developed during the Roman Republic as well as the ideas that influenced the Founders' thinking about limited government. Students learn what republican government meant, and how the example of government during the Roman Republic and the writings of Baron de Montesquieu influenced the Founders' thinking about representative democracy. Students also learn about the fundamental principles of constitutionalism and why the Founders believed that a constitution was necessary for the preservation of republican institutions and political liberty.

Subsequent lessons in the unit examine the ideas about rights developed during the classical periods in Greece and Rome, the Middle Ages, and those that emerged as a result of the economic, social, and political changes brought about by the Renaissance and Reformation. Students learn that the Founders' ideas also were influenced by their experiences as British subjects and by the 150 years of virtual self-government they enjoyed during the colonial period. Students examine the development of rights in England by examining the Magna Carta, the Petition of Right, and the English Bill of Rights. They then review the experiences of the Founders in the colonies and the events that led to the American Revolution. During the final lesson in the unit, students examine how the Founders used their ideas about government and rights during the Revolutionary War period to create their state constitutions.

UNIT OBJECTIVES. At the conclusion of this unit, students should be able to

1. describe the major ideas of the natural rights philosophy, including natural rights, the purpose of government, consent, and the social contract

2. describe the major ideas of republican government, including self-interest, civic virtue, the common good, and representative democracy

3. describe the major ideas of constitutional government, including higher law, constitution, separation of power, and checks and balances

4. explain the evolution of thinking about individual rights beginning with the classical periods in Greece and Rome through the Age of Enlightenment

5. explain the influence of British history on the Founders' thinking about natural rights, republicanism, and constitutional government

6. explain how the differences between colonial America and Europe affected the Founders' beliefs about government and individual rights

7. explain how the state declarations of rights reflected the Founders' ideas about the purpose of government and the protection of individual rights

8. evaluate, take, and defend positions on a number of issues related to natural rights, republicanism, and constitutional government

INTRODUCING THE UNIT. Have the class read the "Purpose of Unit" on p. 1 of the text. Discuss the basic themes students can expect to learn about during their study of this unit and review the objectives of the unit. Ask students how they think a book about ideas, such as this text, might differ from traditional government texts. Why might they think it important to study the ideas and principles of our political system? Ask students to write four or five personal objectives they would like to accomplish during the study of this unit. You may want to ask them, instead, to write four or five basic questions they would like to explore during their study of these lessons. They should keep their personal objectives or questions in a journal or notebook for review at the conclusion of the unit. They may want to expand upon these personal objectives or questions as their study in the unit progresses.

Introduce students to the unit timeline. Each unit in this text contains a timeline illustrating key events relevant to the topics of the lessons. You will find the events discussed in the text on the top of the timeline, other interesting or significant events are on the bottom of the timeline. They may offer additional topics for research and discussion. Students may want to create a similar timeline in their journals or notebooks to track in more detail important events or developments described in each lesson.

LESSON 1: What Would Life Be Like in a State of Nature?

Lesson Overview

This lesson introduces the fundamental ideas of the natural rights philosophy. It helps students understand the influence of these ideas on the Founders and on their thinking about the origins and need for government and the purposes a government should serve. The major ideas described in this lesson include: the state of nature, the law of nature, natural rights, consent, and the social contract. Students learn about these ideas as they were developed by the English philosopher John Locke (1632–1704). During the critical thinking exercise, students experience "thinking like a philosopher" by developing responses to questions similar to those which stimulated the thinking of the natural rights philosophers. Following the exercise, students compare their responses with the basic concepts and principles of John Locke.

Lesson Objectives

At the conclusion of this lesson, students should be able to

1. describe how and why the natural rights philosophers used an imaginary state of nature to think about the basic problems of government

2. explain some of the basic ideas of the natural rights philosophy, including state of nature, law of nature, natural rights, social contract, and consent

3. explain that the purpose of government based on the natural rights philosophy is to preserve our natural rights to life, liberty, and property

4. describe how the natural rights philosophy uses the concepts of consent and social contract to explain the formation of government

5. describe the influence of the natural rights philosophy on the Founders

Preparation/Teaching Materials

Student Text, pp. 2–6

Optional. Chart paper and markers

Optional. Invite a community resource person such as a political science professor to help students understand the ideas of the natural rights philosophy

Teaching Procedures

A. Introducing the Lesson

Ask students what rights come to mind when they hear the term "natural rights." What might be the source of such rights? Who should be responsible for protecting such rights if they are ever threatened?

While students read the "Purpose of Lesson" on p. 2, post the "Terms to Know" on the board. Review with the class what students should be able to do at the completion of the lesson, as explained in the "Purpose of Lesson." Review the vocabulary items listed on the board and remind students to take special note of these terms as they study the material in the lesson.

B. Reading and Discussion

What is the natural rights philosophy?

Have the class read "What is the natural rights philosophy?" on pp. 2–3 of the text. After students have read the material, direct their attention to the excerpt from the Declaration of Independence at the beginning of the reading. Ask students to identify key principles about rights and the purpose of government in the Declaration. Some of the ideas students should

identify are: (1) all human beings are created equal and they are endowed with certain rights; (2) these are the rights to life, liberty, and the pursuit of happiness ("pursuit of happiness" was used by Jefferson rather than the more common term "property" which was used by Locke); (3) government is created for the purpose of protecting the individual's rights to life, liberty, and the pursuit of happiness; and (4) governments derive their power by consent and whenever a government abuses its powers at the expense of the rights of its citizens, the citizens have the right to change or eliminate the government and establish a new one. Check that students understand that these are fundamental philosophical ideas underlying our form of government.

Ask students to identify the person of **John Locke**—who was John Locke and when did he live? You may want to provide additional background information concerning John Locke and the Age of Enlightenment. Stress that Locke's political philosophy is often called the **natural rights philosophy** and that these ideas profoundly influenced the Founder's thinking about government. Check that students understand that the natural rights philosophy derives from thinking about what life might be like in a **state of nature**, that is, an imaginary situation in which no government exists.

Ask students how using an imaginary state of nature might be useful in thinking about government, in justifying the decision to separate from Britain, or in writing constitutions. Lead the class in a general discussion of the questions, p. 3 of the text, raised by John Locke: (1) What is human nature? For example, are all people selfish or do they tend to care for the good of others? (2) What should be the purpose of government? (3) How do the people running a government get the right to govern? (4) How should a government be organized? (5) What kinds of government should be respected and supported? (6) What kinds of government should be resisted and fought?

C. Critical Thinking Exercise
Taking the Position of a Political Philosopher

In preparation for participating in the critical thinking exercise "Taking the Position of a Political Philosopher" on p. 3 of the text, ask students to work with a partner to define what they think a political philosopher does. Have them share their responses with the class. Explain to the class that during this exercise they will experience thinking like a political philosopher to develop responses to important questions about living in an imaginary state of nature.

Divide the class into groups of five students. Distribute to each group a sheet of chart paper and markers, or ask students to provide their own paper and pencils. Ask each group to determine who in the group will assume responsibility for each the following tasks: (1) Reader, to read the questions to the group; (2) First and Second Responders, to initiate the discussion on each question; (3) Recorder, to take notes on the group discussion; and (4) Reporter, to share the groups ideas with the class.

Have the students read the directions for completing the exercise and allow adequate time for students to develop responses to the questions. When the groups have completed their work, have them record their responses on chart paper and prepare for sharing their ideas with the class. Then lead a class discussion on the responses.

D. Reading and Discussion
How do your answers compare with those of John Locke?

Have the class read "How do your answers compare with those of John Locke?" on pp. 3–4 of the text. At the conclusion of the reading ask students to compare the ideas of John Locke with the responses they developed during the preceding exercise. You may want to outline some of Locke's key ideas on the board.

During the discussion, check for students' understanding that in a state of nature there are rules which Locke calls the **law of nature** that oblige everyone not to harm another in his life, health, liberty, or possessions. Locke believed that most people understood the law of nature through reason and followed it because their conscience obliged them to do so. However, not all humans were reasonable or good and, in the absence of government, no one would have a right to interpret or enforce these laws. A legitimate government cannot exist until people have created it by giving their consent to be ruled by it. Review the remaining items in this reading section, similarly stressing key points students should understand. Return to the question posed at the introduction to the lesson: what are the things that all people always need and seek, no matter what they believe, no matter when or where they live? List the terms **Life**, **Liberty**, and **Property** on the board. Have students define each of the terms from the text. Have students classify the items on the list they created during the introduction according to the three rights identified by John Locke.

To summarize the reading and discussion, direct attention to the illustrations on p. 4. Ask students to respond to the questions in the captions: (1) According to Locke, how is personal property protected in a state of nature? (2) Why did Locke believe it was necessary for people to create governments?

Direct attention to the questions in the "What do *you* think?" section on p. 5. Encourage students to express their ideas in response to each of the questions in this section. You may want students to work with a study partner to develop responses to each question. If so, have the students share their responses with the class.

E. Reading and Discussion
What is the significance of Locke's definition of the natural rights to life, liberty, and property?

Have the class read "What is the significance of Locke's definition of the natural rights to life, liberty, and property?" on p. 5. During discussion of the narrative, check that students understand the concept of **rights** and **unalienable** and that students can distinguish between **natural rights**, **civil rights**, and **political rights**. Students also should be able to explain that civil and political rights serve to protect natural rights to life, liberty, and property. Students should understand that the natural rights philosophy represented a departure from traditional ways of thinking about rights. Historically, rights were considered as special privileges enjoyed by certain groups or classes of people. The natural rights philosophers regarded the individual to be more important than a group or class. They viewed society as a collection of individuals, all of whom shared the same rights. The class will learn more about the evolution of ideas concerning the importance of the individual and individual rights in Lesson 4.

Direct attention to the illustration on p. 5. Ask students to respond to the question in the caption: Why are political rights necessary to protect our natural rights?

F. Reading and Discussion
What did Locke mean by the "social contract"?

Have the class read "What did Locke mean by the 'social contract'?" on p. 6. During the discussion, stress that Locke realized that because not all human beings were rational or good, there would always be people who would try to violate the rights of others. The great problem, according to natural rights philosophers, was to find a way to protect each person's natural rights. Locke's answer was the **social contract**, that is, for each individual to agree with others to create and live under a government and to give that government the power to make and enforce laws. In a social contract everyone agrees to give up the absolute right to do anything he or she wants in return for the security that government can provide. Everyone **consents** to obey the limits placed upon him or her by the laws created by the government. Check for student understanding that, according to the natural rights philosophy, the purpose of government is to protect those natural rights that the individual cannot effectively secure in a state of nature.

Direct attention to the questions in the "What do *you* think?" section on p. 6. Have students work individually or with a study partner to develop responses to the questions. At the conclusion, have students share their responses with the class.

G. Concluding the Lesson

To conclude the lesson, ask students to examine the photo on p. 2 and to respond to the question in the caption: Did the end of white rule in South Africa in 1993 result in a state of nature? Why or why not? Can students think of situations or rebellions where the people of a country might have reverted to a hypothetical state of nature, i.e., an absence of government.

Have students respond to the questions in the "Reviewing and Using the Lesson" section on p. 6 of the text. Student responses to these questions can provide them some measure of how well they learned the concepts in this lesson. Finally, have students return to the "Purpose of Lesson" on p. 2. Ask students to describe the extent to which they accomplished the objectives of the lesson.

Optional Activities
Reinforcement, Extended Learning, and Enrichment

1. Ask students to collect clippings from newspapers and periodicals that contain examples of the United States government, or the governments of other nations, protecting or violating citizens' basic rights to life, liberty, and property.

2. Ask students to gather biographical information about John Locke or other Enlightenment thinkers such as Montesquieu, Jean Jacques Rousseau, and David Hume and report their finding to the class.

3. Ask student to read about Thomas Hobbes and compare his view of the state of nature with John Locke's. Students may be asked to do this by writing an intellectual dialogue between the two political thinkers.

LESSON 2: How Does Government Secure Natural Rights?

Lesson Overview

This lesson describes the Founders' ideas about what kind of government is most likely to protect the basic rights of people. Students learn to distinguish between limited and unlimited government, and develop their understanding of concepts such as constitution, and constitutional government. Students also learn that while all nations have constitutions, not all nations have constitutional governments. The essential characteristics that differentiate constitutional government from autocratic or dictatorial government include the idea that in a constitutional government the powers of a person or group in government are limited by a set of laws and/or established customs (a constitution) which must be obeyed. The constitution is a form of higher law that: (1) sets forth the basic rights of citizens to life, liberty, and property; (2) establishes the responsibility of the government to protect those rights; (3) establishes limitations on how those in government may use their power; (4) establishes the principle of a private domain; and (5) may not be changed without the widespread consent of the citizens.

During the lesson, students learn how a constitutional government protects natural rights and how constitutional governments can be organized to prevent the abuse of power, including a system of distributed and shared powers and checks and balances. During the first critical thinking exercise, students explore ideas related to key questions about the purpose of government and the source of governmental authority. In the second exercise students examine selections from writings by the Founders which illustrate why the Founders feared the abuse of power by government.

Lesson Objectives

At the conclusion of this lesson, students should be able to

1. explain the concepts of constitution and constitutional government

2. explain the essential characteristics of constitutional governments that differentiate them from autocratic or dictatorial governments

3. explain the essential characteristics of a constitution or higher law

4. explain how the Founders' fear of abuse of power by government may have motivated them to establish a constitutional government

Preparation/ Teaching Materials

Student text, pp. 7–12

Teaching Procedures

A. Introducing the Lesson

Ask students to suppose that they are dissatisfied with living in a state of nature. They and others agree to a social contract and the creation of a government to protect their natural rights. What kind of government might they create? What authority, or powers, might they assign to their government in order that it provide equal protection for the rights of everyone? How will the persons selected to run the government know what their authority is? How might the citizens protect themselves so that the government they create does not itself violate the rights it is designed to protect?

While students read the "Purpose of Lesson" on p. 7 of the text, post the "Terms to Know" on the board. Review with the class what students should be able to do at the completion of the lesson, as explained in the "Purpose of Lesson." Review the vocabulary items listed on the board and remind student to take special note of these terms as they study the material in the lesson.

B. Critical Thinking Exercise

Examining Government Protection of the Basic Rights of the People

During the critical thinking exercise, "Examining Government Protection of the Basic Rights of the People" on p. 7, the class explores several more questions related to deciding what kind of government to create. In Lesson 1 students learned some of John Locke's ideas about the purpose of government. When introducing this exercise, encourage students to explore some of their own ideas about what they think the purpose of government should be.

Divide the class into groups of five students. Review the instructions for completing the exercise and the three questions the groups are to explore. Students should understand that designing and establishing a government to provide **equal protection** for the rights of everyone is not an easy task. Allow adequate time for the groups to complete their work. At the conclusion, have the groups share their ideas with the class.

C. Reading and Discussion

How do your answers compare with those of John Locke?

Have the class read "How do your answers compare with those of John Locke?" on pp. 7–8 of the text. Then have students compare their responses to the questions in the critical thinking exercise with John Locke's answers listed in this narrative. Discuss with the class how people give their consent to be governed, focusing on **explicit** and **implicit** consent. What do students think Locke meant when he talked about a **right to revolution**? Direct attention to the illustration on p. 8. Ask students to respond to the question in the caption: Under what circumstances would Locke agree that people have the right to take up arms against an established government? Do students think that there are other ways to deal with bad government?

D. Reading and Discussion

How do Americans express consent to their government?

Have the class read "How do Americans express their consent to their government?" on p. 8 of the text. Discuss with the class how Americans in 1787 gave explicit consent to their new government by ratifying the Constitution. Naturalized citizens also give explicit consent when they take the oath of citizenship. Ask students how native-born citizens affirm their consent. Students may cite examples listed in the text, but encourage them to think of additional examples of their own such as obeying the laws and availing themselves of the services government provides.

E. Reading and Discussion

What is constitutional government?

Have the class read "What is constitutional government?" on p. 8 of the text. During the discussion, check that students have learned to distinguish between **limited** and **unlimited government** and that students can cite examples of the types of unlimited governments (dictatorship, totalitarianism, etc.) that might exist. Ask them to cite specific examples of historical and contemporary governments in the world that have exercised unlimited power over the people. Check that students understand the definition of **constitutional government**, that is, the powers of the government are limited by a set of laws and customs called a **constitution**. The term "constitution" is defined in the next section. Help students make the connection between the natural rights philosophy, the Founders' historical experience, and constitutional government. Discuss with the class why the Founders believed that if the purpose of government is to protect natural rights, that government would have to be a constitutional government.

F. Reading and Discussion

What is a constitution?

Have the class read "What is a constitution?" on pp. 8–9 of the text. Check that students understand the definition of the term **constitution**. Ask students to cite examples of the types of questions a constitution should answer concerning the relationship between the government and its citizens. Be sure that students understand that if a constitution provides for unlimited power or does not contain ways to limit the powers of government, it does not form the basis for a constitutional government. You may want to explain, as one example, that the former Soviet Union had a lengthy constitution which did not limit the power of government. You may want to ask students to cite other examples of nations with constitutions that do not form the basis of constitutional government. At the conclusion, stress that a constitution is a form of **higher** or **fundamental law** that everyone must obey, including those in power.

Direct attention to the illustration on p. 8. Ask students to respond to the question in the caption: Are all governments with written constitutions constitutional governments? Why?

G. Reading and Discussion

How did the Founders characterize higher law?

Have the class read "How did the Founders characterize higher law?" on p. 9 of the text. Ask students to explain the characteristics of a constitution or **higher law**. Record their responses on the board. Their responses should include:

- sets forth the basic rights of citizens to life, liberty, and property
- establishes the responsibility of government to protect those rights
- establishes limitations on how those in government may use their power
- establishes the principle of a **private domain**
- can only be changed with the widespread consent of the citizens, and according to established and well-known procedures

Check that students can relate the characteristics of a constitution or higher law to the ideas of the natural rights philosophers and the concept of constitutional government. Discuss with the class how a constitution limits the power of those in government with regard to citizens' rights and responsibilities, distribution of resources, and control of conflict. Ask students to offer examples of limits on the power of our government. Check that students understand the concept of a **private domain** and ask them to cite examples of areas of citizens' lives in which our government cannot interfere. Direct attention to the illustration on p. 9. Ask students to respond to the question in the caption: How does the principle of private domain protect you from government interference?

Finally, you may want to briefly explain the procedures provided for amending the Constitution of the United States as a means of illustrating the last characteristic of a constitution or higher law. Why might the class think it important to have wide-spread consent and established procedures for changing the Constitution?

Direct attention to the "What do *you* think?" section at the end of the reading selection. You may want to use these questions for general class discussion. As an alternative, you may want to divide the class into small groups, have the groups develop responses, and then share their responses with the class.

H. Reading and Discussion

How does constitutional government protect natural rights?

Have the class read "How does constitutional government protect natural rights?" on p. 9. During the discussion, check that students understand that a constitutional government establishes both **legal protection** and **organizational protection** for the rights of citizens. Help students clarify how legal and organizational protections can be used to assure the rights of citizens.

I. Reading and Discussion

How can constitutional governments be organized to prevent the abuse of power?

Have the class read "How can constitutional governments be organized to prevent the abuse of power?" on p. 10. During the discussion, check that students understand that the organizational protections in the Constitution include distribution and sharing of power among the three branches of the national government. Check that students (1) understand the concept of **checks and balances**, (2) can cite examples of checks and balances, and (3) can explain what the Founders thought were the advantages of a system of checks and balances.

Direct attention to the illustration on p. 10. Ask students to respond to the question in the caption: Does a system of checks and balances guarantee that power will not be abused?

J. Critical Thinking Exercise

Examining Why the Founders Feared the Abuse of Power by Government

Divide the class into small groups of five students to complete the critical thinking exercise "Examining Why the Founders Feared the Abuse of Power by Government" on p. 10. The exercise includes quotations from Alexander Hamilton, Benjamin Franklin, and George Mason expressing their views about human nature and why they greatly feared the possible abuse of power by government. Read the directions for completing the exercise with the class. Allow adequate time for the groups to develop responses to the questions. At the conclusion, have the groups share their responses with the class.

K. Reading and Discussion

What kinds of governments may be constitutional governments?

Have the class read "What kinds of governments may be constitutional governments?" on pp. 10–11 of the text. During the discussion stress that constitutional governments may take many forms, including monarchies, republics, and democracies.

L. Reading and Discussion

What alternative models of government could the Founders choose from?

Have the class read "What alternative models of government could the Founders choose from?" on pp. 11–12. During the discussion, check that students understand the concepts **republic** and **democracy**. Stress that the Founders were familiar with both models of government from their knowledge of history and from their own experience in the colonies. During the discussion check that students can define the term **republican government** by citing the following characteristics: (1) government is devoted to promoting the common good; (2) all or most of the citizens share political authority; and (3) political authority is exercised through elected representatives of the people. Direct attention to the illustration on p. 11. Ask students to respond to the question in the caption: How did the Founders' knowledge of ancient Rome shape their views about government?

M. Concluding the Lesson

To conclude the lesson, conduct a general class discussion using the questions in the "What do *you* think?" section on p. 12 of the text.

Have students respond to the questions in the "Reviewing and Using the Lesson" section on p. 12 of the text. Student responses to these questions can provide them some measure of how well they learned the concepts in this lesson. Finally, have students return to the "Purpose of Lesson" on p. 7. Ask students to describe the extent to which they accomplished the objectives of the lesson.

Optional Activities

Reinforcement, Extended Learning, and Enrichment

1. Select students to prepare and present reports on countries in the world which have constitutional governments.

2. Select several students to prepare and present reports on practices of the British government which are a part of its unwritten constitution.

3. Select several students to prepare and present reports on Adolf Hitler's early years of power during which he overturned the German Constitution. The reports should emphasize the specific steps by which constitutional procedures were abolished.

4. Lead a class discussion on the following quote by Judge Learned Hand: "Liberty lies in the hearts of men and women: when it dies there, no court can ever do much to help it. While it lies there, it needs no constitution, no law, no court to save it."

LESSON 3: What Did the Founders Learn about Republican Government from the Ancient World?

Lesson Overview

This lesson introduces the concept of republican government, that is, the theory that the best kind of society is one that promotes the common good instead of the interests of only one class of citizens. Students learn how the Founders were influenced by the example of the Roman Republic. Students learn the four basic ideas of classical republicanism: (1) a republic is devoted to the common good of the state; (2) citizens must possess civic virtue, that is, they must put the common good above their personal interests; (3) citizens must be raised in a manner that develops the right civic habits, that is, citizens must be taught to be virtuous by moral education; and (4) a republican government functions best in small communities—a great degree of diversity should not be tolerated if people are to know and care for each other and their common good. These ideas played a large role in the deliberations of the Founders.

During the lesson, students examine the basic ideas underlying a republican government developed by Montesquieu, a French philosopher whose writings were highly regarded by the Founders. Students learn that Monstesquieu believed that a republican government must be a mixed government, that is, a government in which all the classes of society shared power. This was the only form of government, philosophers argued, that would achieve the common good rather than the welfare of one particular class or group. Finally, students learn how James Madison adapted the classical idea of republicanism to meet the needs of government in eighteenth-century America

and the role of republicanism in the establishment of our constitutional system.

Lesson Objectives

At the conclusion of this lesson, students should be able to

1. describe the major characteristics of republican government as exemplified by the Roman Republic and as discussed by Montesquieu

2. demonstrate an understanding of civic virtue and why it was thought to be important

3. explain in their own terms Montesquieu's argument about the importance and value of mixed government

4. explain how James Madison adapted the ideas of classical republicanism to meet the needs of government in America

Preparation/Teaching Materials

Student text, pp. 13–18

Optional. Photographs of key government buildings in Washington D.C. which illustrate the ancient Greek and Roman style of architecture and a illustration of the statue of George Washington dressed in a toga.

Optional. Chart paper and markers

Optional. Invite a community resource person such as a political science professor to discuss the ideas of republicanism and constitutionalism with the class.

Teaching Procedures

A. Introducing the Lesson

Direct attention to the illustration on p. 13 of the text. Ask students to respond to the question in the caption: How does the architectural style of some government buildings symbolize the influence of ancient Greece and Rome on the Founders? If you have collected additional illustrations of key buildings in Washington D.C., share them with the class.

While students read the "Purpose of Lesson" on p. 13, post the "Terms to Know" on the board. Review with the class what they should be able to do at the completion of the lesson, as explained in the "Purpose of Lesson."

Review the vocabulary items listed on the board and remind students to take special note of these terms as they study the material in the lesson.

B. Reading and Discussion

What ideas about government did the Founders find in classical republicanism?

Have the class read "What ideas about government did the Founders find in classical republicanism?" on pp. 13–15 of the text. Ask students what impressed the Founders about the Roman Republic and what lessons they learned from its example. Ask students to speculate why Americans in the eighteenth century might have thought the example of the Roman Republic applied to them, i.e., did they think that Americans at that time possessed many of the characteristics attributed to the ancient Romans?

During class discussion, check that students can define the term **classical republicanism**, that is, the theory that the best kind of society is one that promotes the common good instead of the interest of only one class of citizens. Check that students can define the term **common good**, that is, what is best for the entire society. Ask students to identify and describe the desirable characteristics citizens in a classical republic should possess:

(1) **civic virtue** which causes citizens to participate fully in their government, promoting the common good rather than personal interests such as making money, caring for families, traveling, and reading or thinking about things that have nothing to do with government. Classical republics often limited individual rights such as privacy, freedom of belief, and nonpolitical expression.

(2) **moral education** through which citizens are taught to be virtuous. Civic virtue is not something that comes automatically to people. Children must be raised in a manner that develops the right habits, such as courage, self-control, and fairness. They should learn the importance of political debate and military service.

(3) **small, uniform communities** where people are not very different in their wealth, moral beliefs, or ways of life. Government works best in a small community where people know and care for each other and the common good. If people differ greatly, they divide into factions more concerned with their own interest than with the common good.

To summarize this section of the reading, direct attention to the illustrations on pp. 14 and 15. Ask students to respond to the questions in the captions: (1) Why did classical republicans believe that republican government could only work in small, uniform communities? (2) Is civic virtue as important in America today as it was in ancient Rome? Why? Why not? (3) Do all Americans have an obligation to practice civic virtue? Why?

Direct attention to the questions in the "What do *you* think?" section on p. 15. Encourage students to express their ideas in response to each of the questions in this section. If time permits, you may want students to work with a study partner to develop responses to each question. If so, have the students share their responses with the class.

C. Critical Thinking Exercise

Understanding the Differences between the Natural Rights Philosophy and Classical Republicanism

Have students work individually, with a study partner, or in small groups to complete the critical thinking exercise, "Understanding the Differences between the Natural Rights Philosophy and Classical Republicanism," on pp. 15–16 of the text. The activities of the exercise engage students in comparing and contrasting differing views of individual rights, the purpose of government, and the role of the citizen in government. Read the directions for completing the exercise with the class and review each of the questions in the exercise. Distribute chart paper and markers to each group. Allow adequate time for students to complete the exercise. Listed on the chart on the next page are items students might include in their own charts.

Natural Rights Philosophy	Classical Republicanism
1. Stressed the rights of the individual to life, liberty, and property	1. Stressed promoting the common good above the rights of the individual
2. Stressed that human nature is such that individual behavior is motivated by self-interest	2. Stressed that individuals should be motivated by civic virtue
3. Stressed that society is a collection of individuals, each sharing the same right to pursue his or her own welfare	3. Limited individual rights to privacy, belief, expression, and opportunities to read, think, and earn money. If people had freedom to do such things, they might stop being reliable and fully dedicated to the common good
4. Stressed that people's opportunities should not be limited by the situation or group into which they are born	4. Discouraged diversity of beliefs, wealth, and ways of life. Stressed small communities where people know and care for each other. Discouraged citizens from traveling, earning money, and reading and thinking about things that had nothing to do with their government.
5. Stressed that the main purpose of government should be to protect natural rights. The state existed to serve the interests of the individual	5. Stressed avoiding the formation of factions or interest groups that might endanger the common good. Stressed that citizens should participate fully in the government to promote the common good
6. To preserve natural rights, governments guarantee specific rights, such as civil rights (freedom of conscience and privacy) and political rights (vote, run for office)	6. Stressed the importance of political rights such as voting, expressing ideas and opinions about government, and serving in public office

At the conclusion of the exercise, ask students to share their work with the class.

D. Reading and Discussion

How did the Founders think a government should be organized to promote the common good?

Have the class read "How did the Founders think a government should be organized to promote the common good? on p. 16 of the text. Ask students to explain how a republican government should be organized according to Montesquieu and why it should be organized that way. During the discussion, check that students understand that Montesquieu advocated dividing and balancing the powers of government among the classes of society. This was the best way to enhance the common good and to ensure that the government would not be dominated by a single group. Ask students to explain the concept of a **mixed government**. You might also ask students to speculate on what might be some problems in trying to establish the mixed government described by Montesquieu (a government that combined royalty, nobility, and commons) in eighteenth-century America. Direct attention to the illustration on p. 16. Ask students to respond to the question in the caption: What important contribution did Montesquieu make to the Founders' ideas about government?

E. Reading and Discussion

What were some problems in transferring the ideas of classical republicanism to eighteenth-century America?

Have the class read "What were some problems in transferring the ideas of classical republicanism to eighteenth-century America?" on p. 16 of the text. During the discussion of this material, direct students to the responses they generated during the critical exercise earlier in the lesson.

F. Reading and Discussion

How did James Madison refine the ideas of classical republicanism?

Have the class read "How did James Madison refine the ideas of classical republicanism?" on p. 17. Have students discuss how James Madison refined the notion of republicanism for a large and diverse nation by distinguishing between a **democracy** and a **republic**. Have students identify the problems, as Madison saw them, of trying to establish a republic in America. Students might refer to the charts they created during the critical thinking exercise to compare their responses with those of James Madison. Have the students explain how Madison reconciled the differences between the natural rights philosophy and classical republicanism. Ask the students how Madison's definition of a republic as a **representative democracy** might have solved some of the problems of having a republican government in a large and diverse nation. Finally have the students speculate about why the Founders thought a written constitution was necessary for a republican government.

G. Reading and Discussion

How did the Founders adapt the ideal of civic virtue to the American republic?

Have the class read "How did the Founders adapt the ideal of civic virtue to the American republic?" on pp. 17–18 of the text. Students should understand that James Madison accepted the natural rights view that people are primarily motivated by self-interest. Madison argued that if each person were free to pursue his or her economic self-interest, each would contribute to the general prosperity of the nation and thereby to the common good.

Direct attention to the illustration on p. 17. Ask students to respond to the question in the caption: Were the Founders more representative of the ideas of the natural rights philosophy or classical republicanism? Why?

Madison realized that as people pursue their self-interest, they sometimes act against the interests of others and against the common good. He argued that people should possess the quality of civic virtue, but at the same time government should guard against those who did not by creating a constitution that included separation of powers and checks and balances.

Direct attention to the illustration on p. 18. Ask students to respond to the question in the caption: Why did James Madison favor a constitution that limited the power of government?

Direct attention to the "What do *you* think?" section on p. 18. Ask the class to respond to the questions in this section. You may want to assign students to work in small groups to develop responses to individual questions or to the entire set of questions included in this section. If so, have the students share their responses with the class.

H. Concluding the Lesson

Have students respond to the questions in the "Reviewing and Using the Lesson" section on p. 18 of the text. Student responses to these questions can provide them some measure of how well they learned the concepts in this lesson. Finally, have students return to the "Purpose of Lesson" on p. 13. Ask students to describe the extent to which they accomplished the objectives of the lesson.

Optional Activities

Reinforcement, Extended Learning, and Enrichment

1. Ask students to bring to class excerpts from newspapers describing recent governmental actions. Ask students to state whether each action promotes the common good and why.

2. Have students write a short essay on Montesquieu in which they explain his political philosophy in more detail.

3. Select two groups of three or five students to debate whether Americans today possess the civic virtue the Founders admired. They should be prepared with examples to support their positions.

LESSON 4: How Did Modern Ideas of Individual Rights Develop?

Lesson Overview

This lesson illustrates how ideas about rights developed throughout history and examines the influence of these developments on the Founders. Students learn that the Founders were heirs to the millennia-old Judeo-Christian tradition which emphasizes the special place humanity occupies in creation. Though of different faiths within this tradition—and some skeptical of certain religious doctrines—most of the Founders had grown up in a religious environment and were familiar with the teachings of the Bible. During the reading and discussion exercises in the lesson, students will learn the ideas about rights held during the Middle Ages, the Renaissance, and the Reformation. Students will examine how the religious, economic, and political changes which followed led to a greater emphasis on individual rights. Students will also examine how the rise of the nation-state, the rise of capitalism, and the Age of Enlightenment influenced the Founders' beliefs about rights.

Lesson Objectives

At the conclusion of this lesson, students should be able to

1. explain the ideas about rights that predominated during the Middle Ages, the Renaissance, and the Reformation

2. explain the difference between the rights of individuals and the rights of groups

3. explain how the Renaissance, the Reformation, the rise of the nation-state, and the rise of capitalism contributed to the growth of individual rights

Preparation/Teaching Materials

Student text, pp. 19–25

Teaching Procedures

A. Introducing the Lesson

Ask students what aspects of contemporary life influence the way Americans today think about rights. In what way might the historical time period in which people live influence their thinking about government and rights?

While students read the "Purpose of Lesson" on p. 19 of the text, post the "Terms to Know" on the board. Review with the class what students should be able to do at the completion of the lesson, as explained in the "Purpose of Lesson." Review the vocabulary items listed on the board and remind students to take special note of these terms as they study the material in the lesson.

B. Reading and Discussion

How did the Judeo-Christian heritage contribute to the Founders' understanding of human rights?

Have the class read "How did the Judeo-Christian heritage contribute to the Founders' understanding of human rights?" on pp. 19–20 of the text. During class discussion of the material, check that students understand the meaning of **Judeo-Christian** heritage and can identify some of the religious beliefs and moral principles which the Founders thought beneficial to developing civic virtue and promoting the common good. Discuss how these beliefs might have strengthened the Founders' commitment to the ideals of justice, liberty, and individual rights.

C. Reading and Discussion

What were the concepts of the individual and society during the Middle ages?

Have the class read "What were the concepts of the individual and society during the Middle Ages?" on pp. 20–21 of the text. During the discussion, stress that medieval society was based on the ideas of unity, social harmony, and other-worldliness. People defined their allegiance as belonging to (1) their local community and (2) to Christendom united in one "universal" church. Students should also understand that in medieval society: (1) classes and groups were divided, such as royalty, nobility, clergy, tradesmen, etc.; (2) classes and groups were hierarchical, that is, they were ranked from most important to least important and there was no equality among them; (3) the individual's role was defined by his or her membership in a class or group and there was little chance of rising above the group into which one had been born; and (4) rights were seen as privileges belonging to particular groups in society.

To summarize this section of the reading, direct attention to the illustrations on pp. 20 and 21. Ask students to respond to the questions in the captions: (1) How were a person's rights and responsibilities determined in the Middle Ages? (2) Why did the Popes and the church attain such important status in the Middle Ages? (3) How were people's understanding of rights shaped by the economic and social structure of the Middle Ages?

Direct attention to the "What do *you* think?" section on p. 21. Ask students to respond to the questions in this section. You may want to have students work individually or in small groups to develop their responses. At the conclusion, have the students share their responses with the class.

D. Reading and Discussion

How did the Renaissance contribute to the development of individual rights?

Have the class read "How did the Renaissance contribute to the development of individual rights?" on p. 21 of the text. During the discussion check that students can define the term **Renaissance** and can describe key features of this historical period. Stress that economic and intellectual pursuits during the Renaissance led to an increased interest in the rights of individuals and contributed to a reexamination of the individual's relationship to religious institutions and governments.

Direct attention to the illustrations on p. 22. Ask students to respond to the question in the caption: How did Michelangelo's statue of David and changes in technology reflect changes in thinking that occurred in the Renaissance?

E. Reading and Discussion

How did the Protestant Reformation advance the cause of individual rights?

Have the class read "How did the Protestant Reformation advance the cause of individual rights?" on p. 22 of the text. During the discussion check that students can identify the characteristics of the Reformation. Stress that during this historical period there was an increased emphasis on the importance of the individual and his or her equality in the eyes of God. The ideas which emerged during the Reformation ultimately posed a threat to all established institutions and authority.

F. Reading and Discussion

What caused the rise of modern nation-states?

Have the class read "What caused the rise of modern nation-states?" on p. 23 of the text. During the discussion, help students understand that the rise of the **nation-state** occurred rather recently in historical terms. The importance of the emergence of the nation-state is that it caused people to think of themselves as citizens of a particular state or country and that, as citizens, they possessed public rights and duties. Thus, people began to focus on the question of what kind of government would be best for these states. The modern state also brought with it national legal systems and representative institutions of government.

G. Reading and Discussion

What was the new economic system of capitalism?

Have the class read "What was the new economic system of capitalism?" on p. 23 of the text. During the discussion check that students can define the term **capitalism** and can describe key features of this economic system. Stress that under capitalism people gained more freedom to choose their occupation and own businesses and property. Capitalism encouraged people to gain property and improve their positions in society. As a result, political and economic power shifted to a newly developed middle class of successful citizens.

Direct attention to the illustration on p. 23. Ask students to respond to the question in the caption: How did the Renaissance, the Reformation, and the emergence of the modern nation-state make the rise of capitalism possible?

Direct attention to the "What do *you* think?" section on p. 24. Ask students to respond to the questions in this section. You may want to have students work individually or in small groups to develop their responses. If so, have them share their responses with the class.

Optional instructional activity. You may want to have students illustrate what they have learned about the development of individual rights described in this lesson by having the class create a timeline similar to the one in the introduction to Unit One on p. 1 of the text. If so, divide the class into seven groups and assign each group one of the following: (1) Roman Republic (previous lesson), (2) Middle Ages, (3) Renaissance, (4) Reformation, (5) rise of the modern nation-state, (6) rise of capitalism, and (7) Age of Enlightenment. Distribute to each group a sheet of chart paper and markers. At the top of the sheet have the group identify their assigned era. On the top half of the sheet have them describe key features of the period. On the lower half ask them to list the influence the period had on the development of individual rights. Have each group share their work with the class.

H. Critical Thinking Exercise

Understanding the Effects of the Renaissance and Reformation on Ideas about Rights

Divide the class into groups of five students to complete the critical thinking exercise, "Understanding the Effects of the Renaissance and Reformation on Ideas about Rights," on p. 24 of the text. The exercise engages students in analyzing each of the historical periods described in the text so that they better understand the evolution of thinking about the role of the individual in society and individual rights. Review with the class the instructions for completing the exercise and the questions in this section. Allow adequate time for students to complete their work. At the conclusion have students share their responses with the class. The chart below illustrates some possible responses students might give to question #1 in the exercise.

Historical period	Ideas about the individual and individual rights
Middle Ages	Stressed harmony between the individual and society

Individual existed for the good of society and each person's role was defined by membership in a group

Rights and duties were defined in terms of the group. Rights were seen as privileges belonging to particular groups

No concept of "natural" rights belonging to all the people. Few individual rights |
| Renaissance | In many areas of life, emphasis was placed on the individual rather than the group into which that individual had been born

Increased interest in the rights of individuals

Individuals began to reexamine their relationship to religious institutions and governments |
| Reformation | Emphasized the direct relationship between the individual believer and God, leading to the increased importance of the individual

Encouraged freedom of conscience

All individuals seen as equals in the eyes of God

Each person was to be respected and held accountable as an individual |
| Rise of Nation-State | People began to think of themselves as citizens of a particular state

Citizens possessed both public rights and public duties |
| Rise of Capitalism | People gained freedom to choose their occupations, start businesses, and own property

People had more control over their lives

People began to pay more attention to their private interests than to the common good |

Direct attention to the "What do *you* think?" section on p. 24. Ask the class to respond to the questions in this section. You may want to do this as a whole class discussion, assign questions individually, or assign them to small groups. If students work individually or in small groups, have them share their responses with the class.

I. Reading and Discussion
What was the Age of Enlightenment?

Have the class read "What was the Age of Enlightenment?" on pp. 24–25 of the text. During the discussion check that students understand that the Age of Enlightenment (or Age of Reason) was an intellectual movement that celebrated human reason and sought to realize human potential in all areas of endeavor. Stress that it was during this period that people began to apply the methods of scientific thinking to the study of society and politics. The Founders belonged to the Age of Reason from which the natural rights philosophy emerged.

Direct attention to the illustration on p. 24. Ask students to respond to the question in the caption: How did increased interest in scientific study relate to the development of the natural rights philosophy?

J. Concluding the Lesson

Have students respond to the questions in the "Reviewing and Using the Lesson" section on p. 25 of the text. Student responses to these questions can provide them some measure of how well they learned the concepts in this lesson. Finally, have students return to the "Purpose of Lesson" on p. 19. Ask students to describe the extent to which they accomplished the objectives of the lesson.

Optional Activities
Reinforcement, Extended Learning, and Enrichment

1. Have students create a series of cartoons to illustrate ideas about individual rights and responsibilities during the historical periods discussed in the lesson.

2. Have students monitor the newspapers or their television viewing during the next several days to find examples of how other societies view the individual and individual rights.

LESSON 5: What Were the British Origins of American Constitutionalism?

Lesson Overview

This lesson describes how the basic rights of Englishmen were established and why such rights were important to the American colonists. As loyal subjects of the British Crown, the Founders enjoyed the rights to trial by jury, security in one's home from unlawful entry, and no taxation without consent. These rights were established by custom and became part of English common law. During the lesson, students learn about the early origins of English government and how the monarchy gradually consolidated its power over the institutions of government. Students learn that under the system of feudalism there emerged an emphasis on contracts between lords and vassals which included mutual rights and responsibilities. Students learn how conflicts between the king and the nobility resulted in the Magna Carta which established three basic principles: (1) the rule of law; (2) that basic rights may not be denied by government; and, (3) that government should be based on an agreement, or contract, between the ruler and the people. To reinforce the importance of the Magna Carta and the origins of constitutional government, students complete a critical thinking exercise in which they examine two articles from the Magna Carta to evaluate how the Great Charter limits the power of the monarchy.

Lesson Objectives

At the conclusion of this lesson, students should be able to

1. explain the development of individual rights in British history and the significance of the rights of Englishmen and of the Magna Carta

2. explain the basic ideas about rights and government contained in the Magna Carta

3. explain what values and interests are protected by the specific rights discussed in the Magna Carta

4. evaluate the importance of specific rights enumerated in the Magna Carta and how those rights placed limitations on the power of the king

Preparation/Teaching Materials

Student text, pp. 26–29

Teaching Procedures

A. Introducing the Lesson

Ask students to think of their earlier years as young children. In what ways might their families, their teachers, and their childhood experiences influence the way they think and behave today? (This might not be a pretty picture!) Remind students that the American colonial period lasted 150 years. Why might they think it important to examine how the English government developed and evolved?

While students read the "Purpose of Lesson" on p. 26, post the "Terms to Know" on the board. Review with the class what students should be able to do at the completion of the lesson, as explained in the "Purpose of Lesson." Review the vocabulary items listed on the board and remind students to take special note of these terms as they study the material in the lesson.

B. Reading and Discussion
How did English government begin?

Have the class read "How did English government begin?" on p. 26 of the text. From this section students should understand that the authority of the English monarch emerged from early tribal conflicts among various groups living on the island. With the arrival of Christianity, the monarch's power was seen as "anointed by God" and all the people became subject to his or her rule. Because of the large size of the territory the monarch governed, local areas were allowed generally to tend to their own affairs according to local custom.

C. Reading and Discussion
What was feudalism?

Direct attention to the timeline in the introduction to Unit One on p. 1 of the text. Help students establish a sense of the chronology for the historical events described in this lesson. Have the class read "What was feudalism?" on pp. 26–27 of the text. During the discussion students should be able to describe the Norman Invasion of 1066 and with this event the arrival of feudalism. Check that students can define the term **feudalism**, that is, a form of political organization in which a lord gave land and protection to other men in return for their personal allegiance and for military and other services. Feudalism was a system of vassalage in which the lord guaranteed protection in exchange for service and loyalty. The key point students should learn from this section is that feudal government was based on agreements, or contracts, between the lord and his vassals that included the mutual rights and responsibilities of the parties. This system introduced the ideas of government based on contracts and is likely the origin of the idea of constitutional government.

To summarize the ideas in this section, direct attention to the illustrations on pp. 26 and 27. Ask students to respond to the questions in the captions: (1) How did feudalism change power relationships between people? (2) How did feudalism change the way people were governed?

D. Reading and Discussion
What do we mean by the "rights of Englishmen"?

Have the class read "What do we mean by the 'rights of Englishmen'?" on p. 27 of the student text. During the discussion check that students understand the term **rights of Englishmen** as being fundamental rights that could not be changed and which all subjects of the monarch were believed to possess. These rights included: (1) trial by jury, (2) security in one's home from unlawful entry, and (3) no taxation without consent. These rights evolved from **custom** and ultimately were confirmed by royal charters and became part of English common law. Help students understand the term **common law**, which consists of accumulated legal opinions arising out of specific court cases which provide precedent for future judgments. The English common law became the basis for the American legal system.

E. Reading and Discussion
What is the British constitution?

Have the class read "What is the British constitution?" on pp. 27–28 of the text. During the discussion check that students understand that the British constitution is not a single document, but rather that it includes the common law, acts of Parliament, and other political customs and traditions. Three important documents in the British constitution include the **Magna Carta** (1215), the **Petition of Right** (1628) and the **English Bill of Rights** (1689). Stress the evolutionary nature of the British constitution, much of it emerging from the struggles between the royalty, the nobility, and the church. Check that students understand the meaning of the term **parliament** and can explain how the English Parliament gradually gained power as a result of the conflicts between the Crown and the nobility. The key point for students to understand is that these struggles resulted in limiting the power of the monarch in order to protect the rights of other groups.

F. Reading and Discussion
What was the Magna Carta and why is it important to us?

Have the class read "What was the Magna Carta and why is it important to us?" on p. 28 of the text. During the discussion students should understand that the Magna Carta resulted from a struggle between the king and nobles because King John attempted to rescind customary rights the feudal nobility had traditionally enjoyed. Students should be able to define **Magna Carta** as the "Great Charter" which limited the power of the king. As an early example of limited government, the Magna Carta established several important principles of constitutional government: (1) those in power must govern according to established rules of law, including **due process of law**; (2) established rights of the governed could not be violated; (3) government should be based on an agreement, or contract, between the ruler and the people to be ruled; and (4) no taxation without representation and consent.

To summarize the reading in this section, direct attention to the illustrations on pp. 28 and 29. Ask students to respond to the questions in the captions: (1) How did the Magna Carta reduce the power of the English monarch? (2) Did the Magna Carta protect the rights of all Englishmen? Why?

G. Critical Thinking Exercise
Analyzing and Evaluating Specific Rights

To complete the critical thinking exercise, "Analyzing and Evaluating Specific Rights" on p. 29, have the students work with a study partner or divide the class into small groups of five students each. During this exercise the class examines two articles from the Magna Carta to analyze what rights they protect and to evaluate what values and interests they promote. Review with the class the instructions for completing the exercise and the questions within the exercise. Allow adequate time for students to complete their responses. At the conclusion, have the students share their responses with the class.

Direct attention to the "What do *you* think?" section on p. 29. You may use these questions to conduct a general classroom discussion or assign students to respond to the questions individually, with a study partner, or in small groups. Have the students share their responses with the class.

H. Concluding the Lesson

Have students respond to the questions in the "Reviewing and Using the Lesson" section on p. 29 of the text. Student responses to these questions can provide them some measure of how well they learned the concepts in this lesson. Finally, have students return to the "Purpose of Lesson" on p. 26. Ask students to describe the extent to which they accomplished the objectives of the lesson.

Optional Activities
Reinforcement, Extended Learning, and Enrichment

1. Ask students to imagine they are reporters observing the events at Runnymede in 1215. Have them write a news account for a fictional newspaper in which they describe the scene, what is happening, who the participants are, and what is said. Interviews with leaders and bystanders may be included to get on-the-scene reactions.

2. Have students work with a study partner to create a list of the pros and cons of having a written constitution. Have them share their ideas with the class.

3. Have students monitor newspapers and television news broadcasts to find contemporary examples of the rule of law, the social contract, basic inviolable rights, and representative government. Have the students share their findings with the class.

LESSON 6: How Did Representative Government Begin in England?

Lesson Overview

This lesson continues to develop understanding about the expansion of individual rights in British history, with specific focus on the Petition of Right (1628), the Habeas Corpus Act (1678), and the English Bill of Rights (1689). Students learn how representative government developed from conflicts between the English monarchy and what was originally an advisory council known as Parliament. During the prolonged struggle between monarch and advisors, Parliament emerged as a representative institution of government because English subjects found Parliament to be an effective way to voice their grievances to the monarch and to limit or check his or her power. The monarchs found Parliament to be an efficient way to make important laws and to raise money. Students learn that the Petition of Right confirmed the principle that taxes could be collected only with the consent of Parliament and that it included a prohibition against requiring people to quarter soldiers in their homes. The Habeas Corpus Act prohibited the government from using unlawful arrest and prolonged imprisonment without trial as a weapon against English subjects. The English Bill of Rights placed the dominant power of government in Parliament, protected subjects from cruel and unusual punishments, and established the rights to petition the government and to bear arms for personal defense. During the critical thinking exercise in the lesson, students closely examine the importance of the rights of habeas corpus and trial by jury.

Lesson Objectives

At the conclusion of this lesson, students should be able to

1. explain the origins of representative government in British history

2. explain the development of individual rights in British history and the significance of the Petition of Right, the Writ of Habeas Corpus, and the English Bill of Rights

3. explain the basic ideas about rights and government contained in the above documents

4. explain what values and interests are protected by the specific rights discussed

5. evaluate, take, and defend positions on the importance of specific rights such as habeas corpus and trial by jury and on what limitations, if any, should be placed on them

Preparation/Teaching Materials

Student text, pp. 30–34

Teaching Procedures

A. Introducing the Lesson

While students read the "Purpose of Lesson" on p. 30, post the "Terms to Know" on the board. Review with the class what students should be able to do at the completion of the lesson, as explained in the "Purpose of Lesson." Review the vocabulary items listed on the board and remind students to take special note of these terms as they study the material in the lesson.

B. Reading and Discussion

How did parliamentary government in England begin?

Have the class read "How did parliamentary government in England begin?" on pp. 30–31 of the student text. During the discussion, remind students that Parliament began during the feudal period as an advisory council to the monarch. Gradually, membership and the role of Parliament expanded to represent the interests of different parts of the realm. Students should understand that Parliament is divided into two houses, **House of Lords** and **House of Commons**, each representing the interests of different classes in English society. Students should also understand that English subjects as well as monarchs found the institution of Parliament to be beneficial: (1) English subjects found that in Parliament they could both voice their grievances and limit the authority of the monarch, and (2) the monarch found Parliament an effective way to enact laws and raise revenue.

Direct attention to the illustration on p. 30. Ask students to respond to the question in the caption: How did the English Parliament come to represent the interests of more people?

C. Reading and Discussion

How did the struggles between the English kings and their subjects develop the British constitution?

Have the class read "How did the struggles between the English kings and their subjects develop the British constitution?" on p. 31 of the text. During the discussion, help students understand that the struggles between the monarch and Parliament centered on a key issue: whether the monarch could exercise power independently of established law and of parliamentary consent, or whether the monarch must govern through Parliament and accept the supremacy of Parliament to make laws. Resolution of this issue ultimately required several confrontations between king and Parliament, beginning with Runnymede and including a civil war and the Glorious Revolution.

D. Reading and Discussion

What was the Petition of Right?

Have the class read "What was the Petition of Right?" on p. 31 of the text. During the discussion stress that the Petition of Right was the culmination of a confrontation between King Charles I and Parliament over money. Charles sent a naval expedition in support of the French Protestants, or Huguenots, against their Catholic ruler. Additionally, Charles wanted to launch an expansion of English colonies in North America and in the Far East. When Charles refused to accept Parliament's conditions for approving the finances, he tried to collect the money directly from his subjects. Those who refused to pay were imprisoned or drafted for the army. Because Charles was short of funds to build barracks for the new draftees, he demanded that they be quartered in civilian homes. To enforce his demands, Charles declared martial law. The response of Parliament was to draw up the Petition of Right to force Charles to recognize the illegality of his acts. Students should understand that the Petition of Right confirmed the principle that taxes could only be raised with the consent of Parliament and it guaranteed other rights such as a prohibition against requiring people to quarter soldiers in their homes.

Direct attention to the illustration on p. 31. Ask students to respond to the question in the caption: How did the Petition of Right of 1628 strengthen the principle of constitutional government?

E. Reading and Discussion

What was the connection between the Petition of Right and the Magna Carta?

Have the class read "What was the connection between the Petition of Right and the Magna Carta?" Students should understand that like the Magna Carta, the Petition of Right was a confirmation of the fundamental rights belonging to all Englishmen.

F. Reading and Discussion

Why is habeas corpus such an important right?

Have the class read "Why is habeas corpus such an important right?" on pp. 31–32 of the text. During the discussion check that students understand the definition of the term **habeas corpus**. Direct attention to the illustration on p. 32. Discuss with the class, "Why is the right to a writ of habeas corpus so important in protecting the rights of a person accused of crimes?"

G. Critical Thinking Exercise

Evaluating the Importance of the Rights to Habeas Corpus and Trial by Jury

To complete the critical thinking exercise, "Evaluating the Importance of the Rights to Habeas Corpus and Trial by Jury" on pp. 31–32 of the text, divide the class into two groups. Assign one group to read section A, Habeas Corpus, and the other group to read section B, Trial by Jury. Each group should develop responses to the questions following their assigned reading selection. To increase interaction and the opportunity to participate in this exercise, you may want to further subdivide each of the two larger groups into groups of five students each. Review with the class the instructions for completing the exercise and the questions in each reading section. Allow adequate time for the groups to complete their work. At the conclusion, have the students share their responses with the class.

H. Reading and Discussion

What led to the English Bill of Rights of 1689?

Have the class read "What led to the English Bill of Rights of 1689?" on p. 33 of the text. During the discussion you may want to give students additional background information on key events of the **Glorious Revolution**. If so, you may want to share some of the following with the class.

James II was determined to make England a Catholic nation by appointing Catholics to high offices in violation of the Test Act. James claimed the right to set aside the law in certain cases and quickly appointed Catholics to head the Irish government, to command the navy, and to serve as justices of the peace and mayors. When certain Anglican bishops protested, James had them arrested and tried for seditious libel. Then James called for a close alliance with Louis XIV of France, a predominantly Catholic nation. In 1688 a son was born to James and his second wife, an Italian Catholic. The newborn child became first in line to inherit the throne, ahead of his adult Protestant half-sister Mary. Members of Parliament now worried that England was likely to have a succession of Catholic rulers. Thus, negotiations began with William of Orange from Holland to secure the succession of his wife Mary, James' daughter, to the English throne. When William and his Dutch force reached English shores, James II fled to France. Parliament declared the throne vacant and agreed that William and Mary should be joint sovereigns. Before bestowing the crown upon the new monarchs, however, William and Mary had to agree to accept a **Declaration of Rights** which Parliament enacted into law as the Bill of Rights of 1689.

I. Reading and Discussion

What protections did the English Bill of Rights include?

Have the class read "What protections did the English Bill of Rights include?" on p. 35 of the text. During the discussion stress that the English Bill of Rights accomplished three important objectives: (1) it placed limits on the power of the king; (2) it established Parliament as the dominant power of government; and (3) it protected the Church of England against a counter revolution by James II or his descendants. The English Bill of Rights also provided for such traditional rights of Englishmen as trial by jury, prohibition against cruel and unusual punishments, the right to petition the government, and the right to bear arms for personal defense. Students should note that the English Bill of Rights did not establish freedom of religion nor freedom of speech and press outside of Parliament. Students should be able to explain that the **Act of Toleration** protected freedom of worship for Protestant dissenters, and that Roman Catholics were generally left alone to practice their faith. The government later repealed the law that permitted censorship of printed materials.

J. Reading and Discussion

How does the English Bill of Rights differ from the U.S. Bill of Rights?

Have the class read "How does the English Bill of Rights differ from the U.S. Bill of Rights?" During the discussion students should note several specific differences between the two documents. (1) The English Bill of Rights was enacted into law by the Parliament, and could be changed by Parliament. The U.S. Bill of rights was ratified by the people and could be changed only with their consent. (2) The English Bill of Rights was intended to limit the power of the king and increase the power of Parliament. The U.S. Bill of Rights was

intended to prohibit the federal government from violating individual rights of all people and to protect the rights of minorities.

During the discussion it is also important to note that the English Bill of Rights reaffirmed several important constitutional principles which influenced the Founders: (1) **rule of law**; (2) **parliamentary supremacy**; and (3) **government by contract and consent**.

Direct attention to the "What do *you* think?" section on pp. 33–34. Have students work individually, with a study partner, or in small groups to develop responses to the questions in this section. At the conclusion have the students share their responses with the class.

K. Reading and Discussion

Why did Montesquieu admire the British constitution?

Have the class read "Why did Montesquieu admire the British constitution?" on p. 34 of the text. Remind students what they learned earlier about Montesquieu's ideas about "mixed government." During the discussion ask students to cite specific examples of mixed government in the British constitution.

L. Concluding the Lesson

To summarize the ideas in this lesson, direct attention to the illustration on p. 34. Ask students to respond to the question in the caption: How did the Glorious Revolution of 1688 and the resulting English Bill of Rights change the balance of power between the king and Parliament? Have students create a cartoon illustrating the importance of one of the rights they learned about in this lesson.

Have students respond to the questions in the "Reviewing and Using the Lesson" section on p. 34 of the text. Student responses to these questions can provide them some measure of how well they learned the concepts in this lesson. Finally, have students return to the "Purpose of Lesson" on p. 30. Ask students to describe the extent to which they accomplished the objectives of the lesson.

Optional Activities

Reinforcement, Extended Learning, and Enrichment

1. Have students begin collecting information from newspapers, magazines, law journals, and Supreme Court reports about contemporary issues concerning habeas corpus and trial by jury. They should plan to present their finding to the class when procedural due process is examined in Unit Four.

LESSON 7: What Basic Ideas about Rights and Constitutional Government Did Colonial Americans Have?

Lesson Overview

This lesson examines the social, economic, and political differences between colonial America and Europe and how those differences shaped the Founders' beliefs about rights. The colonists enjoyed greater economic, social, and political opportunities (cheap land, greater demand for labor, greater equality of opportunity, free elections, and the rights to trial by jury and to petition) than did people in Europe. These advantages led the colonists to believe in the importance of protecting their rights, especially property rights. The American colonies became a fertile ground for constitution-making and many experiments with limiting the power of government. During the lesson students learn that colonial constitutions incorporated the basic principles of limited government developed in England, such as (1) fundamental rights, (2) rule of law, (3) separation of power, (4) checks and balances, (5) representative government, and (6) the right to vote. The content of the lesson should help students to recognize that constitution-building is an evolutionary process based on experience as well as on philosophical concepts. The two critical thinking exercises in the lesson engage students in evaluating an original document from the colonial era and in evaluating the political status of enslaved African-Americans by using the natural rights philosophy.

Lesson Objectives

As the conclusion of this lesson, students should be able to

1. explain how the social, economic, and political differences between colonial America and Europe affected the Founders' beliefs about rights

2. explain the early development of America's own traditions of constitutional government

3. explain why the American colonists attached special importance to such constitutional principles as written guarantees of basic rights and representative government

4. evaluate, take, and defend positions on the Founders' views about property rights

Preparation/Teaching Materials

Student text pp. 35–41

Teaching Procedures

A. Introducing the Lesson

Ask students to what extent they think the American colonists were influenced by constitutional developments in Britain. Might the relative isolation of the colonies from Britain have influenced the way in which colonial Americans thought about government and rights?

While students read the "Purpose of Lesson" on p. 35 of the text, post the "Terms to Know" on the board. Review with the class what students should be able to do at the completion of the lesson, as explained in the "Purpose of Lesson." Review the vocabulary items listed on the board and remind students to take special note of these terms as they study the material in the lesson.

B. Reading and Discussion

How did the colonial settlement of America inspire new experiments in constitutional government?

Have the class read "How did the colonial settlement of America inspire new experiments in constitutional government?" on p. 35 of the student text. During the discussion help students to recognize that the colonial experience lasted more than 150 years. Settlers of the English colonies brought with them customs, laws, and ideas about government. The distance between the colonies and England, however, forced the settlers to improvise, adapt old ideas, and develop new ones if they were to survive. Direct attention to the illustration on p. 35. Ask students to respond to the question in the caption: How does the Mayflower Compact reflect the principle of government by consent or social contract?

C. Reading and Discussion

What was unique about the American experience?

Have the class read "What was unique about the American Experience?" on pp. 35–36 of the text. During the discussion ask students to describe how the abundance of cheap, undeveloped land affected social, economic, and political life in colonial America. Stress that the availability of land created a labor shortage and, as a result, greater opportunities for people to advance their economic condition. Such opportunities increased the possibility that any ambitious white male might acquire 50 acres of land, the basic qualification to obtain the right to vote in most colonies. Property, therefore, became the basis for economic and political power, rather than noble title or class privilege. Equality of opportunity and the chance to better one's position in life became fundamental ideals in the American experience.

D. Critical Thinking Exercise

Examining an Original Document about Colonial Life

Have students work with a study partner or in small groups of five to complete the critical thinking exercise, "Examining an Original Document about Colonial Life," on pp. 36–37 of the text. The questions in the exercise are based on a brief narrative by a colonial farmer, Philip Taylor, describing life in an American colony. Read the instructions for completing the exercise and review the questions that follow. Allow adequate time for students to complete their work. At the conclusion, have the students share their responses with the class. To summarize the exercise, direct attention to the illustration on p. 36. Ask students to respond to the question in the caption: How did life in the American colonies break down the social and economic barriers so common in Europe?

E. Reading and Discussion

What basic ideas of constitutional government did the colonial governments use?

Have the class read "What basic ideas of constitutional government did the colonial governments use?" on pp. 37–38 of the text. During the discussion help students understand that the colonies were founded on the basis of charters or grants from the English government to private groups or individuals. These charters or grants said little about what form of government the colonies should have. As a result, the colonist had to create their own local governments. Students should be able to cite the **Fundamental Orders of Connecticut** (1735) as the first colonial constitution. While varying from colony to colony, colonial constitutions shared some common characteristics: (1) they were written documents; (2) they followed certain basic constitutional principles developed in England, including (a) **fundamental rights**, (b) **rule of law**, (c) **separation of powers**, (d) **checks and balances**, and (e) **representative government and the right to vote**. You may want to post these five principles on the board before students read the material so they can be prepared during class discussion to describe how colonial governments incorporated these principles in their constitutions.

Direct attention to the illustrations on pp. 37 and 38. Ask students to respond to the questions in the captions: (1) Why is it important to protect the right to dissent? (2) How did early colonial governments reflect the ideas of English constitutionalism?

F. Reading and Discussion

Why did colonial governments become more representative than Britain's?

Have the class read "Why did colonial governments become more representative than Britain's?" on p. 39 of the text. During the discussion students should be able to explain that people in England and in the American colonies believed that the security of life and liberty depended on the security of property. Thus, there was a property requirement for the enjoyment of political rights like voting. If one of the purposes of government was to protect property, it seemed reasonable to limit **suffrage** to those who possessed at least a small amount of property. Students should be able to cite the following reasons colonial governments were more representative than Britain's: (1) since land was more easily acquired in America, the body of eligible voters was proportionally larger; (2) elections for colonial legislatures occurred with more frequency; (3) voters were offered a choice of candidates; and (4) legislators came from the district they represented and were considered agents of their constituents' interests; whereas in England, legislators represented the interests of the nation.

Direct attention to the illustration on p. 39. Ask students to respond to the question in the caption: Why did more people in America enjoy the right to vote than in England?

G. Reading and Discussion

What basic rights did most Americans enjoy?

Have the class read "What basic rights did most Americans enjoy?" on pp. 39–40 of the text. During the discussion stress that all Englishmen, wherever they went, enjoyed certain fundamental rights as the class learned in Lesson 5. The first colonial charter of rights was the **Massachusetts Body of Liberties** (1641) which secured the rule of law and protected basic rights against any abuse by the colony's magistrates. Students should be able to cite that the Body of Liberties included the following protections: (1) no man could be arrested, held, banished, or punished in the absence of an express law to that effect; (2) trial by jury; (3) free elections; (4) right to own property; (5) just compensation; (6) prohibition of forced self-incrimination; (7) prohibition by cruel and unusual punishment; and (8) nonvoters possessed the right to petition. Similar guarantees were passed in other colonies, including freedom of conscience. Students should also be able to recognize that most of these rights were later incorporated in the U.S. Bill of Rights.

Direct attention to the illustration on p. 39. Ask students to respond to the question in the caption: Why did the American colonists believe they enjoyed the same rights they had in England?

Direct attention to the "What do *you* think?" section on p. 40. You may want to use these questions to conduct a general class discussion, or you may want to have students work individually, with a study partner, or in small groups to develop their responses. If you elect the latter options, have students share their ideas with the class.

H. Reading and Discussion
Did all Americans enjoy these rights?

Have the class read "Did all Americans enjoy these rights?" on p. 40 of the text. Students should learn that some colonies restricted the right to vote and hold office to Protestant males. Laws limited the right of women to own property and manage their own legal and personal affairs. Ask students to explain why women were denied political rights. Students should be able to explain that under English law, husband and wife were one person. Students should also understand that the colonies recognized two categories of servitude, **indentured servants** and slaves. Enslaved people were treated as property and thus denied basic human rights.

Direct attention to the diagram on p. 41. Ask students to respond to the question in the caption: How does this diagram of a typical slave transport vessel show the inhumanity of the slave trade?

I. Critical Thinking Exercise
Evaluating the Institution of Slavery by Using the Natural Rights Philosophy

To complete the critical thinking exercise, "Evaluating the Institution of Slavery by Using the Natural Rights Philosophy" on pp. 40–41, divide the class into groups of five students each. The brief introduction explains that some free citizens, as well as slaves themselves, were opposed to slavery. The questions in the exercise engage students in applying the ideas of the natural rights philosophy to develop arguments both opposing and justifying slavery in the colonies. Review the questions in the exercise with the class. Allow adequate time for

students to formulate their responses. At the conclusion, have students share their ideas with the class. During the discussion focus on question #3: Is slavery compatible with the natural rights philosophy? You may want to extend the discussion to include evaluating the status of women in colonial America according to the ideas of natural rights.

J. Reading and Discussion
How did the colonial experience prepare Americans for independence?

Have the class read "How did the colonial experience prepare Americans for independence?" on p. 41 of the text. The key idea students should be able to express is that, during the colonial era, Americans adapted the governmental institutions and constitutional principles inherited from England to meet their own special needs. Ask students to summarize the important constitutional principles the colonists used to create their own constitutions.

Direct attention to the "What do *you* think?" section on p. 41. You may want to use these questions to conduct a general class discussion or have the students work individually, with a study partner, or in small groups to develop responses. If students work individually or in small groups, have them share their responses with the class.

K. Concluding the Lesson

To conclude the lesson, have students respond to the questions in the "Reviewing and Using the Lesson" section on p. 41 of the text. Student responses to these questions can provide them some measure of how well they learned the concepts in this lesson. Finally, have students return to the "Purpose of Lesson" on p. 35. Ask students to describe the extent to which they accomplished the objectives of the lesson.

Optional Activities
Reinforcement, Extended Learning, and Enrichment

1. Have students study the governmental structure of the Spanish and French colonies in America. Their reports should stress the differences in organization between these colonies and British colonies.

2. Have students write a petition for full property and political rights for colonial women based on the natural rights philosophy.

LESSON 8: Why Did the American Colonists Want to Free Themselves from Britain? What Basic Ideas about Government Did The Founders Put in the Declaration of Independence?

Lesson Overview

This lesson surveys the events that led to the American Revolution. Britain's efforts to tighten control over the colonies following the French and Indian War led Parliament to adopt policies which the colonists felt threatened cherished principles of constitutional government. Students learn the colonists' concerns about the "corruption" of British government which enabled the king and his ministers to gain so much power they (1) ignored the limitations placed upon them by the British constitution, (2) violated the rights of the people, and (3) favored their own interests at the expense of the common good. Students learn how the colonists resisted British policies and why they finally decided to declare themselves independent of English authority. During the lesson students examine excerpts from the Declaration of Independence in order to identify the basic ideas about constitutional government it contains, including natural law, social contract, consent as the foundation of political authority, and the right to change or abolish government. The critical thinking exercise involves students in evaluating the colonists' experiences to determine whether the actions of the British government violated any of the basic principles studied in earlier lessons.

Lesson Objectives

At the conclusion of this lesson, students should be able to

1. describe British policies toward the colonies which the American colonists believed violated some of the basic principles of constitutional government

2. explain the reasons why Americans resisted particular British policies

3. explain how the Declaration of Independence embodies the concepts of the natural rights philosophy, republicanism, and constitutional government

4. describe the arguments that are found in the Declaration of Independence justifying the separation of the colonies from Great Britain

Preparation/Teaching Materials

Student text, pp. 42–46

Teaching Procedures

A. Introducing the Lesson

Ask the class to recall (from the students' earlier studies in American history) why the American colonists were dissatisfied with British rule and how they expressed their displeasure.

While students read the "Purpose of Lesson" on p. 42 of the text, post the "Terms to Know" on the board. Review with the class what students should be able to do at the completion of the lesson, as explained in the "Purpose of Lesson." Review the vocabulary items listed on the board and remind students to take special note of these terms as they study the material in the lesson.

B. Reading and Discussion

What was Britain's new policy toward the colonies?

Have the class read "What was Britain's new policy toward the colonies?" on page 42 of the text. During the

discussion students should understand that following the French and Indian War Britain tried to increase control of the colonies and to raise revenue. Students should be able to explain the purpose of the **Stamp Act** of 1765 and to explain that, in the colonists' view, the law was flawed because it lacked the consent of the governed. Direct attention to the illustration on p. 42. Ask students to respond to the question in the caption: Why were the colonists angered by the Stamp Act of 1765?

C. Reading and Discussion

Why did the colonists resist British control?

Have the class read "Why did the colonists resist British control?" on p. 42 of the text. During the discussion students should understand that Britain's policy changes toward the colonies meant some would lose money and that the new regulations challenged their belief in representative government. Check that students understand the following terms: **Quartering Act** of 1765, **Writs of Assistance**, **Boston Massacre**, **Tea Act** of 1773, and **Intolerable Acts**. The key issue students should understand is that these measures attacked representative government, gave more power to colonial governors, limited town meetings, weakened the court system, and authorized occupation by British troops. Also check that students understand the terms **Sons of Liberty**, **Stamp Act Congress**, and **Boston Tea Party**. Students should understand that these were ways by which the colonists resisted increased control by the British government. Each time Parliament tried to regain some sort of control over the colonies, the Americans resisted. They complained that the British were plotting to destroy their constitutional liberties. As the conflict grew, the British government began to limit further the rights of the colonists. The British began to restrict the Americans' right to express their opposition. When the colonists disobeyed laws they thought unfair, they found themselves denied the legal protection traditionally enjoyed by Englishmen.

Direct attention to the illustration on p. 43. Ask students to respond to the question in the caption: What basic rights are violated when the government orders private citizens to "quarter" soldiers?

Optional instructional activity. Post the following topics on the board: (1) Taxation without representation, (2) Parliament tightens controls over the colonies, and (3) Colonists resist British controls.

Divide the class into two sections. One section should role-play newspaper editors in Britain during the colonial period who are concerned about the topics listed on the board. The other section will role-play their counterparts in the American colonies. Instruct the class on the function of opinion and editorial pages in newspapers. Stress the point that the purpose of letters to the editors, cartoons, and editorials is to advance a point of view and to convince readers to support that position.

Further subdivide each of the two sections into three groups and assign one of the three topics listed on the board. Each group may write a letter to the editor, an editorial, or draw a cartoon illustrating the group's position on the issue assigned. Allow adequate time for students to complete their work. Then have the groups share their ideas with the class.

D. Critical Thinking Exercise
Identifying Violations of Rights

Have students work with a study partner or in small groups of five students each to complete the critical thinking exercise, "Identifying Violations of Rights," on pp. 43–44 of the text. The exercise contains a number of historical situations experienced by colonial Americans that violated basic rights. Students examine each situation to determine what right(s) is being claimed.

Read the instructions for completing the exercise with the class. Allow adequate time for students to complete the work. Then ask the students to share their responses with the class. As the various rights are noted during the discussion, post them on the board. The list will most likely include the following: (1) freedom of expression, (2) freedom from cruel and unusual punishment, (3) freedom from having troops quartered in one's home, (4) freedom from unreasonable searches and seizures, and (5) due process of law. You may want to have students examine the Bill of Rights in the Reference Section of the student text and note which constitutional amendments were later written to prohibit the federal government from violating these rights. To conclude the discussion, direct attention to the illustration on p. 44. Discuss the question, "Should publishers be prohibited from printing criticisms of government leaders? Why?"

E. Reading and Discussion
How did the colonists organize to resist British control?

Have the class read "How did the colonists organize to resist British control?" on p. 44 of the text. During the discussion check that students understand the terms **Committees of Correspondence**, **First Continental Congress**, and **Minutemen**. The key issue students should understand is that colonial opposition to British policies became organized throughout the colonies.

Optional instructional activity. Before having students read this section, you may want to engage the class in a town meeting to make decisions about how to respond to the abuses of rights by the British government. The class should consider the proposal that the colonies organize and coordinate their resistance to British policies. Divide the class into the following groups: (1) a chairperson, (2) elected official of the community, (3) representative groups favoring the proposal, (4) representative groups opposed to the proposal, and (5) community members at large. Allow adequate time for students to prepare their positions. For detailed instructions on conducting a town meeting, please see p. 21 of this guide.

F. Reading and Discussion
What was the purpose of the Declaration of Independence?

Have the class read "What was the purpose of the Declaration of Independence?" on pp. 44–45 of the text. During the discussion check that students understand the meaning of the term **sovereignty**, that is, authority beyond which there is no appeal, the supreme authority in a state. Sovereignty in Britain rests in the British Parliament. Students should understand that the

American Revolution was a rebellion against the sovereignty of the British government. The purpose of the Declaration of Independence was to justify this action to other nations and to win sympathy and support.

G. Reading and Discussion

What were the main ideas and arguments of the Declaration?

Before assigning this reading, you may want to have students examine the full text of the Declaration of Independence in the Reference Section of the student text. Have the class read "What were the main ideas and arguments of the Declaration?" on pp. 45–46 of the text. During the discussion students should be able to describe the most important ideas and arguments it contains (natural law, higher law, social contract, consent, natural rights, limited government, representative government, right to alter or abolish government).

Direction attention to the illustrations on pp. 44 and 45. Ask students to respond to the questions in the captions: (1) What ideas were used to justify the Revolutionary War? (2) Why did colonial leaders believe a formal declaration of independence was needed?

H. Reading and Discussion

What impact did the experience of the American Revolution have on American constitutionalism?

Have the class read "What impact did the experience of the American Revolution have on American Constitutionalism?" on p. 46 of the text. Students should understand that the experience of revolution made Americans distrustful of strong central government and a strong executive, and it had an effect on how Americans shaped their state and national governments in the years immediately following independence.

I. Concluding the Lesson

To conclude the lesson, have students respond to the review questions in the "Reviewing and Using the Lesson" section of the text. Finally, have students return to the "Purpose of Lesson" on p. 42. Ask students to describe the extent to which they accomplished the objective of the lesson.

Optional Activities

Reinforcement, Extended Learning, and Enrichment

1. Have students research the "pamphlet war" between opponents and supporters of British policies in the colonies and report their findings to the class.

2. Have students research the Stamp Act crisis and report to the class on the principles behind the Americans' objections to that Act.

3. Have the class present a panel discussion in which several of the Founders who signed the Declaration of Independence are represented. Panelists should be asked to explain why they felt they owed an explanation of their actions to world opinion. Why did they feel they had to write a declaration at all?

4. Have students do research on the influence of the Declaration of Independence on colonial people in the 20th century.

5. In 1948 the United Nations General Assembly adopted a Universal Declaration of Human Rights. A copy may be found in the Reference Section of the student text. Have students compare the Universal Declaration of Human Rights with the Declaration of Independence. Do the documents reflect the same basic ideas? What are the similarities and differences in the two documents?

LESSON 9: What Basic Ideas about Government Did the State Constitutions Include? How Did the New States Protect Rights?

Lesson Overview

In terms of the natural rights philosophy, the American Revolution returned the colonists to a state of nature. Colonial governments under British authority ceased to exist. New governments would have to be created, a task the newly independent states initiated soon after the war commenced. This lesson examines the main features of the written constitutions the thirteen new states created using the basic ideas of the natural rights philosophy, republicanism, and constitutional government. Students learn how these ideas were incorporated into the state constitutions and how these constitutions concentrated power in the legislative branch of government. This imbalance of power was thought by some to be largely responsible for the multiple problems that later arose in the new states. During the critical thinking exercise in the lesson, students evaluate the advantages and disadvantages of legislative supremacy. Students also examine the Massachusetts constitution, which sought to establish a more balanced government based on three equal branches. This structure of state government incorporated the idea that representation, separation of powers, and checks and balances were essential for the protection of the rights of the people.

The lesson also examines the declarations of rights which most new state constitutions contained. Students learn that none of the state constitutions relied entirely on the form of their governments to protect individual liberties. Rather, by beginning their constitutions with a declaration of rights, the Founders recognized that citizens possess certain basic rights which exist prior to government and which no government can take away. Students examine in some detail the first of these declarations, the Virginia Declaration of Rights, which served as a model for other states. Students also learn that these state declarations of rights included most of the protections later found in the U.S. Bill of Rights.

Lesson Objectives

At the conclusion of this lesson, students should be able to

1. explain the basic ideas of natural rights, republicanism, and constitutional government contained in the early state constitutions

2. explain the differences between the Massachusetts constitution and the constitutions of the other states in terms of some of the basic ideas about government they have been studying

3. explain the purpose of the state declarations of rights

4. describe the main components of the Virginia Declaration of Rights

5. evaluate, take, and defend positions on legislative supremacy

Preparation/Teaching Materials

Student text, pp. 47–52

Teaching Procedures

A. Introducing the Lesson

Ask students to imagine that they are writing a constitution for your state. What principles of government would they want to emphasize? What rights would they want to protect?

While students read the "Purpose of Lesson" on p. 47 of the text, post the "Terms to Know" on the board. Review with the class what students should be able to do at the completion of the lesson, as explained in the "Purpose of Lesson." Review the vocabulary items listed on the board and remind students to take special note of these terms as they study the material in the lesson.

B. Reading and Discussion

Why were the colonies returned to a "state of nature"?

Before students read this section, direct attention to the illustration on p. 47. Ask them to respond to the question in the caption: Did the Revolution return the colonies to a state of nature? Why? Have the class read "Why were the colonies returned to a 'state of nature'?" on p. 47 of the student text. During the discussion, students should understand that the American Revolution established the need to formulate new governments in the newly independent states. Students also should understand that the Founders' understanding of history and philosophy and their experiences under British rule greatly influenced the constitutions they wrote and the structures of government they created.

C. Reading and Discussion
What six basic ideas did the state constitutions include?

Have the class read "What six basic ideas did the state constitutions include?" on pp. 47–48 of the text. Post the six basic ideas of the state constitutions on the board: (1) **Higher law** and **natural rights**, (2) **Social contract**, (3) **Popular sovereignty** (4) **Representation** and **the right to vote**, (5) **Legislative supremacy**, and (6) **Checks and balances**. During the discussion, ask students to identify how each idea was embodied in the state constitutions. Ask students to identify which of these ideas illustrate how the Founders incorporated the natural rights philosophy, republicanism, and constitutional government in the state constitutions. In what way does the inclusion of these ideas in the state constitutions reflect what the Founders' learned from history and from their experiences under British government?

D. Critical Thinking Exercise
Evaluating Legislative Supremacy

To complete the critical thinking exercise, "Evaluating Legislative Supremacy" on p. 49, divide the class into small groups of five students each. During this exercise students evaluate the advantages and disadvantages of legislative supremacy which most state constitutions adopted. Review with the class the instructions for completing the exercise and the questions included in this section. Allow adequate time for the groups to complete their work. At the conclusion, have the groups share their ideas with the class.

E. Reading and Discussion
How was the Massachusetts constitution different?

Have the class read "How was the Massachusetts constitution different?" on pp. 49–50 of the text. During the discussion check that students understand the essential differences between the way the Massachusetts

constitution was designed to prevent the abuse of governmental power and the means used in the other state constitutions. Students should be able to explain that (1) the Massachusetts constitution emphasized to a greater degree the ideas of **separation of powers** by including a stronger, more independent executive branch elected by the people rather than using the legislative supremacy model followed by other states; (2) it used a system of **checks and balances**, including both appointive and veto powers to limit the authority of the legislative and executive branches; and (3) it provided for **representation of different groups in society**, following a model of mixed government in which different groups in society were represented according to their wealth to prevent any one group from dominating the others.

Direct attention to the illustration on p. 49. Ask students to respond to the question in the caption: How did the Massachusetts constitution differ from those of other states? Why did the Massachusetts constitution provide for a strong executive branch?

Direct attention to the "What do *you* think?" questions at the end of the reading selection on p. 50. You may want to use these questions to conduct a general class discussion, or you may want to have students work individually, with a study partner, or in small groups to develop their responses. If you elect the latter option, have students share their ideas with the class.

Optional instructional activity. This optional activity is a class debate about the best way to prevent the abuse of governmental power—legislative supremacy or the model used by the state of Massachusetts. Divide the class into groups of five students each. Assign half of the groups the task of developing arguments in favor of legislative supremacy; assign the other half arguments in favor of the form of government created by Massachusetts. Debate the issue "Legislative supremacy is the best protection of natural rights" by having the groups present their arguments. Begin with a group assigned the affirmative side; follow by one assigned the negative side; alternating thereafter. For more detailed instructions on conducting a class debate, please see p. 22 of this guide. Allow several minutes for each group presentation. Then lead a class discussion about which arguments the class felt were most convincing and why.

F. Reading and Discussion
What were the state declaration of rights?

Have the class read "What were the state declaration of rights?" on p. 50 of the text. Students should recognize that most of the state constitutions began with a **declaration of rights**, listing certain basic rights that existed prior to government and that no constitution or government could take away. Placing these declarations at the beginning of a constitution represented the belief that only after protecting the basic rights of the people was it proper to form state governments.

G. Reading and Discussion

What important ideas are in the Virginia Declaration of Rights?

Have the class read "What important ideas are in the Virginia Declaration of Rights?" on pp. 50–51 of the text. Students should be able to identify the **Virginia Declaration of Rights** as the first state declaration of rights and the forerunner of the U.S. Bill of Rights. The Virginia declaration incorporates the basic ideas of the natural rights philosophy and classical republicanism. It includes the right to trial by jury, protection against forced self-incrimination and cruel and unusual punishment, freedom of the press, and free exercise of religious beliefs. Ask the students to identify some of the rights not included in the Virginia declaration, such as freedom of speech, petition, right to counsel, and protection from illegal searches and seizures.

Direct attention to the illustration on p. 51. Ask students to respond to the question in the caption: What philosophical ideas and experiences influenced the Virginia Declaration of Rights?

H. Critical Thinking Exercise

Examining Historical Documents

Have students work with a study partner to complete the critical thinking exercise, "Examining Historical Documents," on p. 51 of the text. During the exercise students examine the Virginia Declaration of Rights to find specific examples of the natural rights philosophy and classical republicanism. A copy of the Virginia Declaration of Rights may be found on pp. 221–22 in the Reference Section of the student book. Review the questions in the exercise with the class. Allow adequate time for students to complete their work. At the conclusion, have students share their responses with the class.

I. Reading and Discussion

What rights were protected by the other states?

Have the class read "What rights were protected by the other states?" on pp. 51–52 of the text. During the discussion students should recognize that while most state declarations of rights resembled that of Virginia, there was some diversity in the rights different states chose to emphasize. Students should note that some states included **political guarantees**, such as the right to vote and the right to petition the government. Some included **procedural guarantees of due process**, such as the right to counsel and protection from illegal searches and seizures. Ask students to cite other examples of political and due process guarantees offered in the state declarations.

Direct attention to the illustration on p. 52. Ask students to respond to the question in the caption: How did the state constitution balance fear of military tyranny with recognition of a need for defense?

J. Reading and Discussion

In what ways were the state declarations different from the U.S. Bill of Rights?

Have the class read "In what ways were the state declarations different from the U.S. Bill of Rights?" on p. 52 of the text. Students should recognize that the state declarations had a great influence on the later drafting and adoption of the U.S. Bill of Rights. During the discussion ask students to identify some of the differences between the declarations and the Bill of Rights. For example, the state declarations resemble the Declaration of Independence, they were written as preambles to state constitutions, they describe the purpose of government, and set forth the principles of the natural rights philosophy and classical republicanism. The U.S. Bill of Rights, on the other hand, specifically lists the rights that should be protected from the national government. It includes the establishment and free exercise of religion clauses which protect both **equality** and **freedom of religion**.

Direct attention to the "What do *you* think?" section on p. 52. You may want to use these questions to conduct a general class discussion, or you may want to have students work individually, with a study partner, or in small groups to develop their responses. If you elect the latter options, have students share their ideas with the class.

K. Concluding the Lesson

To conclude the lesson, have students respond to the review questions in "Reviewing and Using the Lesson." Finally, have students return to the "Purpose of Lesson" on p. 47. Ask students to describe the extent to which they accomplished the objectives of the lesson.

This lesson concludes the study of Unit One. If you had students develop personal objectives or a list of questions during the introduction of the unit, students should now review those objectives or questions and determine to what degree they achieved their goals. In addition, you may want to use the questionnaire, "Reflecting on Your Experience," on p. 28 of this guide to engage students in an evaluation of their participation in the lessons in this unit.

Optional Activities

Reinforcement, Extended Learning, and Enrichment

1. Have students examine the governmental structure of a country that has a parliamentary system of government. How does this kind of government compare with those of the states during the immediate post-Revolutionary period?

2. Have students prepare reports on the nations in the world which are in transition—designing new governments, writing new constitutions, or struggling with human rights issues. The report should describe the situation in each nation and the ideas about rights and government under debate.

3. Have students analyze a copy of your state bill of rights and compare it to the Virginia Declaration of Rights or to the U.S. Bill of Rights. In what ways are the documents similar? What are some of the differences? What factors might help explain the differences?

Unit Two: How Did the Framers Create the Constitution?

UNIT OVERVIEW. After declaring their independence from Great Britain, the colonists had to decide how they would govern themselves. This unit begins with a lesson describing the national government created under the Articles of Confederation, the problems Congress had financing the national government and protecting natural rights, and the reasons the Founders wanted to change the Articles. Students learn how events following the Revolutionary War convinced Congress to convene the Philadelphia Convention. In the next lesson, students learn about the people who attended the Philadelphia Convention, why the delegates decided to create a new constitution, and the rules they developed for conducting their deliberations.

In studying the Philadelphia Convention, students learn about the Virginia and New Jersey Plans and the conflicting views about how best to organize a republican government in a large and diverse nation. Students learn why the Framers favored the Virginia Plan as a framework for their deliberations.

The next lesson describes how the Framers organized the legislative branch, the issues that arose concerning representation, and how the Framers resolved those issues by creating a bicameral legislature with representation in the House based on population and equal representation in the Senate. Students learn what powers were delegated to the legislative branch and the limitations the Framers set forth on the exercise of legislative authority by national and state governments. The lesson also describes the disagreements that separated the northern and southern states and the compromises the Framers reached over the issue of slavery.

The lesson on the executive and judicial branches describes the difficulties the Framers experienced in creating these two branches of the national government. Students learn how the Framers organized the executive and judicial branches, what powers they assigned to each, and the limitations they placed on the exercise of executive authority. Students learn that while the Framers probably intended for the Supreme Court to have the power of judicial review, they did not explicitly include it in the Constitution.

The concluding lesson in the unit describes why the Framers decided to have the people of the states ratify the Constitution rather than state legislatures. Students discuss the disagreements during the ratification debates between the Anti-Federalists, the opponents of the new Constitution, and the Federalists, its proponents. Students learn that these disagreements centered on differing views of the requirements of the natural rights philosophy, republicanism, and constitutionalism. Finally, students learn that the Anti-Federalists pledged support for the new Constitution if the Federalists agreed to add a bill of rights.

UNIT OBJECTIVES. At the conclusion of this unit, students should be able to

1. describe the weaknesses in the Articles of Confederation and explain why the Founders decided to change the Articles

2. describe who attended the Philadelphia Convention and the plan the Framers used to create the Constitution

3. describe how the Framers designed the Constitution to limit the powers of the national government and protect the rights of the people, including separation of power, checks and balances, and enumerated powers

4. describe how the Framers organized the legislative, executive, and judicial branches of the national government, the powers delegated to each branch, and the limitations imposed on their exercise of authority

5. explain why the Framers wanted the new Constitution ratified by the people rather than by state legislatures

6. explain how the differences between the Federalists and Anti-Federalists were related to differing interpretations of the requirements of the natural rights philosophy, republicanism, and constitutionalism

7. evaluate, take, and defend positions on issues related to the creation of the Constitution and on the controversies between the Federalists and Anti-Federalists

INTRODUCING THE UNIT. Have the class read the "Purpose of Unit" on p. 53 of the text. Discuss the basic themes students can expect to learn about during their study of this unit and review the objectives of the unit. Ask students how they think a book about ideas, such as this text, might differ from traditional government texts. Why might they think it important to study how the Framers created the Constitution? Ask students to write four or five personal objectives they would like to accomplish during the study of this unit. You may want to ask them, instead, to write four or five basic questions they would like to explore during their study of these lessons. They should keep their personal objectives or questions in a journal or notebook for review at the conclusion of the unit. They may want to expand upon these personal objectives or questions as their study in the unit progresses.

Introduce students to the unit timeline. Each unit in this text contains a timeline illustrating key events relevant to the topics of the lessons. Students may want to create a similar timeline in their journals or notebooks to track in more detail important events or developments described in each lesson.

LESSON 10: Why Did the Founders Want to Change the Articles of Confederation of 1781?

Lesson Overview

This lesson describes the need for a national government after the colonies declared their independence from Great Britain. Students learn that the Founders feared creating too strong a national government because of their belief that government should be close to the people so they could control it and make certain it did not violate their rights. The colonists also feared that in a national government some states would have more power than others, thereby threatening states' interests. These fears prompted the Founders to develop a weak national government under the Articles of Confederation. The Articles organized the national government on the basis of a central legislature, the Confederate Congress, with limited authority and no executive or judicial branches. The Articles granted each state one vote, with nine states having to agree on important matters like declaring war. During the critical thinking exercise in the lesson, the class analyzes and evaluates the advantages and disadvantages of government under the Articles of Confederation.

The lesson also describes the major weaknesses in the government under the Articles of Confederation: (1) no money and no power to get it; (2) no power over state governments and their citizens; (3) unenforceable trade agreements; (4) unfair competition among the states; and (5) threats to citizens' right to property. Eventually, the problems under the Articles led to the movement to create a new constitution that would provide for a stronger national government. Finally, the lesson briefly describes Shays' Rebellion and the argument that state legislatures were being used by majorities, or "factions" with special interests, to deprive minorities of their rights.

Lesson Objectives

At the conclusion of this lesson, students should be able to

1. explain why Americans needed a national government after the colonies declared independence from Great Britain

2. explain why the Founders created their first constitution, the Articles of Confederation, as they did and identify the basic ideas about government involved

3. describe the problems of the United States under the Articles of Confederation and how the Founders' concerns led to a proposal to revise the Articles

4. evaluate, take, and defend positions on advantages and disadvantages of the Articles of Confederation

Preparation/Teaching Materials

Student text, pp. 54–59

Teaching Procedures

A. Introducing the Lesson

Direct attention to the map on p. 54 of the text. Ask students to respond to the question in the caption: How did independence create a need for a national government? Then ask students to anticipate some of the problems the Founders might encounter in trying to unite the states into a nation.

While students read the "Purpose of Lesson" on p. 54, post the "Terms to Know" on the board. Review with the class what students should be able to do at the completion of the lesson, as explained in the "Purpose of Lesson." Review the vocabulary items listed on the board and remind students to take special note of these terms as they study the material in the lesson.

B. Reading and Discussion

How were the Articles of Confederation created?

Have the class read "How were the Articles of Confederation created?" on pp. 54–55 of the text. During the discussion check that students understand that the newly independent states needed a national government to (1) manage trade and solve disputes among the states, (2) unite the states in diplomatic and trade relations with other nations, (3) help the states cooperate in their struggle against the powerful British army and navy, and (4) perform all the activities of government.

C. Reading and Discussion

What problems were addressed in the Articles of Confederation?

Have the class read "What problems were addressed in the Articles of Confederation" on pp. 55–56 of the text. During the discussion students should understand that once the war with Great Britain commenced, each state was like an independent nation. The Founders faced two basic problems that made it difficult for the Continental Congress and the states to accept the Articles of Confederation:

(1) **fear of a strong national government**

Americans believed that the British government had deprived people of their rights and thought this was likely to happen with any central government that was both powerful and far away. They believed that republican government could only succeed in small communities where people shared common ideas and beliefs.

(2) **fear that some states would dominate others in a national government**

In a national government, some feared that those states with greater population or wealth might dominate the other states. Others feared that because issues before the Congress would be decided by majority vote, the seven smaller states might dominate the six larger states. Thus, a majority might use its power for its own interest at the expense of those states that were in the minority.

Students should also understand that the solutions the Founders crafted to address these problems determined the structure and characteristics of the national government under the Articles of Confederation.

(1) **Solution to problem #1, fear of a strong national government**

Create a weak national government with a central legislature and no executive or judicial branches. Restrict the authority of the central legislature by giving it little power over the states and their citizens.

(2) **Solution to problem #2, some states might dominate others**

Give each state one vote in Congress, regardless of its population. On important matters, like declaring war, require nine states to agree, thus preventing the smaller states from outvoting the larger states.

During the discussion, encourage students to cite examples of specific provisions in the Articles of Confederation that kept the national government from becoming too strong.

You may want to use the illustrations on pp. 55 and 56 to summarize the discussion. Ask students to respond to the questions in the captions: (1) Why did the Founders create a weak national government? (2) What problems might result from each state issuing its own currency?

D. Critical Thinking Exercise

Examining the Advantages and Disadvantages of the Articles of Confederation

Have students work with a study partner to complete the critical thinking exercise, "Examining the Advantages and Disadvantages of the Articles of Confederation," on p. 56 of the text. During the exercise students examine several provisions in the Articles of Confederation and evaluate their advantages and disadvantages. Read the instructions for completing the exercise with the class and check for understanding of the tasks involved. Allow adequate time for students to complete their work. At the conclusion, have students share their work with the class. The chart on the next page illustrates how students might organize their work and possible advantages and disadvantages to the states and national government they might cite.

Articles of Confederation	Advantages		Disadvantages	
	to the states	to the national government	to the states	to the national government
Article II	States retained sovereignty and independence. They retained every power not expressly delegated to Congress.			Since the states retained their independence, Congress could not pass laws governing their behavior. Since the states retained sovereignty, Congress did not have any power over any person in any state.
Article V		Issues decided by majority vote.		
Article VIII	States assessed fees in proportion to the value of its land. Only the state legislatures could levy taxes to pay for the national government. Limited the spending authority of the national government to common defense and general welfare.			Depended on the states to supply money for the national government. Congress had no power to tax. State legislatures decided whether, and what amount, to pay to support the national government. Congress could spend money only for the common defense and the general welfare.
Article IX	States could seek the assistance of Congress in settling their disputes. States did not have to accept the decisions of Congress.		Judicial questions to be settled by Congress, a political body. No appeal for disputes between states and other nations or between citizens of different states.	Congress did not have the power to make states or their citizens live up to their agreements.
Article IX	States could continue to issue their own currency.		Made it difficult to conduct commerce among the states.	Congress could only regulate the value of its own currency and that of the states. It did not have the power to prevent states from issuing their own currency.
Article XIII	The Articles of Confederation could not be changed without the consent of the states.			Since every state had to agree, it would be extremely difficult to change the Articles of Confederation.

E. Reading and Discussion

What were weaknesses in the Articles of Confederation?

Have the class read "What were weaknesses in the Articles of Confederation?" on pp. 57–58 of the text. Students should understand that the national government created by the Articles of Confederation had very limited power.

(1) The national government had **no money and no power to get it**. Congress had no power to tax. All it could do was request that states pay certain amounts to support the costs of the national government. During the Revolutionary War the government borrowed the money it needed, but it had no way to pay its debts.

(2) The national government had **no power over state governments** and their citizens. Congress could not make laws governing the behavior of states or their citizens. Although Congress had the power to enter into trade agreements with foreign nations, it did not have the power to make the states or their citizens live up to these agreements. As a result, Americans were unable to buy or sell goods abroad.

(3) The national government could not prevent **unfair competition among the states**. Congress had no power to regulate trade among the states. As a result, some states taxed goods passing through to other states, preventing efficient and productive trade among the states and worsening the economy.

(4) This lack of power created **threats to citizens' right to property**. In the state legislatures **factions** were able to form majorities that violated the rights of minorities and the common good. They passed laws that canceled debts, confiscated property, and created inflationary paper money. Many complained that **majority rule**, when the majority pursued its own selfish interests, was another form of tyranny.

Direct attention to the illustration on p. 57. Ask students to respond to the question in the caption: How was Congress' ability to govern hurt by not being able to collect taxes from the states?

Direct attention to the questions in the "What do *you* think?" section on p. 58. You may want to have students respond to these questions during a general class discussion or by having students work individually, with a study partner, or in small groups. However you elect to engage the class in this activity, have students share their responses with the class.

F. Reading and Discussion

How did Shays' Rebellion sow the seeds of change?

Have the class read "How did Shays' Rebellion sow the seeds of change?" on p. 58 of the text. During the discussion students should be able to cite the cause for Shays' Rebellion and the effect this event had in convincing people of the need to strengthen the national government.

Direct attention to the illustration on p. 58. Ask students to respond to the question in the caption: Why did Shays' Rebellion force people to examine the weaknesses of the national government?

Optional instructional activity. Shays' Rebellion provides a dramatic setting for examining some basic ideas about representative democracy and constitutional government. To help students understand the conflict involved in Shays' Rebellion, you might want to conduct the following simulation. Ask students to imagine that they were taking part in a television interview of some of the major personalities who were involved in, or commented on, the rebellion. Assign the roles of TV interviewers to two or three students. Divide the rest of the class into small groups. Each group can represent a historical personality, such as Daniel Shays or one of his followers, or Abigail Adams or other citizens of Massachusetts opposed to the rebellion. Students should conduct research to determine the positions of the persons they represent. After each group prepares a position statement, conduct the simulated television interview, asking the interviewers to question the groups on their points of view. Each interviewee should be asked whether he or she favors a stronger national government, and why or why not.

G. Reading and Discussion

What were the achievements of the first national government?

Have the class read "What were the achievements of the first national government?" on p. 59 of the text. Students should understand that some important things were accomplished by the national government under the Articles of Confederation: (1) the Revolutionary War was conducted under the leadership of this government; (2) its diplomats secured recognition of American independence by European governments; and (3) Congress passed the **Northwest Ordinance** of 1787.

Direct attention to the map on p. 59. Ask students to respond to the question in the caption: How did problems that arose in the Northwest Territory demonstrate the weaknesses of the new national government?

H. Concluding the Lesson

To conclude the lesson, have students respond to the review questions in the "Reviewing and Using the Lesson" section of the text. Finally, have students return to the "Purpose of Lesson" on p. 54. Ask students to describe the extent to which they accomplished the objectives of the lesson.

Optional Activities

Reinforcement, Extended Learning, and Enrichment

1. Have students compare the government under the Articles of Confederation with one of the contemporary confederations of nations, e.g., the United Nations, the European Union, Organization of American States, or the Organization of African States.

2. Have students write an essay in which they speculate about what the United States might be like today if the Articles of Confederation had been kept as the constitution.

3. Have students research additional information on the Northwest Ordinance and the difficulties related to governing the Northwest Territory.

LESSON 11: Who Attended the Philadelphia Convention? What Did They Agree to Do?

Lesson Overview

Dissatisfied with the national government, the Founders asked Congress to call a meeting of state representatives in Philadelphia to suggest ways to change the Articles of Confederation in order to strengthen the central government. In this lesson students learn that Congress only gave the Philadelphia Convention authority to amend the Articles; however, once the delegates assembled, they decided to develop the best constitution they could. The delegates agreed that the deliberations of the Convention should be conducted in secret to protect the free exchange of ideas and to increase chances that the people would accept the new constitution. This lesson also describes the background and characteristics of some of the leading Framers of the Constitution. During the critical thinking exercise, the students take and defend positions on (1) whether the constitution should be developed by Congress and then submitted to the states for approval or (2) whether the constitution should be developed at a special national convention of delegates from the states and then submitted to the people for approval.

Lesson Objectives

At the conclusion of this lesson, students should be able to

1. describe the steps leading to the calling of the Philadelphia Convention and the initial purpose of the Convention

2. describe the characteristics of the Framers who attended the Convention

3. describe the Framers' agreements on how to conduct the business of the convention

4. evaluate, take, and defend positions on how the constitution should be developed—by Congress or by a special national convention

Preparation/Teaching Materials

Student text, pp. 60–64

Optional. Provide the class with biographical sketches and copies of paintings illustrating the delegates who attended the Philadelphia Convention.

Teaching Procedures

A. Introducing the Lesson

Introduce the lesson by asking students who they think should attend a constitutional convention if one were being held today. How might delegates to a contemporary constitutional convention differ from those who attended the Philadelphia Convention in 1787?

While students read the "Purpose of Lesson" on p. 60, post the "Terms to Know" on the board. Review with the class what students should be able to do at the completion of the lesson, as explained in the "Purpose of Lesson." Review the vocabulary items listed on the board and remind students to take special note of these terms as they study the material in the lesson.

B. Reading and Discussion

What attempts were made to solve the problems of the Articles of Confederation?

Have the class read "What attempts were made to solve the problems of the Articles of Confederation?" on p. 60

of the text. During the discussion students should understand that the idea of holding a special meeting or convention of all the states was a departure from the traditional method of having legislatures write constitutions. The first state to hold a constitutional convention was Massachusetts. James Madison and others decided that since it had been successful in Massachusetts, it would be worth trying at the national level. In 1786 a meeting was held in Annapolis, Maryland to discuss commercial problems. Disappointed by a low attendance of state representatives, Madison submitted a report to Congress requesting a special meeting in Philadelphia to suggest ways to change the Articles of Confederation to strengthen the national government. Congress authorized the Philadelphia Convention only to propose amendments to the Articles. Adopting them would have required the consent of Congress and all the states.

C. Critical Thinking Exercise

Evaluating Alternative Political Strategies

To have students complete the critical thinking exercise, "Evaluating Alternative Political Strategies" on p. 61 of the text, divide the class into two groups. During the exercise students imagine they want to develop a plan to change the Constitution. Students develop and present positions on whether such a plan should be developed by Congress or by a special national convention of delegates from the states. Assign Group 1 to develop arguments favoring position number one: the plan to change the Constitution should be developed by Congress and then submitted to state governments for approval. Assign Group 2 to develop arguments favoring position number two: the plan to change the Constitution should be developed at a special national convention of delegates from the states selected by their legislatures. Review the instructions for completing the exercise with the class. Allow adequate time for the groups to develop their positions. To maximize participation in this exercise, you may want to further subdivide the two larger groups into smaller groups of five students each.

After the groups have completed their work, ask them to present their positions to the class. Following each presentation allow time for questions from the opposing group. At the conclusion, ask the students to evaluate the arguments presented. What were the merits of the arguments presented by each group? What might be some of the problems with the arguments presented? During the discussion you may want to direct attention to Article V of the Constitution (see the Reference Section of the student text) to help students understand the procedures the Framers established for amending the Constitution.

Optional instructional activity. You may want to use this critical thinking exercise to conduct a simulated legislative debate. If so, please see p. 16 for detailed instructions on structuring a legislative debate in your classroom.

D. Reading and Discussion
Who attended the Philadelphia Convention?

Have the class read "Who attended the Philadelphia Convention?" on pp. 61–62 of the text. During the discussion students should understand that the fifty-five delegates to the convention are now often called the Framers of the Constitution. You may want to ask the students to explain some of the characteristics of the most prominent members of the convention, such as George Washington, James Madison, Alexander Hamilton, and John Jay. Students should also be able to identify *The Federalist* as a published series of 85 articles written for newspapers in New York explaining the basic principles and ideas underlying our constitutional government. For additional information on the delegates to the Philadelphia Convention, you may want to have students

reference Max Farrand's *The Framing of the Constitution of the United States*. Chapter 2 contains William Pierce's descriptions of many of his fellow delegates.

E. Reading and Discussion
What other important delegates attended?

Have the class read "What other important delegates attended?" on pp. 62–63 of the text. Students should be able to identify James Wilson, Gouverneur Morris, Edmund Randolph, George Mason, and Elbridge Gerry.

During the discussion ask students to identify those traits the Framers had in common. Then ask them why they think these people were chosen as delegates to the convention. The students may identify some of the following attributes of the Framers: (1) they were experienced in colonial, state, and national government; (2) they were accorded a high level of respect for their talents, knowledge, civic virtue, and patriotism; (3) they had great understanding of the principles of government; (4) they were reasonably affluent; and (5) they were familiar with the history of English government and the writings of political philosophers.

F. Reading and Discussion
What important Founders did not attend the convention?

Have the class read "What important Founders did not attend the convention?" on p. 63 of the text. Students should be able to identify Thomas Jefferson, John Adams, Patrick Henry, John Hancock, Samuel Adams, and Richard Henry Lee.

Direct attention to the "What do *you* think?" section on p. 63. Use these questions to conduct a general class discussion about whether the delegates to the Philadelphia Convention were representative of the American people in 1787.

G. Reading and Discussion
What happened when the convention began?

Have the class read "What happened when the convention began?" on p. 64 of the text. During the discussion students should understand that the delegates selected George Washington president of the Convention and that a committee was appointed to draw up the rules for the meeting. The delegates decided to keep the deliberations secret from the public to encourage a free exchange of ideas during the meetings. They agreed that each state should have one vote and that a member could not be absent from the convention without permission if his absence would deprive his state of its vote.

Direct attention to the illustration on p. 64. Ask students to respond to the question in the caption: Why did the delegates to the Constitutional Convention decide to keep their deliberations secret?

Direct attention to the "What do *you* think?" section on p. 64. Use the questions in this section to conduct a general class discussion about the procedural rules established by the delegates.

H. Concluding the Lesson

To conclude the lesson, have students respond to the questions in the "Reviewing and Using the Lesson" section on p. 64 of the text. Finally, have students return to the "Purpose of Lesson" on p. 60. Ask students to describe the extent to which they accomplished the objectives of the lesson.

Optional Activities
Reinforcement, Extended Learning, and Enrichment

1. Article II of the Constitution provides that only native born citizens can serve as president and vice president of the United States. Ask students: (1) to find out who was the first president of the United States who was born after the Declaration of Independence, and (2) which of the Framers about whom biographical data is given in the lesson was not even born in the colonies.

2. In recent years there have been calls for a constitutional convention. If such a convention were to be held today, what should be the make-up of its members? In small groups, have students suggest lists of characteristics for members of a contemporary constitutional convention.

3. Have students research additional information on the delegates to the Philadelphia Convention who are pictured in this lesson. Have students share their information with the class.

LESSON 12: Why Did the Framers Use the Virginia Plan to Create the Constitution?

Lesson Overview

Some of the Framers were convinced that the defects of the Articles of Confederation were so serious that it would be better not to use them as a starting point of the convention. In this lesson students learn that James Madison of Virginia arrived at Philadelphia with a draft plan for a new national government. After disagreement developed over representation, William Paterson of New Jersey led the small states in proposing their own plan.

During the lesson, students study the basic elements of two plans of government—the Virginia Plan and the New Jersey Plan—which the delegates submitted to the convention for consideration. Both plans embodied the important ideas about government the Framers understood from political philosophy and history, the British constitutional system, and their own experiences in politics. The Virginia Plan and the New Jersey Plan differed only in the application, emphasis, and relative importance placed on these ideas. During the critical thinking exercise in the lesson, students evaluate the advantages and disadvantages of both plans for a national government. Students learn why the Virginia Plan was eventually adopted as the basis for the Constitution of the United States. The lesson also includes information about the disagreements among the delegates regarding representation and the extent of power that the proposed national government should have.

Lesson Objectives

At the conclusion of this lesson, students should be able to

1. describe the basic elements of the Virginia Plan and the New Jersey Plan and the differences between them

2. relate the elements of the Virginia and New Jersey plans to the basic ideas of government they have been studying, such as natural rights, republican government, and constitutional government

3. explain the reasons for the disagreements among the delegates regarding representation

4. evaluate the advantages and disadvantages of the Virginia and New Jersey Plans for a national government

5. explain why the Virginia Plan was used as the basis for the new Constitution rather than the New Jersey Plan

Preparation/Teaching Materials

Student text, pp. 65–67

Teaching Procedures

A. Introducing the Lesson

To introduce the lesson, ask students to anticipate some of the issues over which there might be some disagreement among the delegates to the Philadelphia Convention. Might there be some issues on which they would all agree?

While students read the "Purpose of Lesson" on p. 65, post the "Terms to Know" on the board. Review with the class what students should be able to do at the completion of the lesson, as explained in the "Purpose of Lesson." Review the vocabulary items listed on the board and remind students to take special note of these terms as they study the material in the lesson.

B. Reading and Discussion
What was the Virginia Plan?

Have the class read "What was the Virginia Plan?" on p. 65 of the text. During the discussion students should understand that some of the delegates thought the defects in the Articles of Confederation so serious, that it would be better not to use them as a starting point of the convention. James Madison, before the convention began, had drafted a plan for a new national government, the **Virginia Plan**, which the delegates agreed to put forward as a basis for discussions. Students should understand the following six characteristics of the Virginia Plan. The Virginia Plan proposed:

(1) a strong national government with the power to make and enforce its own laws and to collect its own taxes;

(2) a **federal system** whereby each citizen would be governed under the authority of a national and a state government;

(3) three branches of government—legislative, executive, and judicial;

(4) a bicameral national legislature—a House of Representatives elected by the people and a Senate elected by the members of the House;

(5) a system of **proportional representation in the Congress**; and

(6) Congress would have the power to make laws that states were not able to make, strike down state laws considered to violate the national constitution or interest, call forth the armed forces against a state if necessary to enforce laws passed by Congress, and elect people to serve in the executive and judicial branches.

Direct attention to the "What do *you* think?" section on p. 66. Have students work with a study partner or in small groups of five students each to develop responses to the questions in this section. Allow adequate time for students to complete their work. At the conclusion, have students share their work with the class.

C. Reading and Discussion

How did the Framers react to the Virginia Plan?

Have the class read "How did the Framers react to the Virginia Plan?" on p. 66 of the text. Students should understand that the issue of representation in Congress created a crisis for the convention. The larger states wanted proportional representation in both houses, while the smaller states wanted equal voting power for each state. Delegates from the smaller states asked for time to develop an alternative plan.

Direct attention to the illustration on p. 66. Ask students to respond to the question in the caption: Why were delegates from small states suspicious of the Virginia Plan?

D. Reading and Discussion

What was the New Jersey Plan?

Have the class read "What was the New Jersey Plan?" on pp. 66–67 of the text. Students should understand that the plan developed by the smaller states is called the **New Jersey Plan**. The plan resembles the Articles of Confederation because the smaller states did not want to create a national government in which they had little power. Students should understand the three central characteristics of the New Jersey Plan. The New Jersey Plan proposed:

(1) a one house **legislative branch**, as in the Confederation, but with increased powers. Congress would have the power to levy import duties and a stamp tax, and the power to collect money from the states. Congress would have the power to regulate trade among the states and with other nations. The laws and treaties made by Congress would be the supreme law of the land.

(2) an **executive branch** made up of several persons appointed by Congress. The executive would have the power to administer the laws, appoint officials, and direct the military.

(3) a **judicial branch** comprised of a supreme court appointed by the executive. The court would have the power to settle disputes involving treaties, trade among the states or with other nations, and the collection of taxes.

E. Critical Thinking Exercise

Developing and Defending Positions

Have the class work in small groups of five students each to complete the critical thinking exercise "Developing and Defending Positions," on p. 67 of the text. During the exercise students analyze the benefits and costs of both the Virginia and New Jersey Plans. Read the instructions for completing the exercise with the class. Allow adequate time for students to complete their work. At the conclusion have the groups share their work with the class. During the concluding discussion ask students to select the plan they have determined to be more effective and to explain the reasoning behind their decisions.

Optional instructional activity. You may want to have the students present their analysis of the two plans to a selection committee to decide which plan best suits the purposes of the convention. If so, use the legislative hearing format described on p. 14 of this guide.

F. Reading and Discussion

Why was the Virginia Plan used?

Have the class read "Why was the Virginia Plan used?" on p. 67 of the text. Students should understand that after two weeks of debating the Virginia Plan, many delegates had become convinced that the national government needed both new powers and a new organization for exercising those powers. Adoption of the Virginia Plan did not resolve two important issues—representation in Congress and the powers the national government should have. Disagreement over these issues nearly caused the convention to fail.

G. Concluding the Lesson

To conclude the lesson, have students respond to the questions in the "Reviewing and Using the Lesson" section on p. 67 of the text. Finally, have students return to the "Purpose of Lesson" on p. 65. Ask students to describe the extent to which they accomplished the objectives of the lesson.

Optional Activities
Reinforcement, Extended Learning, and Enrichment

1. Select several students to read detailed treatments of the Philadelphia Convention and report to the class on subjects that were extensively debated at the convention.

2. Have students research the history of proportional representation in the United States.

3. Have students report to the class on anecdotal material from the convention.

LESSON 13: What Powers Were Granted to the Legislative Branch?

Lesson Overview

During this lesson students examine (1) the controversies over representation and the compromises included in Article I of the Constitution; (2) the controversies over slavery and the compromises reached to gain adoption of the Constitution; and (3) the powers which the Constitution grants the national government over the states and the people, and the powers it denies to both national and state governments. During the first critical thinking exercise students work in committees to propose and defend plans on how to structure representation in Congress. Students learn that the Great Compromise combined the ideas of both equal and proportional representation. Students learn that the Framers intended the new government to be one of enumerated powers so there would be no confusion about what government could and could not do. Students examine in some detail the powers that the Constitution places in the legislative branch of government as well as the limits the Constitution places on both state and national governments.

Students also examine another critical disagreement at the Philadelphia Convention—the conflict between the northern and southern states over the issue of slavery. During the second critical thinking exercise students work in small groups to develop positions on the issues of slavery from both a northern and southern perspective.

Lesson Objectives

At the conclusion of this lesson, students should be able to

1. explain how and why the Framers developed the present system of representation in Congress and the advantages and disadvantages of this system

2. describe how Article I of the Constitution delegates explicit powers to the Congress and limits the powers of both the national and state governments

3. describe the "three-fifths clause" and the "fugitive slave clause" and explain what issues they were intended to resolve

4. evaluate, take, and defend positions on disagreements at the Philadelphia Convention over representation and slavery

Preparation/Teaching Materials

Student text, pp. 68–73

Teaching Procedures

A. Introducing the Lesson

To introduce the lesson, ask students to imagine they are delegates to the Philadelphia Convention. How would you structure the legislative branch of government? What powers would you give to the Congress? What limits would you place on the power of the Congress?

While students read the "Purpose of Lesson" on p. 68, post the "Terms to Know" on the board. Review with the class what students should be able to do at the completion of the lesson, as explained in the "Purpose of Lesson." Review the vocabulary items listed on the board and remind students to take special note of these terms as they study the material in the lesson.

B. Reading and Discussion

How should the legislative branch be organized?

Have the class read "How should the legislative branch be organized?" on p. 68 of the text. Students should understand that the Framers believed the most important role in government would be held by the legislative

branch. Article I of the Constitution describes how Congress should be organized and sets forth the duties and powers given to Congress.

C. Reading and Discussion

What were the disagreements about representation?

Have the class read "What were the disagreements about representation?" on p. 68 of the text. The delegates accepted the Virginia Plan's proposal for a two-house legislature. The controversy was about **proportional representation**. The larger states thought representation should be based on the number of people in each state because the new government would operate directly on people. States with larger populations should have a greater voice in the national government. The smaller states feared proportional representation would result in a national government dominated by the more populous states. The smaller states supported **equal** representation. They argued that people in their states would not approve a constitution that did not preserve equality among the states. The Framers formed a special committee of one member from each state to develop a plan to resolve the controversy.

D. Critical Thinking Exercise
Developing and Defending Plans for Representation

Divide the class into groups of five students each to complete the critical thinking exercise, "Developing and Defending Plans for Representation," on p. 69 of the text. During the exercise students simulate the special committee of the convention charged with finding a solution to the disagreement over representation. Read the directions for completing the exercise and review the questions with the class. Allow adequate time for students to complete their work and then have the groups present their decisions to the class. Encourage students to ask questions about the various plans as they are being presented. After students read the next section of the text, they can compare their plans with the compromise reached by the convention.

E. Reading and Discussion
What was the Great Compromise?

Have the class read "What was the Great Compromise?" on pp. 69–70 of the text. Students should understand that the results of the special committee's work is known as the **Connecticut Compromise** or the **Great Compromise**. The Great Compromise contained the following: (1) members of the House of Representatives would be elected on the basis of proportional representation; (2) membership in the Senate would be based on equal representation and the state legislatures would each select two senators; (3) the House would be given the power to develop bills on taxing and spending. Taxation would be **apportioned** among the states on the basis of population. The Senate would only be given the power to accept or reject taxing and spending legislation. The result was that larger states would pay a greater share of the direct taxes, but they would have greater influence over laws on taxing and government spending. The compromise was passed by one vote.

Direct attention to the illustration on p. 69. Ask students to respond to the question in the caption: How did the Connecticut Compromise resolve differences in the Virginia and New Jersey Plans?

Direct attention to the "What do *you* think?" section on p. 70. Have students work with a study partner or in small groups to respond to the questions in this section. At the conclusion, have students share their work with the class.

F. Reading and Discussion
What powers did the Constitution give to Congress?

Have the class read "What powers did the Constitution give to Congress?" on p. 70 of the text. Before students read this section, you may want to have them examine Article I, Section 8 of the Constitution (see Reference Section in student text). Students should understand that the Framers created a government of **enumerated powers** so that there could be no confusion about what each branch of government could and could not do. Ask students to cite examples of the enumerated powers of Congress. Students should also understand that the Framers wanted a government of **separated powers** and **shared powers**, each branch of government would have powers that would enable it to check the use of power by the other branches. Ask students to cite an example of a power in the legislative branch that enables Congress to check the power of the other branches of the national government. Finally, check that students understand the meaning and purpose of the **necessary and proper clause**.

G. Reading and Discussion
What power did the national government have over state governments and the people?

Have the class read "What power did the national government have over state governments and the people?" on pp. 71–72 of the text. Remind students that the initial purpose of the convention was to respond to concerns about some of the things state governments were doing. The Framers wanted a national government that was not dependent on the states for its revenue or for law enforcement. They also wanted a national government with the authority to act directly on the people, in certain areas. The state governments, however, would retain important powers over education, family law, property regulation, and most aspects of daily life. The remainder of this section describes the powers of the national government as well as the limits on the powers of both the national and state governments. During the discussion check that students are able to explain some of the powers and limits described in the text:

■ **powers of the national government**. (1) The **supremacy clause** makes the Constitution and all laws and treaties approved by Congress the supreme law of the land; (2) state judges must follow the Constitution, or federal laws and treaties, when there is a conflicting state law; (3) Congress has the power to organize the militia of the states and call them into national service; (4) national government guarantees to each state a republican form of government; (5) national government must protect the states from invasion or domestic violence.

- **limits on powers of the national government**. The national government may not: (1) ban the slave trade before 1808; (2) suspend **habeas corpus**, except in emergencies; (3) pass any **ex post facto** law; (4) pass any **bill of attainder**; (5) tax anything exported from a state; (6) take money from the treasury without an appropriation law; (7) grant titles of nobility; (8) punish a descendant of a person convicted of treason; or (9) require public officials to hold any particular religious belief.

- **limits on powers of state governments**. The state governments may not:(1) create their own money; (2) pass laws that enable people to violate contracts; (3) pass ex post facto laws or bills of attainder; (4) enter into treaties or declare war; (5) unfairly discriminate against citizens of other states; or (6) refuse to return fugitives from justice to the state from which they have fled.

Direct attention to the illustration on p. 72. Ask students to respond to the question in the caption: Why was it important to have only one monetary system for the nation?

H. Reading and Discussion

What issues separated the northern and southern states?

Have the class read "What issues separated the northern and southern states?" on p. 72 of the text. Students should understand that another controversy of the convention was the disagreement on issues of slavery. Many Framers were opposed to slavery. Delegates from the southern states argued that the people in their states would not approve a constitution that denied citizens the right to import and keep slaves. Three southern states made it clear they would not become part of the new nation.

I. Reading and Discussion

What compromises were made to persuade the southern states to sign the Constitution?

Have the class read "What compromises were made to persuade the southern states to sign the Constitution?" on p. 72 of the text. Students should understand that the compromise over slavery (1) gave Congress the power to regulate commerce between the states, which the northern states wanted; (2) prevented the national government from interfering with the slave trade earlier than 1808; (3) required that a slave be counted as three-fifths of a person when determining how many representatives a state could send to the House of Representatives and when computing direct taxes; and (4) required a fugitive slave clause providing that slaves who escaped to other states must be returned to their owners.

J. Critical Thinking Exercise

Examining Northern and Southern Positions on Slavery

Have the class work in small groups of five students each to complete the critical thinking exercise, "Examining Northern and Southern Positions on Slavery," on pp. 72–73 of the text. During the exercise students examine issues related to the convention's compromise over slavery. Read the instructions for completing the exercise with the class and review the questions in the exercise. Allow adequate time for students to develop their responses, then have them share their work with the class.

Direct attention to the "What do *you* think?" section on p. 73. You may want to use these questions to conduct a general class discussion or have students work individually or with a study partner to develop their responses. Have students share their responses with the class.

K. Concluding the Lesson

To conclude the lesson, have students respond to the questions in the "Review and Using the Lesson" section on p. 73 of the text. Finally, have students return to the "Purpose of Lesson" on p. 68. Ask students to describe the extent to which they accomplished the objectives of the lesson.

Optional Activities
Reinforcement, Extended Learning, and Enrichment

1. Refer students to Article I, Section 8 of the Constitution (see Reference Section in student text). Ask them to list any powers of Congress that are not included that they believe should be. Students should also suggest which powers, if any, that are included should not be. Students should support their suggestions for each addition and deletion.

2. Ask students to relate each of the powers listed in Article I, Section 8 to the general purposes of government which are found in the Preamble.

3. Select students to read a detailed treatment of the Philadelphia Convention and to report to the class on George Mason's speech on the evils of slavery.

LESSON 14: What Powers Were Granted to the Executive and Judicial Branches?

Lesson Overview

This lesson describes why the Framers thought the executive and judicial branches were needed in the new government and examines the development of Articles II and III of the Constitution which establish the executive and judicial authority of the national government. Students learn of the Framers' fears of creating too strong an executive branch and the difficulties the Framers had in deciding how best to control the power of the executive. Students examine how the Framers relied on a system of separated powers and checks and balances so that an executive could not destroy the balance of power among the branches and thus endanger the rights of the people. Students also examine the issues raised in developing a method for selecting the president and that unique solution devised by the Framers—the electoral college. During the critical thinking exercise on the executive branch, students take and defend positions on the evolving influence of the presidency over legislation.

Finally, students examine how the Framers established the federal judiciary and its powers under Article III. The lesson focuses particular attention on an issue the Framers did not address in the Constitution itself—whether the federal judiciary should have the power of judicial review over the actions of the other branches of the national government.

Lesson Objectives

At the conclusion of this lesson, students should be able to

1. explain the basic organization of the executive and judicial branches set forth in Articles II and III of the Constitution

2. describe the limitations on the powers of the executive and judicial branches

3. explain why the Framers developed the electoral college as the method for selecting the president

4. evaluate, take, and defend positions on the influence of the presidency over legislation

Preparation/Teaching Materials

Student text, pp. 74–79

Teaching Procedures

A. Introducing the Lesson

To introduce the lesson, ask students what concerns they might have about creating an executive branch of government. What powers would they give the executive? What limitations would they place on the exercise of executive power? What power would they give to the judicial branch? Why?

While students read the "Purpose of Lesson" on p. 74, post the "Terms to Know" on the board. Review with the class what students should be able to do at the completion of the lesson, as explained in the "Purpose of Lesson." Review the vocabulary items listed on the board and remind students to take special note of these terms as they study the material in the lesson.

B. Reading and Discussion

Why did the Framers want to limit executive power?

Have the class read "Why did the Framers want to limit executive power?" on p. 74 of the text. Students should recall the Founders' experiences under British rule to understand why the Framers wanted to limit the power of the executive. They believed that the king had been able to exercise too much influence over Parliament, upsetting the balance of power. However, the Founders' experiences in their states was that weak executives were unable to check the power of the legislature. The problem for the Framers was how to strengthen the executive to balance the power of the legislature without making the executive so powerful that it would endanger the rights of the people.

C. Reading and Discussion

What basic questions did organizing the executive branch raise?

Have the class read "What basic questions did organizing the executive branch raise?" on pp. 74–75 of the text. The Framers had to decide three basic issues: (1) whether to create a **single or plural** executive; (2) the **term of office**; and (3) whether the executive should be **eligible for reelection**.

D. Reading and Discussion
What powers should be given to the president?

Have the class read "What powers should be given to the president?" on pp. 75–76 of the text. Before reading this section, you may want students to examine Article II of the Constitution (see the Reference Section in the student text). In keeping with their belief in separation of powers, the Framers wanted to be sure that the president had only those powers that were executive in nature. Students should understand that the executive powers include responsibility for (1) carrying out and enforcing laws made by Congress; (2) nominating people for federal offices; (3) negotiating treaties with other nations; and (4) conducting wars. In addition, the president has the power to pardon people convicted of crimes and to send and receive ambassadors to and from other counties. The Framers limited the power of the executive by having the president share powers with the Congress, including: (1) the president can veto legislation passed by Congress; (2) the Senate approves or disapproves the president's nominees for federal positions; (3) the Senate must approve treaties the president negotiates with other nations; (4) although the president is commander in chief, only Congress has the power to declare war and to authorize spending the money necessary to wage war; (5) the president has a duty to suggest legislation; and (6) Congress may impeach the president.

Article II of the Constitution does not define "executive power." Executive departments are mentioned, but there are no provisions for creating them, deciding how many there should be, or how they should operate.

Direct attention to the illustration on p. 76. Ask students to respond to the question in the caption: Why did the Framers limit the power of the president to wage war?

Optional instructional activity. To help students understand the responsibilities of the president, you may want to use the following activity. Have students work in pairs to write a job description for the office of president of the United States. Using the copy of the Constitution in the Reference Section in the student text, have students locate Article II. Explain to the class that in exercising their responsibility as citizens, voters also assume the responsibility of knowing the tasks a president must perform so they can determine whether a candidate possesses the characteristics desirable in a person seeking to fill that office. Instruct students that the job description they write should detail the duties, powers, privileges, and limitations of the position. After they have written their job description, ask students to create a list of the essential characteristics a person should possess to be president of the United States. Have students share their ideas with the class. At the conclusion, have students examine the presidential oath of office in Article II of the Constitution.

E. Critical Thinking Exercise
Identifying the Powers of the President to Influence Legislation

Have students work with a study partner to complete the critical thinking exercise, "Identifying the Powers of the President to Influence Legislation," on p. 76 of the text. During the exercise students consider the multiple ways the executive can influence legislation pending before Congress. Read the instructions with the class for completing the exercise. Allow adequate time for students to complete their work, then have them share their responses with the class.

F. Reading and Discussion
How should presidents be selected?

Have the class read "How should presidents be selected?" on pp. 76–77 of the text. The Framers knew that whoever selected the president would have great power over the person who held the office. That power might be used to benefit some people at the expense of others. The Framers had two alternatives: (1) select the president **indirectly** through either the Congress, the state legislatures, the state governors, or a temporary group elected specifically for this purpose; or (2) select the president **directly** by a majority vote of the people. During the discussion, ask students what they think are the advantages and disadvantages of the two alternatives. Students should understand that the Framers trusted no one group (the people, Congress, state legislatures, or governors) to make the selection for fear they might upset the balance of power between the legislative and executive branches or between the national government and the state governments. Instead, the Framers, by committee, designed what we now call the **electoral college**. During discussion, help students understand the operation of the electoral college as originally proposed by the Framers. You may want to have students do additional research to learn how the electoral college operates today.

Direct attention to the illustration on p. 77. Ask students to respond to the question in the caption: How did the Framers' expectation that George Washington would be the first president affect their writing of Article II of the Constitution?

Direct attention to the "What do *you* think?" section on p. 77. You may want to use these questions to conduct a general class discussion. As an alternative, you may want students to work individually, with a study partner, or in small groups to develop responses to each question. If so, have students share their work with the class.

G. Reading and Discussion
What questions did organizing the judicial branch raise?

Have the class read "What questions did organizing the judicial branch raise?" on pp. 77–78 of the text. Before reading this section, you may want to have students examine Article III of the Constitution (see Reference Section in student text). During the discussion students should understand that the national government needed some system for resolving disputes involving its laws. If the judicial function were left to state courts, each state might apply federal law differently. Also, a judicial branch was needed to complete the system of separation of powers, e.g., trials by jury were an important check on the power of the government.

The Framers vested judicial authority in "...one **supreme court** and in such interior Courts as the Congress may from time to time ordain and establish." In order to protect the judiciary from political pressures, federal judges are nominated by the president and approved by the Senate. Additionally, judges hold their "offices during good behavior," meaning they cannot be removed unless impeached and convicted of "treason, bribery, or other high crimes and misdemeanors." During discussion, ask students why the Framers thought it important that judges be independent of political pressures. Are the methods devised by the Framers effective ways of maintaining the neutrality of the courts? What other factors might influence the independence of the courts?

The judicial power of the national government "extends to all cases in law and equity" that involve (1) the Constitution, (2) the laws of the United States, or (3) treaties.

The federal courts have authority to hear cases involving (1) ambassadors and public ministers and consuls, (2) admiralty and maritime jurisdiction, (3) controversies to which the United States shall be a party, (4) controversies between two or more states, (5) controversies between a state and citizens of another state, (6) controversies between citizens of different states, (7) controversies between citizens of the same state claiming lands under grants of different states, and (8) controversies between a state, or the citizens thereof, and foreign states, citizens or subjects.

The Framers gave the Supreme Court authority to decide the following types of cases:

- **original jurisdiction**. These are cases that go directly before the Supreme Court without first having been heard by the lower courts. These are cases "... affecting ambassadors, other public ministers and consuls, and those in which a state shall be party...."

- **appellate jurisdiction**. These are cases first heard in the lower federal courts and in state courts. The Supreme Court has authority to review these cases on appeal of the parties involved.

Direct attention to the "What do *you* think?" section on p. 79. You may want to use these questions to conduct a general class discussion on the judicial branch. As an alternative, you may want to have students work individually or with a study partner to develop responses to the questions in this section. If so, have students share their responses with the class.

H. Reading and Discussion
Why was the question of judicial review left unanswered?

Have the class read "Why was the question of judicial review left unanswered?" on p. 79 of the text. During the discussion check that students understand the meaning of the term **judicial review**. Ask students why they think the power of judicial review might be important in the system of separation of powers and checks and balances. How might judicial review limit the power of the government and protect the rights of the people?

Direct attention to the illustration on p. 78. Ask students to respond to the question in the caption: Why did the Framers think it was important to protect the independence of the judicial branch?

I. Concluding the Lesson

To conclude the lesson, have students respond to the questions in the "Reviewing and Using the Lesson" section on p. 79 of the text. Finally, have students return to the "Purpose of Lesson" on p. 74. Ask students to describe the extent to which they accomplished the objectives of the lesson.

Optional Activities

Reinforcement, Extended Learning, and Enrichment

1. Have students go to the library to find out about some of the alternatives to the electoral college that have been suggested. Their reports should explain how the alternatives would work and their advantages and disadvantages.

2. Have students locate in the library some of the suggested alternatives to the present term of office of the president. What advantages and disadvantages do the alternatives have?

3. Have students research changes in the way the electoral college operates, limitations on the number of terms a president may serve, or changes in presidential succession in cases involving incapacitation or death of an executive while still in office.

4. Have students debate whether they think Supreme Court justices should be elected and restricted to a fixed term of office.

LESSON 15: What Conflicting Opinions Did the Framers Have about the Completed Constitution?

<table>
<tr>
<td>

Lesson Overview

In this lesson students learn some of the disagreements about the Constitution which set the stage for the debates over its ratification. These are significant because many have to do with issues that are still discussed and debated today. Students read a statement by Benjamin Franklin defending the work of the Philadelphia Convention and supporting the adoption of the Constitution. Then students examine a list of objections which George Mason, who opposed the Constitution, wrote on his copy of the draft Constitution. Students learn that George Mason focuses on the basic ideas of constitutional governments, republicanism, and representative government to make his case against adopting the Constitution. Finally, students read the last notes on the convention written by James Madison.

</td>
<td>

Lesson Objectives

At the conclusion of this lesson, students should be able to

1. explain the comments made by Benjamin Franklin and James Madison who favored the adoption of the Constitution

2. explain the position of George Mason and give arguments in support of and in opposition to his criticisms of the Constitution

Preparation/Teaching Materials

Student text, pp. 80–83

</td>
</tr>
</table>

Teaching Procedures

A. Introducing the Lesson

While students read the "Purpose of Lesson" on p. 80, post the "Terms to Know" on the board. Review with the class what students should be able to do at the completion of the lesson, as explained in the "Purpose of Lesson." Review the vocabulary items listed on the board and remind students to take special note of these terms as they study the material in the lesson.

Ask students to anticipate what opposition the Framers might anticipate in persuading the country to adopt and ratify the Constitution.

B. Reading and Discussion
What did the Framers think when the Philadelphia Convention ended?

Have the class read "What did the Framers think when the Philadelphia Convention ended?" on p. 81 of the text. Ask students what they think it means when the Constitution is described as "a bundle of compromises." Ask students to support this characterization by citing examples of the compromises they learned in earlier lessons. Direct attention to the quotations from Alexander Hamilton and Elbridge Gerry. What positions did the two participants at the Philadelphia Convention take concerning the Constitution? In what way might these two positions foreshadow the debate over the ratification of the Constitution?

C. Reading and Discussion
How did Franklin defend the work of the convention?

Have the class read "How did Franklin defend the work of the convention?" on p. 81 of the text. You may want to divide the class into two groups. Have one group read and present Franklin's position on the completed Constitution. Have the other group read Franklin's position and respond to it critically.

D. Reading and Discussion
Why did George Mason object to the Constitution?

Have the class read "Why did George Mason object to the Constitution?" on pp. 81–82 of the text. Again, you may want to divide the class into two groups, one group reads and presents Mason's position and the other reads and responds critically. Ask the class to identify which of Mason's objections they find most persuasive. What relevance, if any, do Mason's objections have to today's government under the Constitution?

Have students work with a study partner. Ask students to re-read each of George Mason's objections and identify for each objection the principle of government Mason believed the Constitution may have violated. Have students share their ideas with the class.

Direct attention to the illustration on p. 82. Ask students to respond to the question in the caption: What changes in the Constitution would have satisfied George Mason's objections?

E. Reading and Discussion

How did Franklin describe the significance of the convention?

Have the class read "How did Franklin describe the significance of the convention?" on pp. 82–83 of the text. Ask students whether they agree with Franklin's assessment of the work of the convention.

Direct attention to the illustration on p. 83. Ask students to respond to the question in the caption: During convention sessions, why might Franklin have had trouble telling if the "sun behind the president" was "rising or setting"?

F. Concluding the Lesson

To conclude the lesson, have students respond to the questions in the "Reviewing and Using the Lesson"

section on p. 83 of the text. Finally, have students return to the "Purpose of Lesson" on p. 80. Ask students to describe the extent to which they accomplished the objectives of the lesson.

Optional Activities

Reinforcement, Extended Learning, and Enrichment

1. Ask students to write a paragraph speculating on what might have happened if the Constitution had not been ratified.

2. Select students to read from a biography of John Hancock of Massachusetts and report to the class on how he was persuaded to support the Constitution.

3. Have students read studies of the convention and selected speeches by George Mason and report to the class.

LESSON 16: What Was the Anti-Federalists' Position in the Debate about Ratification?

Lesson Overview

This lesson presents the Anti-Federalists' criticisms of the Constitution which are illustrated by the arguments of Mercy Otis Warren. The Anti-Federalists' position was based on traditional ideas about the requirements for republican government. These included ideas stated by Montesquieu and others: the need for a small community of citizens, each possessing civic virtue, with common interests that facilitate agreement on the common good; representative government; widespread suffrage; the effective separation of powers; and checks and balances. Students learn the Federalists' response to the criticisms of the Anti-Federalists, and how the debate between the two groups led to the development and adoption of the Bill of Rights. An optional instructional activity combining Lessons 16 and 17 includes additional student materials and recommended teaching procedures for conducting a class debate on the ratification of the Constitution.

Lesson Objectives

At the conclusion of this lesson, students should be able to

1. explain the arguments of the Anti-Federalists and how those arguments were based upon traditional ideas of republican government

2. explain the responses of the Federalists to the criticisms of the Anti-Federalists

3. explain how the debate between the Federalists and Anti-Federalists led to the development and adoption of the Bill of Rights

Preparation/Teaching Materials

Student text, pp. 84–86

Optional. Invite a scholar from a local college or university to work with the class in preparing a debate on the ratification of the Constitution. Please see p. 22 of this guide for instructions.

Optional. Prepare to conduct a class debate on the ratification of the Constitution using the material in Lessons 16 and 17.

Optional. For each student in the class, prepare a copy of Student Handouts – 16 and 17, "The Anti-Federalist Position on Ratification of the Constitution," on pp. 86–88, "The Federalist Position on Ratification of the Constitution" on pp. 92–95 of this guide.

Teaching Procedures

A. Introducing the Lesson

To introduce the lesson, direct attention to the illustration on p. 86 of the text. Ask students to respond to the question in the caption: What do you think are the most compelling arguments for and against ratification of the Constitution?

While students read the "Purpose of Lesson" on p. 84, post the "Terms to Know" on the board. Review with the class what students should be able to do at the completion of the lesson, as explained in the "Purpose of Lesson." Review the vocabulary items listed on the board and remind students to take special note of these terms as they study the material in the lesson.

B. Reading and Discussion

How did the Anti-Federalists view the importance of representative government and civic virtue?

Have the class read "How did the Anti-Federalists view the importance of representative government and civic

virtue?" on p. 84 of the text. Students should understand that most Americans were mistrustful of government in general and of a strong national government in particular. Have students identify the three basic questions raised during the ratification debates:

■ Would the new Constitution maintain a republican government?

■ Would the federal government have too much power?

■ Was a bill of rights needed in the Constitution?

Students should be able to identify the Anti-Federalists' ideas about government. The Anti-Federalists believed in the basic ideas of **representative government** and that it would only work in small communities of citizens who held similar interests and beliefs. They believed that people living in small agrarian communities would be more likely to possess civic virtue and be willing to set aside their self-interest when necessary for the common good. The Federalists were proposing the opposite—a large, powerful national government located far from the diverse communities of citizens it represented. This system, the Anti-Federalists believed, would inevitably identify some of the prominent Anti-Federalist leaders: George Mason, Mercy Otis Warren, Richard Henry Lee, Patrick Henry, Elbridge Gerry.

D. Reading and Discussion

What were the arguments of Anti-Federalists?

Have the class read "What were the arguments of Anti-Federalists?" on pp. 84–85 of the text. Students should understand the Anti-Federalist position on the three basic questions raised during the ratification debates:

■ **Would the new Constitution maintain a republican government?**

The Constitution would undermine a republican form of government.

■ **Would the federal government have too much power?**

The Constitution gave too much power to the national government at the expense of the state governments.

It gave too much power to the executive branch of the national government at the expense of the other branches.

It gave Congress too much power because of the "necessary and proper" clause.

It did not adequately separate the powers of the executive and legislative branches of government.

It allowed the national government to keep an army during peacetime.

■ **Was a bill of rights needed in the Constitution?**

The Constitution did not include a bill of rights.

It should have been developed in meetings that were open to the public.

Ask students to explain the relationship between the Anti-Federalists' objections to the Constitution and the natural rights philosophy, republicanism, and constitutionalism.

E. Reading and Discussion

Why did the Anti-Federalists fear a strong national government?

Have the class read "Why did the Anti-Federalists fear a strong national government?" on p. 85 of the text. Students should understand that the Anti-Federalists believed that the only safe government was one that was

■ local and closely linked with the will of the people

■ controlled by the people through yearly elections and by replacing people in key positions often

Direct attention to the "What do *you* think?" section on p. 85. During a general class discussion, have students respond to the questions in this section.

F. Reading and Discussion

Should there be a bill of rights?

Have the class read "Should there be a bill of rights?" on pp. 85–86 of the text. Students should understand that this was the strongest argument the Anti-Federalists had in opposition to the Constitution. They believed that

■ the way the government was organized under the proposed Constitution did not adequately protect rights. The federal government was too far removed from the people and could use its power to violate citizens' rights.

■ the powers of the federal government were so general and vague (the "necessary and proper" and "general welfare" clauses) that they gave the government almost unlimited power. The federal government had the power to act directly on citizens.

■ some rights were included in the Constitution, others were not (religion, speech, press, assembly). There was nothing to stop the federal government from violating all the rights that were not mentioned.

■ since Americans had just fought a revolutionary war to secure their fundamental rights, they did not want a constitution that placed those rights in jeopardy.

■ a bill of rights was necessary to remind the people of the principles of our political system.

G. Reading and Discussion

How did the demand for a bill of rights unite the Anti-Federalists?

Have the class read "How did the demand for a bill of rights unite the Anti-Federalists?" on p. 86 of the text. The Anti-Federalists were not a well-organized group; however, they were well organized in their opposition to the new federal government. The lack of a bill of rights became the focus of their campaign against ratification of the Constitution. Some Anti-Federalists, like George Mason, hoped to defeat the proposed Constitution so that a second constitutional convention would be held and they might have more influence in creating the new government.

Direct attention to the "What do *you* think?" section on p. 86. Use the questions in this section to conduct a general class discussion evaluating the position of the Anti-Federalists.

Optional Instructional Activity. Lessons 16 and 17 offer an excellent opportunity to conduct a full class debate on the ratification of the Constitution. To do so, divide the class into two groups, one representing the position of the Federalists and the other the position of the Anti-Federalists. Each group should study the corresponding lesson (16 or 17) in this text in more detail. Distribute to each student a copy of the student materials, "The Federalist Position on Ratification of the Constitution" on pp. 92–95 and "The Anti-Federalist Position on Ratification of the Constitution" on pp. 86–88 of this guide.

To encourage full participation in the class debate, further subdivide both the Federalist and Anti-Federalist groups according to the topic headings in the student material: (1) Republican Government, (2) Federalism, (3) Separation of Power and Checks and Balances, (4) The Congress, (5) The President, (6) The Judiciary, and (7) The Bill of Rights. Assign each of the smaller groups to prepare arguments on their topic for the debate.

Post the following resolution on the board: *Resolved: that the people, by convention assembled in each state, should adopt and ratify this Constitution of the United States.* Allow adequate time for each group to prepare affirmative and rebuttal arguments. During the presentations, have the Anti-Federalists present their positions first. For more detailed instructions on conducting a class debate, please see p. 22 of this guide. Allow adequate time for students to prepare and present their arguments. At the conclusion, discuss with the class the strengths and weaknesses of the arguments presented. Ask students to explain how their arguments relate to the principles of the natural rights philosophy, republicanism and representative democracy, and constitutional government. Have the class take a vote on whether to ratify the Constitution. Finally, discuss the following question with the class. Both the Federalists and the Anti-Federalists believed in the natural rights philosophy, republicanism, and constitutionalism. If this is so, how can you explain the fact that the Federalists supported ratification of the Constitution while the Anti-Federalists bitterly opposed it?

H. Concluding the Lesson

To conclude the lesson, direct attention to the illustrations on p. 85 of the text. Ask students to respond to the question in the caption: Why did the Anti-Federalists demand a bill of rights? Then have students respond to the questions in the "Reviewing and Using the Lesson" section on p. 86 of the text. Finally, have students return to the "Purpose of Lesson" on p. 84. Ask students to describe the extent to which they accomplished the objectives of the lesson.

Optional Activities
Reinforcement, Extended Learning, and Enrichment

1. Have students conduct research on Mercy Otis Warren, George Mason, and other prominent Anti-Federalists and report their findings to the class.

2. Have the students write a letter to Abigail Adams in which they comment on her statement:

   Excluded from Honours and office, we cannot attach ourselves to the State of Government…. Even in the freest country, our property is subject to the control and disposal of our partners…. Deprived of a voice in legislation, obligated to submit to laws imposed on us, is it not sufficient to make us indifferent to the Publick Welfare?

3. Students should explain why they think women should or should not have been given full political and property rights under the proposed Constitution.

The Anti-Federalists' Position on Ratification of the Constitution

Unlike the Federalists, the Anti-Federalists' position was not set forth in a single group of essays. Many speeches and pamphlets by a large number of opponents to the Constitution contain the various objections that were made.

I. Republican Government

*T*he Anti-Federalists agreed that republican government was the only form of government suited to the United States. They, however, insisted that it was impossible to create and maintain a republican government in a territory as large and containing as many people as the thirteen states. One opponent wrote, "The idea of a...republic on an average one thousand miles in length and eight hundred in breadth, and containing six millions of white inhabitants...is in itself an absurdity, and contrary to the whole experience of mankind." It was true that a large republic was contrary to the experience of mankind as well as the teaching of writers such as Montesquieu.

Republican government clearly requires the active support of the people. The Anti-Federalists argued that the government provided by the Constitution was too distant from the people to gain this support. The alternative was too horrible to contemplate, and was described by one opponent in the following words: "Nothing would support the government... but military coercion." And a writer in *The Independent Gazeteer* of Philadelphia warned, "From the moment we became one great Republic...the period is very shortly removed, when we shall sink finally into monarchy, and then into despotism."

Most of the writers on republicanism had assumed republican government was possible only when the people had roughly the same economic status, pursued similar economic activities, lived their lives in similar ways, and had the same religious and moral points of view. The Anti-Federalists argued that this clearly was not the case in the United States. A New Englander observed, "The inhabitants of warmer climes are more dissolute in their manners, and less industrious, than in colder countries.... It is impossible for a code of laws to suit Georgia and Massachusetts." And a southerner expressed a similar view when he wrote, "We see plainly that men who come from New England are different from us." He made it clear that he did not wish to be governed by or to govern with these different men.

Finally, many of the Anti-Federalists continued to insist that republican government required citizens who were virtuous. Writing under the name "Centinel," one argued that a government of checks and balances could not attain the common good. In a republic, he insisted, the people are sovereign and for sovereign people to make good decisions, they must be virtuous. Moreover, they must be relatively equal, and that was less likely in a large nation than a small state.

II. Federalism

*T*he Anti-Federalists were almost unanimous in the opposition to a "national" or "consolidated" government, and that, they insisted, was precisely the kind of government established by the Constitution. They were not impressed with the argument that the new federal government was a limited government of delegated powers, with the states retaining sovereignty over local matters. They based their opposition on four provisions of the Constitution: (1) the taxing power, (2) the provision for maintaining a standing army, (3) the necessary and proper clause, and (4) the supremacy clause.

Article I, Section 8 of the Constitution gave the federal government power to levy taxes. Congress had not possessed this power under the Articles of Confederation. In the minds of the Anti-Federalists, to give the government the power of the purse was to make it dangerously independent of the people.

Worse, they believed the power to tax was the power to destroy, and conjured horrible images of the people being bled dry. And the taxing power of the federal government may be used to destroy the state governments. In Pennsylvania, one person warned, "...the Congress may monopolize every source of revenue, and thus indirectly demolish the state government, for without funds they could not exist."

At least as bad as the taxing power was the provision in Article I, Section 8 which authorized Congress to raise and support armies. Not content with the power to bleed the states dry financially, the Framers had given the Congress the ultimate means of suppression. A standing army, according to Centinel, is "that grand engine of oppression." And he appeared to have few doubts about the potential willingness of the federal government to use that engine.

The Anti-Federalists viewed both the "general welfare" and the "necessary and proper" clause of the Constitution with deep suspicion. Centinel asked of the "general welfare" clause, "Now what can be more comprehensive than these words?... The Congress may construe every purpose...to be for the general welfare, and thereby seize upon every object of revenue." As for the "necessary and proper" clause, it seemed to be such a sweeping grant of power, the Anti-Federalists could see no logical limits to the powers of the national government.

Their fears were confirmed, in their eyes, by the "supremacy clause." Were there any doubts about the end result of ratification of the Constitution in light of this clause? Luther Martin sought to enlighten the voters of Maryland. "[I]f the system is adopted, it will amount to a total and unconditional surrender to that government, by the citizens of this state, of every right and privilege secured to them by our Constitution...."

All of these objections reflected the conviction of most Americans in 1787 that men are seldom content to use less power than they are authorized to use. Human beings' lust for power knows no limits. People who are given power will seek to expand and abuse that power. And particularly in the absence of a bill of rights, these provisions of the Constitution seemed especially dangerous.

III. Separation of Powers and Checks and Balances

*T*he Anti-Federalists did not accept James Madison's argument that a blending of separated powers was essential if there is to be an effective system of checks and balances. The sharing of power between the president and the Senate in the appointive and treaty-making power simply made the president and Senate "partners in crime." The blending of power meant, for the Anti-Federalists, a breakdown of checks and balances.

An obscure opponent of the Constitution made the following speech at the Virginia Convention: "That the legislative, executive, and judicial power should be separate and distinct is a political fact so well established, that I presume I shall not be thought arrogant when I affirm that no country ever did, or even can, long remain free, where they are blended. All the states have been in the sentiment when they form their state constitutions, and therefore have guarded against the danger; and every schoolboy in politics must be convinced of the propriety of the observation; and yet, by the proposed plan, the legislative and executive powers are closely united...."

An opponent in Pennsylvania observed, "This mixture of legislative and executive...highly tends to corrupt where the legislative and executive powers are united in the same person, or in the same body of magistrates, there can be no liberty."

IV. The Congress

*T*he major criticisms of the Congress were the length of terms, re-eligibility for election, and the claim that it would be unrepresentative and aristocratic.

George Clinton of New York wrote, "The most general objections to the first article, [is] that biennial elections for representatives are a departure from the safe democratic principle of annual ones...." And the terms of senators, as well as their mode of selection would lead inevitably to an aristocracy, he added. This view was widely held. The republican principle required, so the Anti-Federalists thought, the representatives of the people to stand for elections every year, or at the very most two years. This was the major means of keeping them responsible to the people.

In addition to frequent elections, rotation of office was important in order to prevent the emergence of a governing class, that is, an aristocracy. By allowing officials to be re-elected, the Constitution invited corruption in the government. Once or, at most, two years was quite enough for any man to be entrusted with power. For once men have tasted power, they develop aristocratic pretensions and become dangerous.

The Constitution provided one representative for every 30,000 inhabitants. The Anti-Federalists believed that it was not possible to represent adequately that many people. The best form of government was one in which men governed themselves, as in a town meeting. This, however, is not practical, so representative government is necessary. It is a substitute for self-government.

Hence, these representatives should act to the greatest possible degree as the individual citizen would act were he governing himself. The condition was most likely to be realized through frequent elections, in eligibility for re-election, and small electoral districts.

Moreover, a small number of representatives representing large districts, and in the case of senators, entire states, would probably be drawn from the upper classes since only they would have the means and the inclination to run for election. Melancton Smith of New York claimed that few men of middle class would choose to run for Congress because the office would be "highly elevated and distinguished." Such circumstances would "render

the place of a representative not a desirable one to sensible, substantial men, who have been used to walking in the plain and frugal life."

This situation described by Smith—the likelihood that the Congress would not be made up of ordinary men—was precisely the opposite of what most Anti-Federalists thought it should be. George Mason said of the representatives that "they ought to mix with the people, think as they think, feel as they feel—ought to be perfectly amenable to them and thoroughly acquainted with their interests and conditions." If they were not, there was the danger, according to the Anti-Federalists, of aristocratic domination and the destruction of representative government.

V. The Presidency

*L*uther Martin warned that a president elected for a four-year term, eligible for re-election, equipped with power to nominate judicial officers, to fill vacancies during the recess of the Senate, to pardon for the offense of treason, and with the armed forces at his disposal would, in fact, be an "elective King." "A King in substance," he would be able, when he chose, to become a "King in name" as well; and if he chose he could perpetuate the kingship in his family.

George Clinton dwelt with relish on the dissolute ambition, baseness, and perfidy that would

characterize the ten square miles of the Federal District. The president would surround himself with "flatterers," "minions and favorites." He would preside over a court that would be an "asylum of the base, idle, avaricious and ambitious." All of this, he concluded would certainly lead to "a vile and arbitrary aristocracy or monarchy." The Anti-Federalists were, of course, reflecting and appealing to the worst fears shared by many Americans as a result of their experience with the British monarchy and the royal governors.

VI. The Judiciary

*T*he Anti-Federalists objected to the absence of a guarantee of trial by jury in civil cases and in criminal cases that reach the Supreme Court. They were also convinced that the federal judiciary "would eventually absorb and swallow up the state judiciaries...." All of this represented a serious threat to the liberties of the people.

Interestingly, not all Anti-Federalists opposed judicial review. Robert Yates of New York preferred the legislature, being accountable to the people, to be the final governmental interpreter of the Consti-

tution. Patrick Henry boasted that the judges in Virginia "opposed the acts of the legislature." He went on, "They had the fortitude to declare that they were the judiciary, and would oppose unconstitutional acts. Are you sure that your federal judiciary will do this? Is that judiciary as well constructed, and as independent of the other branches, as our state judiciary?" In short, for Henry the question was whether the courts as constructed would, not whether they should, exercise the power of judicial review.

VII. The Bill of Rights

*T*he issue of the Bill of Rights was the issue on which the Anti-Federalists were victorious. It was as a result of their efforts that the Bill of Rights was adopted. They were not persuaded by Federalist arguments that a bill of rights was only necessary to protect the people from a king. Nor did they accept the proposition that the Constitution established a limited government of enumerated and delegated powers. Many of those delegations of power, they insisted, were extremely broad and vague. The

"general welfare" and "necessary and proper" clauses as well as the war-making powers were merely a few examples. While it might be true that the Constitution prohibited ex post facto laws, why, they asked, did it not provide guarantees for other important liberties and rights? These rights are too important, and the lust for power with which all officeholders are bound to be infected means that the natural rights of the people must receive specific and extraordinary protection if they are not to be violated.

LESSON 17: What Was the Federalists' Position in the Debate about Ratification?

Lesson Overview	Lesson Objectives
This lesson describes the strategy and the arguments the Federalists used to get the Constitution ratified. These include their use of (1) the concepts of the social contract and consent, and (2) the argument that it is unrealistic, in an extended republic, to rely on the traditional notion of a small nation of citizens possessing civic virtue as the best means of protecting natural rights and promoting the common good. Instead, the Federalists argued, in a large and diverse nation, these goals are best served by a federal system consisting of complex provisions for representation, separation of powers, and checks and balances to make it impossible for self-interested factions to form a majority at the expense of minority rights and the common good. Students also learn that in the larger states like New York and Virginia the debates were very close and, to win some Anti-Federalist support, the Federalists agreed that when the first Congress was held it would draft a bill of rights to be added to the Constitution. The bill was to list the rights of citizens that were not to be violated by the federal government. An optional instructional activity suggests combining Lessons 16 and 17 to conduct a class debate on the ratification of the Constitution.	At the conclusion of this lesson, students should be able to 1. explain why the Federalists wanted the Constitution to be ratified in state conventions, and the arguments they used to justify this procedure which is included in Article VII of the Constitution 2. explain the arguments made by the Federalists in support of the Constitution, including how the Federalists' arguments differed from classical arguments about republican government **Preparation/Teaching Materials** Student text, pp. 87–90 **Optional**. Prepare to conduct a class debate on the ratification of the Constitution. Please see p. 22 of this guide for instructions. **Optional**. For each student in the class, prepare a copy of Student Handouts – 16 and 17.

Teaching Procedures

A. Introducing the Lesson

While students read the "Purpose of Lesson" on p. 87, post the "Terms to Know" on the board. Review with the class what students should be able to do at the completion of the lesson, as explained in the "Purpose of Lesson." Review the vocabulary items listed on the board and remind students to take special note of these terms as they study the material in the lesson.

B. Reading and Discussion

Why did the Federalists ask voters to approve the Constitution?

Have the class read "Why did the Federalists ask voters to approve the Constitution?" on p. 87 of the text. During the discussion, help students understand why the Federalists preferred having the voters approve the Constitution in ratifying conventions rather than having the Congress or state governments approve it. Students should be able to explain how the Federalists used the ideas of the social contract and consent in justifying their

position and the relationship of this position to the natural rights philosophy. Students should also understand that the Federalists were better organized than their opponents, the Anti-Federalists.

Students should understand that the Constitution would go into effect after being ratified by nine of the thirteen state conventions. Ask students how they think this rule is related to representative democracy and majority rule. Students should also understand that the Federalists wanted the ratification process to move quickly, giving the opposition little time to organize support against the Constitution.

C. Reading and Discussion

What methods were used in the struggle for ratification?

Have the class read "What methods were used in the struggle for ratification?" on pp. 87–88 of the text. Students should understand that in some states the political struggle to ratify the Constitution was intense and occasionally acrimonious. Students should also understand that *The Federalist* is a series of essays written by Alexander Hamilton, James Madison, and John Jay as part of the debate over ratification in the state of New York. *The Federalist* was also used in Virginia and today provides an important source of information about the Constitution.

D. Reading and Discussion
How did the Federalists respond to the Anti-Federalists?

Have the class read "How did the Federalists respond to the Anti-Federalists?" on pp. 88–89 of the text. The class should examine the following arguments in detail:

■ **The civic virtue of the people could no longer be relied on as the sole support of a government that would protect the people's rights and promote their welfare.**

The Federalists argued that the greatest danger to the common good and the natural rights of citizens in republics had been groups of citizens who ignored the common good in the selfish pursuit of their own interests. Experiences with state governments had led them to believe they could not rely on the civic virtue of citizens to promote the common good and natural rights.

■ **The way in which the Constitution organized the government, including the separation of powers and checks and balances, was the best way to promote the goals of republicanism.**

The national government as set forth in the Constitution did not have to rely on the civic virtue of citizens to promote the common good and protect natural rights. This would be accomplished by the complicated system of representation, separation of power, and checks and balances. The Constitution's strength was that it provided for different branches of government to represent the different interests of the people. This complicated system would make it impossible for any individual or faction to take complete control of the government to serve its own interests. The large size of the nation and the diversity of interests would make it less likely that any one faction would dominate. The Federalists saw an advantage in making it difficult to get legislation passed. They believed that the best way to prevent bad laws from being passed was to make it difficult to pass any law at all.

■ **The representation of different interests in the government would protect basic rights.**

The House of Representatives would protect the people's local interests. The Senate would protect the people's state interests. The presidents would protect the people's national interests. The Supreme Court would protect the people's fundamental interests since it was responsible only to the Constitution.

Direct attention to the "What do *you* think?" section on p. 89. You may want to use these questions to conduct a general class discussion. Alternatively, you may want students to work individually, with a study partner, or in small groups to develop responses to the questions in this section. If so, have students share their responses with the class.

E. Reading and Discussion
Did the national government have too much power?

Have the class read "Did the national government have too much power?" on p. 89 of the text. The Federalists admitted that the Constitution gave the national government much more power. However, it was a government limited to enumerated powers. The system of checks and balances would ensure that those limits would not be violated.

F. Reading and Discussion
Should there be a bill of rights?

Have the class read "Should there be a bill of rights?" on pp. 89–90 of the text. Students should understand that the Federalists made the following arguments defending the fact that the Constitution did not include a bill of rights:

■ the complexity of the national government and the diversity of the nation protect rights

■ the Constitution itself includes protections against a number of abuses, including the right to habeas corpus, prohibitions against ex post facto laws and bills of attainder, protection from violations of contracts, a guarantee to trial by jury, and protection against accusations of treason

■ in a government based on popular sovereignty, the people have the power to remove elected officials from office

■ the Constitution gives the government limited power and there is no need to list rights the government has no power to violate

■ declarations of rights are ineffective and dangerous because there is no way to create a comprehensive list of rights and the government might feel free to violate rights not specifically listed

G. Reading and Discussion

Why did the Federalists give in to the demand for a bill of rights?

Have the class read "Why did the Federalists give in to the demand for a bill of rights?" on p. 90 of the text. Students should understand that the ratification debates in important states such as New York and Virginia were very close. To gain some Anti-Federalist support, The Federalists agreed that when the first Congress met, it would draft a bill of rights to be added to the Constitution. This agreement deprived the Anti-Federalists of their most powerful argument.

Direct attention to the "What do *you* think?" section on p. 90. You may want to use these questions to conduct a general class discussion on the argument that the Constitution did not need a bill of rights.

H. Concluding the Lesson

To conclude the lesson, have students respond to the questions in the "Reviewing and Using the Lesson" section on p. 90 of the text. Finally, have students return to the "Purpose of Lesson" on p. 87. Ask students to describe the extent to which they accomplished the objectives of the lesson.

This lesson concludes the study of Unit Two. If you had students develop personal objectives or a list of questions during the introduction of the unit, students should now review those objectives or questions and assess to what degree they achieved their goals. In addition, you may want to use the questionnaire, "Reflecting on Your Experience," on p. 28 of this guide to engage students in an evaluation of their participation in the lessons in this unit.

Optional Activities

Reinforcement, Extended Learning, and Enrichment

1. Have students obtain a copy of *The Federalist* and read one of the essays. They should explain the position taken in the essay to the class in their own terms.

2. If your state is one of the original thirteen, have students do research on the ratification convention in your state.

3. Have students study in detail the ratification battle in New York and account for the Federalist victory there.

4. Have students prepare a report for the class in which they explain why Rhode Island took so long to join the Union under the Constitution.

The Federalists' Position on Ratification of the Constitution

The following information summarizes the arguments presented for the Federalists' position in a series of essays entitled *The Federalist*. These essays were written by Alexander Hamilton, John Jay, and James Madison using a common pen-name, Publius, a patriot of ancient Rome.

I. Republican Government

*M*ost people had thought that republican government could only exist in a small territory populated by people who possessed civic virtue. The Federalists maintained that it is possible to have republican government in a territory as large as that represented by the thirteen original states even if the people lack civic virtue. Moreover, such a republic, an extended republic, as they called it, would be superior to the classical republics of small city-states which depended on the civic virtue of the citizens.

In "Federalist No. 10," they describe what they thought was the major problem of the classical republics, that is, factions. Factions are made up of people of common interests or beliefs who try to get the government to do things that are desirable for them but which are contrary to the common good.

Classical republicanism had held that the main way of preventing this kind of behavior was for the citizens to possess civic virtue, encouraged by education, religion, and the good example of those who exercised political authority. The Federalists argued, however, that history demonstrated that this does not work. The old republics had been destroyed because people preferred their own interests to the good of the community.

A larger state could avoid these problems because the people would be dispersed over a large territory. A larger number of people would produce a greater number of interest groups. These interest groups, scattered over a large territory, would find it impossible to cooperate with one another in order to form majorities, get the government to do what they wanted, and obtain laws that were favorable to their own interests instead of the common interest. In addition, representation and checks and balances would also help to ensure that the common interest rather than private interests would influence the policy of the government. Thus, the extended republic solved one of the most important problems of the old republics and clearly represented a superior form of republican government.

II. Federalism

*T*he Constitution established a new kind of political system: a federal system. In such a system, there are two governments, each sovereign in its own sphere and each with the authority to act directly upon the people. Previously there had been confederations consisting of a group of sovereign states held together for purposes of mutual defense or trade. The other form of government had been national or consolidated, in which all authority had been located in one central government.

The United States under the Articles of Confederation had been, as the name suggests, a confederation. The central government, such as it was, had very little authority. The Federalists argued that this had made the United States weak and disreputable abroad and disunited at home. In order to solve these problems, there was a need for a national government with the authority to deal with those problems common to all of the states. These included foreign affairs, i.e., treaty and war-making powers. There is a clear need, they also argued, for a common authority to regulate commerce, coin money, and enforce contracts in order to restore the economy of the United States. All of this was necessary, if the government was to be able to provide for the general defense and security as well as the common welfare of the United States.

This did not mean that the state governments were to be eliminated or made entirely subordinate to the government of the United States in regard to matters of purely local jurisdiction. Under the Constitution, the laws passed by Congress are the supreme law of the land, but only in those matters over which Congress is given authority by the Constitution, and these are the powers enumerated in Article I, Section 8 of the Constitution.

These enumerated powers should not be feared because in any contest between the states and the national government, the advantage is on the side of the state governments. The state governments, being closer to the people than the national government, will have a greater claim to their loyalty and support.

In fact, they argued, the greatest problem under the new Constitution will not come from the power of the national government but from the powers retained by the states. This is so in spite of the supremacy clause of the Constitution.

III. Separation of powers and checks and balances

*V*irtually all Americans in 1787 agreed that the separation of powers is the keystone of constitutional government. In "Federalist No. 47," the Federalists wrote, "The accumulation of all powers, legislative, executive, and judiciary, in the same hands, whether of one, a few, or many, and whether hereditary, self-appointed, or elective, may justly be pronounced the very definition of tyranny."

However, critics of the Constitution pointed out that while the powers of government were indeed placed in three separate branches, these powers were not completely distinct. Through the veto, the executive was involved in the legislative power. Through the authority to approve appointments and treaties, the legislative branch was involved in the executive powers.

The Federalists argued that if the three branches of government were totally separate, it would be impossible for them to check and balance each other. Hence, they must be armed with the power to do so. The new Constitution gives them this power. The executive can check the legislative branch through the use of the veto power. The legislative branch can check the executive by over-riding the veto by a two-thirds vote in the House and Senate. These and other devices provided by the Constitution ensure that the three branches of government will be kept in balance.

IV. The Congress
House of Representatives

*M*ajor objections were voiced to the two-year term and the relatively small number of representatives. Many believed that annual elections were required to keep the representatives responsible to their constituents. They also argued that one representative for 30,000 people was insufficient to provide for representative government.

The Federalists argued that elections every two years are sufficient to protect the safety of the people. They also maintained that two-year terms are desirable because they would enable the representatives to get more experience without making them so independent of the people's judgment as to become dangerous.

In answer to the claim that there are too few representatives, they argued that the limited power given to Congress makes it safe to entrust the legislative authority of the lower house to a fairly small number of persons. Finally, they defended the number of representatives by arguing that the larger the assembly, the smaller the number of people who actually direct its affairs. This is so because large groups are more susceptible to the appeal of emotion and are more likely to be swayed by the appeals of clever and unscrupulous demagogues.

Senate

*T*he following four objections had been raised regarding the Senate:

1. The qualification for senators were more advanced age and a longer period of citizenship. (Senators are required to be at least 30 years of age and citizens for 9 years preceding election. Members of the House of Representatives must be 25 years old and citizens for 7 years.) The Federalists argued that the office of senator requires greater knowledge and stability of character. Since senators deal with foreign nations through the treaty-making power, they should be free of foreign influences, and this is more likely if they have been citizens for a longer period of time.

2. Senators were appointed by state legislatures. The Federalists claimed that this was the method favored by pubic opinion and also is useful as a means of linking the state governments to the federal government.

3. Each state is equally represented in the Senate. The Federalists defended equal representation in the Senate by candidly admitting that this was a compromise between the claims of the large states and the small states. They went on to claim that it is desirable for laws to require approval by a majority of the people and a majority of the states. They admitted that this might seem an inconvenience, making it more difficult to pass laws. But this may be a good thing because "the facility and excess of law-making seem to be the diseases to which our governments are most liable...."

4. The number of senators is small. The Federalists insisted that this would result in greater stability and dignity in the government. They argued that large assemblies are susceptible to sudden and violent passions. A small body, elected for six-year terms, would be more sober and better informed in its deliberations. The resulting stability would be advantageous both in terms of domestic politics and foreign relations.

V. The President

*T*he Federalists had harsh words for critics of the presidency. They first addressed the selection of the president by the electoral college, a group of men chosen specifically for the purpose. This method, they claimed, would remove the selection of the president from tumult and disorder. Meeting in their several states, members of the electoral college would be less susceptible to intrigues and conspiracies. Describing the process by which the selection of the president might be made by the House of Representatives, they concluded, "This process of election affords a moral certainty that the office of president will seldom fall to the lot of any man who is not in an eminent degree endowed with the requisite qualifications." The result will be "a constant probability of seeing the station filled by characters pre-eminent for ability and virtue."

To those who argued that a strong executive is incompatible with republican government, The Federalists retorted that energy in the executive is the first prerequisite of good government. "It is essential to the protection of the community and against foreign attacks; it is not less essential to the steady administration of the laws; to the protection of property . . .; to the security of liberty against the enterprises and assaults of ambition, of faction, and anarchy." A feeble executive, they insisted, leads to weak government and such a government, "whatever it may be in theory, must be, in practice, a bad government."

There were some people who argued in favor of a plural executive. The Federalists held that a plural executive is deficient in performing the executive functions, necessarily lacking secrecy, dispatch and decisiveness. Moreover, a plural executive tends to conceal faults and destroy responsibility. Finally, they pointed out, a plural executive is more expensive than a single executive.

Defending the four-year term of the presidency, the Federalists claimed that it would give the executive a certain independence from the transient whim and passing opinions of the people, which is desirable. The people always intend the public good, but sometimes they are led astray. A statesman, and especially the executive, should be able to resist these momentary impulses and act on the basis of long-term calculations of the public good, unswayed by the passion of the moment.

They defended re-eligibility for election on similar grounds. They also argued that it lends stability to the government, providing a degree of continuity in its administration which is advantageous from the point of view of both domestic and foreign policy.

The people of the United States, given their experience with the British monarch and the royal governors, were naturally suspicious of executive power. The Federalists assured them that the executive power established by the Constitution is not only effective, but it is also safe. The president is chosen every four years by persons (electoral college) "immediately chosen by the people for that purpose," and he is liable to impeachment, trial, and dismissal from office. Moreover, effective controls upon the executive power are provided by the system of checks and balances, in which some of the most important powers (treaty-making and appointive) are shared with the Senate. These measures provide assurance that executive power would not be successfully abused.

VI. The Judiciary

*Q*uestions were raised by opponents of the Constitution regarding the way in which judges were appointed and their lifetime tenure in office during good behavior.

The Federalists dismissed the first by pointing out that while judges are appointed by the president, his appointments require the advice and consent of the Senate. This is sufficient to regard against foolish appointments.

The Federalists defended life tenure by first arguing that the judicial power, having access to neither the sword nor the purse, is the least dangerous branch of the government. "The judiciary is beyond comparison the weakest of the three departments of power...."

Having argued that it is safe to entrust the judicial power to judges with life tenure, they also said it is necessary in order to guarantee their independence. The independence of the judiciary is especially important under a Constitution providing for a government of limited powers. Such a Constitution stipulates that there are certain kinds of laws, for example ex post facto laws, that the legislature cannot pass. "Limitations of this kind," they wrote, "can be preserved in practice no other way than through the medium of courts of justice, whose duty it must be to declare all acts contrary to the manifest terms of the Constitution void. Without this, all the reservations of particular rights or privileges would amount to nothing."

Life tenure, the Federalists emphasized, is essential if the judges are to possess the independence necessary for performing the "arduous" task of enforcing the limits imposed by the Constitution on the other branches of government. Moreover, the duties of judges require great amounts of knowledge and experience which would be enhanced by lengthy terms of service.

VII. Bill of Rights

*T*he Federalists responded to complaints that the Constitution does not contain a bill of rights. They argued that the Constitution contains protections for those rights usually mentioned in bills of rights. These included the guarantee of habeas corpus, the prohibition of ex post facto laws, the guarantee in criminal cases of trial by jury in the state where the crime was committed, protection of persons and their descendants accused of treason, and the prohibition of titles of nobility.

Most bills of rights, such as the Magna Carta, were between kings and their people, and are unnecessary in a political system where sovereignty resides in the people and the members of the government are only the people's servants. Moreover, a Constitution which delegates only limited powers to the government does not require a minutely detailed list of the rights maintained by the people.

Finally, the Federalists suggested that such a list of protected rights is in fact dangerous to the rights of the people. Why provide protection against powers not granted? This might afford the pretext for the government to claim power it doesn't have on the ground that if protection is offered against the misuse of a particular power, that power must have been granted.

Unit Three: How Did the Values and Principles Embodied in the Constitution Shape American Institutions and Practices?

UNIT OVERVIEW. The Constitution was a plan for creating and operating the new government. The lessons in this unit describe some of the more important developments under the new Constitution, including organizing the executive and judicial branches, adding the Bill of Rights to the Constitution, establishing the power of judicial review, dealing with controversies over the powers of Congress and the relationship between the national and state governments, and developing political parties.

The first lesson in the unit describes how the First Congress organized the executive and judicial branches and drafted the Bill of Rights. Students learn how the electoral college selected the president and how Congress established the first executive departments and enacted the Judiciary Act of 1789, creating the federal district courts and circuit courts.

The next lesson focuses on the issues related to drafting the Bill of Rights and deciding whether it should be placed at the beginning of the Constitution or added as a series of amendments. Students learn why the Framers included certain rights, such as habeas corpus, in the body of the Constitution. Students examine the reasons the Anti-Federalists pressured for a bill of rights during ratification. They learn about the first draft James Madison submitted to Congress and the modifications Congress made before sending the Bill of Rights to the states.

Next, the text describes a development the Framers had not anticipated, the rise of political parties. Students learn about the Framers' admonitions against factions and their hope that the influence of factions would be limited by a complicated system of government and a vast diversity of interests in the country. Students examine the conflicting ideas about the powers of the national government that led to the rise of the Federalist and Republican parties.

The concluding two lessons in the unit describe the power of judicial review and the system of federalism created by the Constitution. Students learn how the Supreme Court, in the landmark case *Marbury v. Madison*, acquired the power of judicial review. Students examine different methods judges use to interpret the Constitution and continuing controversies over the application of judicial review. Students learn about the supremacy clause and how the Supreme Court applied judicial review over state governments in the case *McCulloch v. Maryland*.

UNIT OBJECTIVES. At the conclusion of this unit, students should be able to

1. describe how Congress used the Constitution to organize the executive and judicial branches

2. describe the rights included in the body of the Constitution and how and why Congress drafted the Bill of Rights

3. describe the controversies that led to the rise of political parties and explain why this was an important development

4. explain judicial review and describe how the Supreme Court acquired the power of judicial review over federal and state actions

5. explain different methods judges use to interpret the Constitution and the continuing controversies over judicial review

6. describe the importance of the supremacy clause and explain how the Constitution divides power between the national and state governments

7. evaluate, take, and defend positions related to differing opinions about how to interpret the powers which the Constitution delegates to the national government

INTRODUCING THE UNIT. Have the class read the "Purpose of Unit" on p. 91 of the text. Discuss the basic themes students can expect to learn about during their study of this unit and review the objectives of the unit. Ask students how they think a book about ideas, such as this text, might differ from traditional government texts. Why might they think it important to study the ideas and principles of our political system? Ask students to write four or five personal objectives they would like to accomplish during the study of this unit. You may want to ask them, instead, to write four or five basic questions they would like to explore during their study of these lessons. They should keep their personal objectives or questions in a journal or notebook for review at the conclusion of the unit. They may want to expand upon these personal objectives or questions as their study in the unit progresses.

Review the unit timeline. Encourage students to create a similar timeline in their journals or notebooks to track in more detail important events or developments described in each lesson.

LESSON 18: How Was the Constitution Used to Organize the New Government?

Lesson Overview

The First Congress met in New York in April 1789 to begin the task of organizing the new government under the Constitution. This lesson describes how, using the guidelines provided in the Constitution, the First Congress (1) named the new president and vice president, (2) provided funding for the new government, (3) organized the executive and judicial branches, and (4) drafted a bill of rights. Students learn that the Constitution provided a general framework for the government, leaving many necessary details to be worked out later by the Congress and the other branches. Students also learn of one of the events not foreseen by the Framers, the significant growth of the executive branch and the federal bureaucracy.

Lesson Objectives

At the conclusion of this lesson, students should be able to

1. explain that the Constitution provides a general framework outlining how the government should be organized and should operate, and that details are added by the government as the need arises

2. explain how Congress used Article II of the Constitution to name the new president and vice president

3. explain the importance and the methods of raising revenue to fund the new government

4. describe how Congress organized the executive branch and the unforeseen growth of this branch and of the federal bureaucracy

5. describe the federal court system that was established by Congress in the **Judiciary Act of 1789**

Preparation/Teaching Materials

Student text, pp. 92–95

Teaching Procedures

A. Introducing the Lesson

To introduce the lesson, ask the class to imagine that they are members of the First Congress. What might be some important issues they should discuss and act upon? Direct attention to the illustration on p. 92 of the text. Ask students to respond to the question in the caption: Why was it so important for the First Congress to succeed?

While students read the "Purpose of Lesson" on p. 92, post the "Terms to Know" on the board. Review with the class what students should be able to do at the completion of the lesson, as explained in the "Purpose of Lesson." Review the vocabulary items listed on the board and remind students to take special note of these terms as they study the material in the lesson.

B. Reading and Discussion
What were the tasks of the First Congress?

Have the class read "What were the tasks of the First Congress?" on p. 92 of the text. Post the five tasks on the board:

- naming the new president and vice president
- providing money for the new government
- organizing the executive branch of government
- organizing the judicial branch of government
- drafting a bill of rights

Use these five tasks to assign the reading of the next section. You may want to assign individual segments to small groups of students to read and report to the class.

C. Reading and Discussion
How did Congress accomplish these tasks within constitutional guidelines?

Have the class read "How did Congress accomplish these tasks within constitutional guidelines?" on pp. 92–93 of the text. During discussion, check that students understand the following points:

- **Naming the new president and vice president**

  Article II, Section 1 sets forth the way the president and vice president are to be selected. Students should understand the role of the electoral college and that the task of the First Congress was not to select the president and vice president, but merely to count the votes and announce the results of the election.

- **Providing money for the new government**

  Because the federal government had no income, this was a high priority. Article I, Section 8 gave Congress the power to raise money by collecting "taxes, duties, imposts and excises." Congress had to decide what taxes and duties to collect and how to collect them.

You may want to have students examine Article I, Section 8 of the Constitution (see Reference Section in student text) to determine what powers Congress has to collect and spend money.

■ **Organizing the executive branch of government**

The Constitution gives Congress the power to organize the executive branch of government. The First Congress created the State Department, the War Department, and the Treasury Department. In addition, they selected an attorney general to handle all Supreme Court cases involving the federal government and to advise the president on legal questions.

■ **Organizing the judicial branch of government**

The Constitution also gives Congress the power to organize the judicial branch of government. The First Congress passed the **Judiciary Act of 1789** which established a **federal district court** in each state for hearing trials in cases involving the Constitution, federal laws, and disputes between citizens of different states. The law also established the **circuit courts** to try serious cases and to hear appeals from the district courts.

■ **Drafting a bill of rights**

James Madison wanted to fulfill the promise, which the Federalists had made during the debates about ratification of the Constitution, to add a bill of rights. He began his task by examining the proposals for amendments offered during the ratification debates. These proposals either placed additional limits on the powers of the federal government or protected individual rights.

Direct attention to the charts illustrating the contemporary structure of the executive and judicial branches on pp. 93 and 94. Ask students to respond to the questions in the captions: (1) Why has the executive branch grown so much larger than originally envisioned by the Framers? (2) Why has the court system grown so much more complex than originally outlined by the Framers?

D. Concluding the Lesson

To conclude the lesson, have students respond to the questions in the "Reviewing and Using the Lesson" section on p. 95 of the text. Finally, have students return to the "Purpose of Lesson" on p. 92. Ask students to describe the extent to which they accomplished the objectives of the lesson.

Optional Activities
Reinforcement, Extended Learning, and Enrichment

1. Have students conduct research on changes in the way the president and vice president are selected today.

2. Have students conduct research on how the executive branch is organized today.

3. Have students conduct research on how cases on appeal reach the U.S. Supreme Court and the procedures the Court applies in reaching its decisions. Have students find newspaper articles on cases currently before the Court.

4. Ask students to select from newspapers or magazines examples of actions taken by departments of the federal executive. Ask them to explain how these actions relate to the purposes of republican government.

LESSON 19: What Rights Did the Constitution Protect? How Was the Bill of Rights Added to the Constitution?

Lesson Overview

The Framers included provisions in the new Constitution that prohibited both the federal and state governments from violating several important rights, e.g., prohibitions against the passage of ex post facto laws and bills of attainder. This lesson helps students understand that these provisions were designed to protect individuals from the abuses of rights that had occurred under both the British government and the various state legislatures prior to 1787. Students learn why the Anti-Federalists thought it was necessary to add a bill of rights to the Constitution. The lesson describes the amendments James Madison proposed during the First Congress to additionally limit the powers of the federal government and to protect individual rights. The lesson also describes why Madison feared the states were a greater threat to individual rights than the federal government and students examine the two amendments he proposed to limit the power of state governments. Students learn that Congress proposed that the Bill of Rights be adopted as a series of amendments rather than adding it at the beginning of the Constitution to deprive the Anti-Federalists of an opportunity to rewrite the Constitution. During the critical thinking exercise, the class develops and defends positions on the importance of the Second Amendment, the right of the people to keep and bear arms.

Lesson Objectives

At the conclusion of this lesson, students should be able to

1. describe and explain the importance of the rights the Framers included in the body of the Constitution to limit the powers of the federal government and protect the rights of the people

2. explain why the Anti-Federalists wanted a bill of rights added to the Constitution

3. explain why Madison proposed adding a bill of rights to the beginning of the Constitution, and why the Bill of Rights was added as a series of amendments instead

4. describe the amendments Madison proposed to protect individual rights from abuse by state governments

5. evaluate, take, and defend positions on the importance of the Second Amendment, the right of the people to keep and bear arms

Preparation/Teaching Materials

Student text pp. 96–101

Optional. Invite a community resource person, such as an attorney, to work with the class during the critical thinking exercise on the Second Amendment

Teaching Procedures

A. Introducing the Lesson

To introduce the lesson, ask students to suggest three or four rights they consider so important that they would include them in the body of the Constitution, assuming that there was no bill of rights.

While students read the "Purpose of Lesson" on p. 96, post the "Terms to Know" on the board. Review with the class what students should be able to do at the completion of the lesson, as explained in the "Purpose of Lesson." Review the vocabulary items listed on the board and remind students to take special note of these terms as they study the material in the lesson.

B. Reading and Discussion

What rights were specifically protected in the Constitution?

Have the class read "What rights were specifically protected in the Constitution?" on pp. 96–97 of the text. Students should understand that the specific protection of rights included in the Constitution were intended to prevent abuses the Framers had seen in British history, in colonial and state governments, and under the Articles of Confederation. These rights can be organized into three categories:

■ **Protection of the political independence and other rights of public officials.**

These rights include (1) freedom of speech for members of Congress, (2) freedom from arrest for anything said on the floor of Congress, (3) freedom from arrest for minor crimes committed while Congress is in session, (4) freedom from religious tests as a requirement for holding public office, and (5) the right to a fair hearing in impeachment cases.

■ **Protection of individual rights against violation by the state governments.**

These rights include (1) protection for citizens who have entered into agreements regarding property or other economic matters ("impairing the obligation of contracts"), (2) the property rights of slave owners, (3) protection from ex post facto laws, and (4) protection from bills of attainder.

■ **Protection of individual rights against violation by the federal government.**

These rights include (1) habeas corpus, (2) trial by jury in criminal cases, (3) providing a specific definition of treason that can only be changed by amending the Constitution, and (4) prohibiting Congress from requiring any religious test for holding federal office.

Ask students whether these were the same rights they offered earlier during the introduction to the lesson. Have students explain how each of the rights incorporated in the Constitution would limit the power of government and facilitate the protection of individual rights. Ask them to give examples from history or their own experience to support their views.

Direct attention to the illustrations on pp. 96 and 97. Ask students to respond to the questions in the captions: (1) Should members of Congress have immunity for statements made in Congress? (2) Why did the Framers believe it was necessary to protect the obligation of contracts?

C. Critical Thinking Exercise

Examining the Importance of Rights Guaranteed in the Constitution

Divide the class into four groups to complete the critical thinking exercise, "Examining the Importance of Rights Guaranteed in the Constitution," on pp. 97–98 of the text. During the exercise students examine the rights written into the body of the Constitution: (1) no bill of attainder may be passed, (2) no ex post facto law may be passed, (3) treason is narrowly defined, and (4) no religious test for holding public office is allowed. Assign each group one of the four topics. If, in your opinion, the groups are too large to adequately involve all students, divide the class into eight groups. Have two groups work separately on each issue. Review the instructions for completing the

exercise and the questions with the class. After students have completed their work, have them report their responses to the rest of the class.

D. Reading and Discussion

What amendments to the Constitution did Madison propose?

Have the class read "What amendments to the Constitution did Madison propose?" on pp. 98–99 of the text. Students should note that James Madison wanted to move quickly to fulfill the promise the Federalists had made to add a bill of rights to the Constitution. Madison was in a particularly difficult position because he had to convince his fellow Federalists that he was not a traitor to the cause of a more powerful federal government while fulfilling his pledge to the Anti-Federalists to add a bill of rights. Students should note that Madison's suggestions for a bill of rights fell into two categories: (1) limitations on federal government power and (2) protection of individual rights. Have the class examine the first ten amendments to the Constitution (see Reference Section in student text). Examine the First Amendment. In what ways does the amendment limit the power of the federal government? What individual rights does it protect? Have students examine the other amendments in the Bill of Rights. In what ways do they limit the power of the federal government? What individual rights do they protect?

Madison, however, was convinced that the greatest danger to individual rights came from groups who might use the government to serve their selfish interests. He thought that state governments were more easily used by factions than the national government. Have students carefully examine the amendment in the text:

> No state shall violate the equal rights of conscience, or the freedom of the press, or the trial by jury in criminal cases.

Why might Madison have considered this amendment limiting the power of state governments to be "the most valuable amendment in the whole list"? Why was this necessary given that most states had declarations of rights?

Have students examine the Ninth Amendment:

> The enumeration in the Constitution of certain rights shall not be construed to deny or disparage others retained by the people.

Why did Madison think the Ninth Amendment was necessary? What rights does it protect? Ask students to cite examples.

Students should also note that Madison suggested an introductory statement to be added to the Constitution containing the basic ideas about government found in the Declaration of Independence. He also argued that the amendments he had drafted should be included in the Constitution itself, not added as a separate list. Madison concurred with Jefferson that placing rights directly in the body of the Constitution would make clear that the federal courts would have the duty to see that these rights were protected. In Madison's words, "the guardians of those rights…an impenetrable bulwark against the assumption of power in the legislative and executive branches; they will…resist every encroachment upon rights stipulated in the Constitution." Opponents of the position argued that to add language to the Constitution itself would imply that a new constitution had been created, one which had not been ratified by the people. It also might set a dangerous precedent, opening the door to other structural changes which many Anti-Federalists wished to make, but which the Federalists opposed.

Optional instructional activity. Have students work in small groups role-playing congressional representatives to analyze the amendments (discussed in the text) that Madison proposed. After each group has discussed the proposed amendments and decided whether to support their passage, have a spokesperson make a majority and minority report to Congress. Afterwards, hold a vote. During the follow-up discussion, have students summarize the arguments on both sides. Why might Madison have wished to specifically protect these particular rights? What important interests, such as state sovereignty, should be considered when deciding whether or not to support this amendment? What fundamental values, such as individual liberty, should be considered when deciding whether or not to support this amendment?

E. Reading and Discussion
How did Congress respond to Madison's proposals?

Have the class read "How did Congress respond to Madison's proposals?" on pp. 99–100 of the text. Students should note that members of the House of Representatives appeared uninterested in Madison's suggestions. When Madison called for a vote on his amendments, the House sent them to committee instead. Finally, the House made some changes and sent the amendments to the Senate. Roger Sherman insisted that the amendments be added at the end of the Constitution rather than in the body of the document as Madison had suggested. The Senate eliminated the amendment that would have prohibited state governments from violating freedom of conscience, speech, and press, and guaranteed trial by jury in criminal cases.

Direct attention to the illustration on p. 99. Ask students to respond to the question in the caption: Why were members of the House of Representatives not interested in Madison's speeches in support of a bill of rights? Do students think Madison's persistence was justifiable?

Direct attention to the "What do *you* think?" section on p. 100. Use these questions to conduct a general class discussion on the adoption of the Bill of Rights.

Optional instructional activity. Have students work in small groups to examine the Bill of Rights (see Reference Section in student text). Ask them to select the amendments they would apply to the states. They should develop arguments in favor of the rights they have selected, justifying their positions both on philosophical and historical grounds. During the discussion ask students to project what they think might happen if these rights were not protected from state governments? Does their state constitution prohibit their state government from violating these rights? Consider other rights, not specifically listed in the Bill of Rights, which they would like protected from violation by government. Note that in Unit Four students learn about the Fourteenth Amendment and how the Bill of Rights has been selectively incorporated to prevent abuses by state governments.

F. Reading and Discussion
What did people think of the Bill of Rights in 1791?

Have the class read "What did people think of the Bill of Rights in 1791?" on p. 100 of the text. Students should note that initially, the Bill of Rights had little effect. In 1833 the Supreme Court ruled in *Barron v. Baltimore* that the Bill of Rights applied only to the federal government. In *Barron v. Baltimore* the city of Baltimore diverted several streams in order to pave the city's streets. The resulting deposits of sand made the water surrounding Barron's Wharf shallow, preventing the approach of vessels and rendering the wharf useless. Barron claimed that the city's actions violated the Fifth Amendment clause prohibiting the taking of private property for public use without just compensation. The Supreme Court disagreed. The Constitution was established by the people of the United States for their own government, not for the government of the individual states. The powers of the national government were to be exercised only by the national government. Limitations on that power apply only to that government and not to the states, unless directly mentioned.

Students should note that the Anti-Federalists were not pleased with James Madison or the Bill of Rights. It spoiled their chances to rewrite the Constitution. The protections regarding individual rights were narrowly written and so displeased the Anti-Federalists who wanted broader, more open-ended prohibitions. The

Anti-Federalists did manage to defeat the amendment which would have placed prohibitions on the state governments.

G. Critical Thinking Exercise
Developing and Defending Positions on the Second Amendment

To introduce this exercise, direct attention to the illustration on p. 100 of the text. Ask students to respond to the question in the caption: Why is the question of a person's right to bear arms more controversial today than when the Constitution was written?

Have the class work in small groups of five students to complete the critical thinking exercise, "Developing and Defending Positions on the Second Amendment," on pp. 100–101 of the text. During the exercise the class analyzes the Second Amendment and defends positions on what limitations, if any, they would place on the right to bear arms. Ask students to read the introductory material, then review the instructions for completing the exercise and the questions. Allow adequate time for students to complete their work, then have them share their responses with the class.

Optional instructional activity. Have students simulate a legislative hearing on a proposed bill which would place further limits on the right to bear arms. Base the hearing on current federal or state legislation, such as attempts to establish waiting periods or proposed bans on military assault weapons. Students should play the roles of legislators, individual citizens who support further gun control, citizens opposed to further or current limits, and lobbyists for various groups organized to oppose or promote gun control legislation. For detailed instructions on conducting a simulated legislative hearing, please see p. 14 of this guide.

H. Reading and Discussion
Were the Framers aware of other threats to rights?

Have the class read "Were the Framers aware of other threats to rights?" on p. 101 of the text. The key point for students to understand from this section is that during the twentieth century the Bill of Rights has become the most important single document protecting individual rights. Students will learn more about the expansion of rights in Unit Four.

I. Concluding the Lesson

To conclude the lesson, have students respond to the questions in the "Reviewing and Using the Lesson" section on p. 101 of the text. Finally, have students return to the "Purpose of Lesson" on p. 96. Ask students to describe the extent to which they accomplished the objectives of the lesson.

Optional Activities
Reinforcement, Extended Learning, and Enrichment

1. Have students imagine that, as members of the First Congress, they are writing a newsletter to mail to their constituents. The newsletter should report the accomplishments of the First Congress.

2. Have students create a poster convincing others that, in regard to slavery, protecting liberty is more important than protecting property. Students may want to approach the topic from the point of view of a higher natural law. You may wish to share with them this argument from a pamphlet circulated during the ratification debates by a former Harvard classmate of John Adams:

   *There is a great distinction in not taking part in the most barbarous violation of the sacred laws of God and humanity and our becoming guarantees for its exercise for a term of years....
   It is our purpose to wash our hands clean of it.*

LESSON 20: What Caused the Rise of Political Parties?

Lesson Overview

In this lesson students learn that the Framers were opposed to political parties, which they believed were factions concerned with selfish interests at the expense of the common good. James Madison believed that the size and diversity of the nation and the complexity of the government would limit the ability of any single faction to form a majority. Instead, the different groups would have to work together to bargain and compromise. Disagreements soon arose, however, between the Federalists, who were followers of Alexander Hamilton, and the Republicans, whose leader was Thomas Jefferson. These disagreements focused on how Congress should interpret the "necessary and proper" and "general welfare" clauses of the Constitution. This dispute reflected the fundamental division between the two groups on how much power the Constitution delegated to the federal government. Other issues separating the two groups involved questions of foreign policy and the Alien and Sedition Acts. Students learn that by 1800, two identifiable political parties had emerged. Students also examine the role of political parties in American politics today. During the critical thinking exercise, the class applies the "necessary and proper" and "general welfare" clauses to student government in your school.

Lesson Objectives

At the conclusion of this lesson, students should be able to

1. explain why the Framers opposed the development of political parties

2. explain the basis of the disagreement between the Federalists and the Republicans over the interpretation of the Constitution, and the relationship of this disagreement to the emergence of political parties

3. explain the arguments between Jefferson and Hamilton over the establishment of the Bank of the United States, foreign relations, and the Alien and Sedition Acts

4. explain the significance of the presidential election of 1800 and the reasons for the demise of the Federalist Party after the War of 1812

5. explain the role of political parties today

Preparation/Teaching Materials

Student text, pp. 102–106

Teaching Procedures

A. Introducing the Lesson

While students read the "Purpose of Lesson" on p. 102, post the "Terms to Know" on the board. Review with the class what students should be able to do at the completion of the lesson, as explained in the "Purpose of Lesson." Review the vocabulary items listed on the board and remind students to take special note of these terms as they study the material in the lesson.

B. Reading and Discussion

What did Madison say about factions?

Have the class read "What did Madison say about factions?" on pp. 102–103 of the text. Students should understand that James Madison believed one of the advantages of the way the Constitution structured government was that it would control factions. Check that students understand the term **faction**, a group of citizens, either a majority or minority, that pursues its own selfish interests at the expense of other citizens' interests or the

common good. Madison believed that diversity in a large commercial society and the complicated system of government created by the Constitution would limit the influence of factions. Instead, he saw different groups working together through bargaining and compromise to create coalitions that would promote the interests of the majority. Check that students understand the basis for the Framers' resistance to political parties and the relationship of that resistance to their views of the purpose of republican government.

Direct attention to the illustration on p. 103. Ask students to respond to the question in the caption: What has been the role of political parties in elections?

C. Reading and Discussion

What conflicting ideas led to the development of political parties?

Have the class read "What conflicting ideas led to the development of political parties?" on p. 103 of the text. Students should understand that Thomas Jefferson and Alexander Hamilton each had very different ideas about what the government's policies should be. Hamilton and his followers became known as the **Federalists**, while Jefferson and his followers were called **Republicans**.

- The **Federalists** argued that the Constitution created a government designed to solve national problems. If a problem was a national one, the federal government could and should deal with it, even if the power to do so was not specifically mentioned in the Constitution.

- The **Republicans** argued that if government were free to define its own power, the liberty of the people would be threatened. The federal government should be limited strictly to enumerated powers.

The differences of opinion between the two groups on how to interpret the power of the national government played a large role in the development of political parties.

Direct attention to the illustration on p. 103. Ask students to respond to the question in the caption: Why is there no mention of political parties in the Constitution?

D. Reading and Discussion

Why was Jefferson concerned about the interpretation of the Constitution?

Have the class read "Why was Jefferson concerned about the interpretation of the Constitution?" on pp. 103–104 of the text. Students should understand that Jefferson was deeply concerned about interpretations of the general welfare clause and the necessary and proper clause in Article I, Section 8. It was the "energetic" use of these powers that Jefferson and others feared.

E. Critical Thinking Exercise

Identifying Jefferson's Concern

Have the class work in small groups of five students to complete the critical thinking exercise, "Identifying Jefferson's Concern," on p. 104 of the text. Read the instructions and review the questions with the class. Allow adequate time for students to complete their work, then have them share their responses with the class. During the discussion help students understand why the Framers included the necessary and proper and general welfare clauses in the Constitution and the problems raised by these clauses concerning the principle of limited government.

F. Reading and Discussion

What conflicts arose between the Federalists and the Republicans?

Have the class read "What conflicts arose between the Federalists and the Republicans?" on p. 104 of the text.

Students should understand that the disagreement between Jefferson and Hamilton centered on whether Congress had the power to create the Bank of the United States. Hamilton claimed the bank was "necessary and proper" to carrying out the responsibilities given to Congress in the Constitution. Jefferson disagreed. He claimed that the necessary and proper clause should be interpreted to mean "absolutely and indispensably necessary." George Washington accepted Hamilton's interpretation, increasing the power of the federal government.

G. Reading and Discussion

Why did the Federalists and Republicans take opposing views on the war between Great Britain and France?

Have the class read "Why did the Federalists and Republicans take opposing views on the war between Great Britain and France?" on p. 104 of the text. Students should understand that the Federalists wanted to help Great Britain because of trade relations and general opposition to the French Revolution of 1789. The Republicans wanted to assist the French in return for the help they had given during the American Revolutionary War and they generally supported the revolution against the French monarch. To avoid a division in his administration, President Washington declared neutrality in the conflict between Great Britain and France. By the time George Washington left office, party conflict was becoming a fixture in American politics, despite the departing president's warnings.

H. Reading and Discussion

What were the Alien and Sedition Acts?

Have the class read "What were the Alien and Sedition Acts?" on pp. 104–105 of the text. Students should note that the election of 1796 resulted in a Federalist president, John Adams, and a Republican vice president, Thomas Jefferson. Jefferson was critical of the way the Federalists were running the government. A Federalist Congress passed the **Alien and Sedition Acts**, giving the president power to force foreigners to leave the country if he considered them dangerous and making it a crime for editors, writers, or speakers to attack the government. Jefferson and the Republicans were outraged. They knew the laws were aimed at them. They responded with the **Virginia and Kentucky Resolutions** which claimed that the states had a right to decide if the federal government had exceeded its powers and, further, they had the power to declare the laws of Congress null and void.

Direct attention to the illustration on p. 105. Ask students to respond to the question in the caption: Why did the Federalists try to silence criticism of the government in the press?

I. Reading and Discussion
What was the "revolution of 1800?"

Have the class read "What was the 'revolution of 1800'?" on p. 105 of the text. The importance of the election of 1800 is that it was the first to feature candidates for president and vice president from rival parties and it was the first time in modern history that control of a government was given over to new leaders as the result of a "democratic revolution" rather than by hereditary succession or violent overthrow. The election of 1800 was a bitter one, with both Federalists and Republicans accusing the other of wishing to destroy the Constitution.

J. Reading and Discussion
What part do political parties play in today's political system?

Have the class read "What part do political parties play in today's political system?" on p. 106 of the text. During the discussion students should note the role political parties have in our contemporary political process: (1) provide a means to organize support for a political candidate, (2) persuade more people to participate in elections, (3) provide a means to show support or opposition to the policies of the party in power, (4) provide an outlet for popular passions and forums for deliberating public policy, and (5) provide a means to change government and not the Constitution.

Direct attention to the "What do *you* think?" section on p. 106. You may want to use these questions to conduct a general class discussion. Alternatively, you may want to have students work individually, with a study partner, or in small groups to develop responses to the questions. If so, have students share their responses with the class.

K. Concluding the Lesson

To conclude the lesson, direct attention to the illustration on p. 106 of the text. Ask students to respond to the question in the caption: Have political parties advanced or inhibited representative democracy? Then have students respond to the questions in the "Reviewing and Using the Lesson" section on p. 106 of the text. Finally, have students return to the "Purpose of Lesson" on p. 102. Ask students to describe the extent to which they accomplished the objectives of the lesson.

Optional Activities
Reinforcement, Extended Learning, and Enrichment

1. Have students do additional research on the election of 1800 and report their findings to the class.

2. Have students research and develop a time chart illustrating the development and evolution of political parties from 1800 to the Civil War.

3. Have students illustrate the development and evolution of political parties from the Civil War to the present.

4. Have students research third party movements in the United States describing their influence and policies that have resulted.

5. Assign the class to read "Federalist No. 10" and to summarize and discuss the argument it contains. Ask them how this argument is related to the question of political parties.

6. Have students get copies of the Republican and Democratic party platforms from a recent election. Ask them to read them and discuss whether these platforms confirm the Framers' view that political parties were simply factions pursuing their own interests rather than the common good.

LESSON 21: What Is Judicial Review? Why Is It Controversial?

Lesson Overview

This lesson deals with the power of the United States Supreme Court to exercise judicial review over the actions of the executive and legislative branches of the federal government. One new idea about government that developed in this nation was the idea that the Supreme Court and lower courts should have the power to interpret the Constitution and decide what it means. However, there have been great differences of opinion about whether the Constitution gave the judicial branch this power and about how the courts should use it. Students learn that this controversy raises basic questions about representative government and majority rule, on one hand, and constitutional government and the protection of basic rights and unpopular minorities on the other. Students learn how, in the case of *Marbury v. Madison*, Chief Justice John Marshall claimed the power of judicial review for the Supreme Court. He believed that if the Court did not have the power of judicial review there would be no effective way to enforce the limitations the people placed on the powers of government in the Constitution. The powers of government, therefore, would be unlimited and we would no longer have a constitutional government.

Although most Americans today agree that judicial review is a necessary power of the Court, many do not agree on how the Court should exercise that power. During the lesson, students examine differing opinions on how best to interpret the meaning of the words in the Constitution: (1) using the literal words or plain meaning of the Constitution, (2) using the intentions of the Framers, (3) using basic principles and values in the perspective of history, or (4) using contemporary social values in terms of today's policy needs. During the critical thinking exercise the class examines the issues and takes and defends positions on whether the Supreme Court should have the power of judicial review.

Lesson Objectives

At the conclusion of this lesson, students should be able to

1. explain the differing arguments on whether the Supreme Court should have the power of judicial review

2. explain the relationship of judicial review to representative democracy and constitutional government

3. describe how Chief Justice Marshall claimed the power of judicial review for the Supreme Court in the case of *Marbury v. Madison* and explain his argument

4. explain the various methods of constitutional interpretation that influence the way the Supreme Court arrives at a decision and the arguments for and against each of them

5. explain a variety of factors that may influence the justices' opinions

Preparation/Teaching Materials

Student text, pp. 107–112

Optional. Invite a community resource person, such as an attorney or judge, to work with students during the critical thinking exercise or the optional instructional activity in the lesson.

Teaching Procedures

A. Introducing the Lesson

Introduce the lesson by asking the class to recall any cases they have heard about in which a court declared a legislative or executive act unconstitutional. Do students think the courts should have the power to declare acts of the president and Congress unconstitutional? Who should decide when the national or state governments have violated the limits of their authority as defined in the Constitution?

While students read the "Purpose of Lesson" on p. 107, post the "Terms to Know" on the board. Review with the class what students should be able to do at the completion of the lesson, as explained in the "Purpose of Lesson." Review the vocabulary items listed on the board and remind students to take special note of these terms as they study the material in the lesson.

B. Reading and Discussion
What is judicial review?

Have the class read "What is judicial review?" on p. 107 of the text. Check that students understand that the term **judicial review** is the power of the judicial branch to decide if acts of the legislative or executive branch violate the Constitution. Once a court declares a law or act "null and void" it can no longer be enforced.

Direct attention to the illustration on p. 107. Ask students to respond to the question in the caption: How does judicial review strengthen the judicial branch of government?

C. Reading and Discussion

Should the Supreme Court have the power to declare acts of the president and Congress unconstitutional?

Have the class read "Should the Supreme Court have the power to declare acts of the president and Congress unconstitutional?" on pp. 107–108 of the text. Students should understand that the Founders were familiar with the ideas of judicial review since under British rule the Privy Council had the power to veto laws passed by the colonial legislatures. After the Revolution, some state courts had declared laws to be unconstitutional. The Framers, however, did not mention the power of judicial review in the Constitution.

D. Reading and Discussion

How did the Supreme Court establish its power of judicial review?

Have the class read "How did the Supreme Court establish its power of judicial review?" on p. 108 of the text. Students should understand that although the Constitution does not explicitly give the Court the power of judicial review, the Founders believed that some part of government should be given power to decide if other parts of government had violated the higher law. The issue was discussed during the Philadelphia Convention and the ratification debates and is mentioned in "Federalist No. 78."

E. Critical Thinking Exercise

Evaluating, Taking, and Defending a Position on the Power of Judicial Review

Have the class work in small groups of five students to complete the critical thinking exercise, "Evaluating, Taking, and Defending a Position on the Power of Judicial Review," on p. 108 of the text. During the exercise, students examine two choices, and the potential consequences of each choice, to determine whether the Supreme Court should have the power of judicial review. Allow adequate time for students to complete their work. At the conclusion, have students share their work with the class.

F. Reading and Discussion

What events led to the Supreme Court case *Marbury v. Madison*?

Have the class read "What events led to the Supreme Court case *Marbury v. Madison*?" on pp. 108–109 of the text. During the discussion students should understand that following the election of 1800, the Federalists passed legislation creating a number of new federal courts. The Federalists attempted to fill the new courts with Federalist judges before handing power over to the new Republican president, Thomas Jefferson. Jefferson did not want more Federalists serving as judges, so he ordered Secretary of State James Madison not to deliver the commissions. As a result, William Marbury did not receive his commission to serve as a justice of the peace for the District of Columbia. Marbury asked the Supreme Court to issue a **writ of mandamus**, a power granted to the Court in the Judiciary Act of 1789. Students should understand that a writ of mandamus is a court order forcing a public official to do something that he or she is supposed to do. In this case, Madison was supposed to deliver the commission to Marbury. Chief Justice Marshall was faced with a difficult problem. If the Court ordered President Jefferson to deliver the commission and he refused, the Court would appear weak and powerless. The Court must rely on the executive branch to enforce its orders. If the Court did not order Jefferson to deliver the commission, though, it would also appear weak.

Optional instructional activity. To help students better understand the basic issues and importance of the case *Marbury v. Madison*, you may want to engage the class in a moot court. First, review the facts and issues in the case. Then divide the class into five groups: (1) justices of the Supreme Court, (2) attorneys for Marbury, (3) rebuttal attorneys for Marbury, (4) attorneys for Madison, and (5) rebuttal attorneys for Madison. Have the groups prepare arguments to present to the justices. The opposing sides should address the following issues in the case: (1) Does Marbury have a right to the appointment? (2) If Marbury has a right to the appointment and his right has been violated, do the laws of the country give him a way to have things set right? (3) If the laws of the country give Marbury a way to deal with this problem, is that way a writ of mandamus from the Supreme Court? During their preparation, students should carefully examine Article III of the Constitution (see Reference Section in the student text). The justices should examine the issues and Article III and prepare a set of questions to ask each side during the presentation of arguments. Allow adequate time for preparation. At the conclusion, the justices should deliberate and announce their decision and the reasoning which supports it. Then have students evaluate the strengths and weaknesses of the arguments presented and the possible consequences of the court decision. To understand how the Supreme Court decided the case, have students read the next section of the text. For detailed instructions on conducting a moot court, please see p. 19 of this guide.

G. Reading and Discussion

What were the major issues in *Marbury v. Madison*?

Have the class read "What were the major issues in *Marbury v. Madison*?" on p. 109 of the text. Students should understand the three key issues raised in the case: (1) Does Marbury have a right to the appointment? (2) If Marbury has a right to the appointment and his right has been violated, do the laws of the country give him a way to set things right? (3) If the laws of the country give Marbury a way to deal with this problem, is that way a writ of mandamus from the Supreme Court?

H. Reading and Discussion

What was Marshall's decision?

Have the class read "What was Marshall's decision?" on p. 109–110 of the text. During discussion students should analyze Marshall's decision in the case.

- Marshall reasoned that the appointment had been signed by the president and sealed by the secretary of state; therefore, Marbury had the right to hold the office as provided by law.

- Marshall reasoned that the secretary of state is an officer of the government directed by the Constitution and the laws made by Congress to perform certain duties such as delivering the commissions. When the secretary of state refused to do so, he broke the law and violated Marbury's rights. Marbury had the right to go before a court and request that the secretary of state deliver his commission.

- Marshall reasoned that the Constitution clearly limits the Supreme Court's original jurisdiction to "cases affecting ambassadors, other public ministers and consuls, and those in which a state shall be a party." Marbury was not an ambassador, a minister, consul, or a state, so the Supreme Court did not have the power to hear his case unless it was first heard in a lower court and then appealed to the Supreme Court. That part of the Judiciary Act which gave Marbury the right to have his case heard by the Supreme Court

changed the Constitution. Since Congress did not have the authority to change the Constitution, that part of the Judiciary Act was unconstitutional.

By refusing to issue a writ of mandamus, the Court avoided a direct confrontation with the president.

I. Reading and Discussion

What was the significance of the Supreme Court's decision in *Marbury v. Madison*?

Have the class read "What was the significance of the Supreme Court's decision in *Marbury v. Madison*?" on p. 110 of the text. Students should understand that Thomas Jefferson opposed the idea of judicial review. Jefferson believed that no one branch of government should have the power to determine constitutionality for the others. Marshall said that when the people adopted the Constitution, they agreed that it would be the supreme law of the land. The Constitution places certain limitations on the powers of Congress. When Congress violates those limitations, it violates the will of the people as expressed in the Constitution. If the Supreme Court did not have the power of judicial review, there would be no effective way to enforce the limitations the people have placed on the powers of Congress. Its powers would be limited only by elections. Ask students what they think might be the relationship of judicial review to the natural rights philosophy, republicanism, and constitutional government.

J. Reading and Discussion

Why has judicial review remained controversial?

Have the class read "Why has judicial review remained controversial?" on p. 110 of the text. Americans do not always agree on how the courts should use their power. People disagree over the methods used to interpret the Constitution.

K. Reading and Discussion

What are four methods used to interpret the Constitution?

Have the class read "What are four methods used to interpret the Constitution?" on pp. 110–11 of the text. Students should understand that judicial review is not an active power. The Court does not seek out laws to declare unconstitutional, nor does the Court advise the other branches of government. Cases must be real disputes over laws or actions of government which the Court can settle. Most cases must reach the Court on appeal from the lower courts. Students should understand that deciding whether the federal or state governments have violated the Constitution is not always easy because parts of the Constitution are not clear. Ask students to cite passages from the Constitution or Bill of Rights where the meaning is not entirely clear. Students should be able to explain the following methods the Court might use in interpreting the meaning of the Constitution:

■ **Using the literal words or plain meaning of the Constitution**. Judges should consider the literal or plain meaning of the words in the Constitution. Their interpretation should not contradict other parts of the Constitution or make them meaningless. The problem with this method is that Congress must still interpret the meaning of such words like "general welfare" and there are certain questions that the Constitution does not address.

■ **Using the intentions of those who wrote the Constitution**. The Constitution, by itself, does not reveal its own meaning. Instead we should look at the intentions of those who framed it. The problem is that each of the signatories to the Constitution may have had different views of what its various provisions meant.

■ **Using basic principles and values in the perspective of history**. Besides enumerating the powers of government, the Constitution is based on basic principles of natural rights, republican government, and constitutionalism. The problem is that our understanding of these principles change as the nation matures. Judges have a responsibility not to hold back social progress by sticking to outmoded interpretations.

■ **Using contemporary social values in terms of today's policy needs**. The justices should use contemporary social values in interpreting the Constitution. The problem is that this gives the Court too much power to change the Constitution. Controversial decisions are better left to the elected branches, who represent the will of the people, or to the amending process.

Direct attention to the illustration on p. 111. Ask students to respond to the question in the caption: What problems might arise in trying to discover the intentions of the Framers?

L. Critical Thinking Exercise
Evaluating, Taking, and Defending Positions on Judicial Review

Divide the class into four groups to complete the critical thinking exercise, "Evaluating, Taking, and Defending Positions on Judicial Review," on pp. 111–12 of the text.

The exercise involves students in analyzing a number of quotations about the power of judicial review and methods of interpreting the meaning of the Constitution. Assign each group one of the quotations listed in the exercise. If your groups are too large, you may want to divide the class into eight groups, instead. If so, assign two groups to work on each quotation. Review the instructions for completing the exercise and the questions with the class. After students have completed their work, have them share their ideas with the class.

M. Reading and Discussion
How has judicial review worked in practice?

Have the class read "How has judicial review work in practice?" on p. 112 of the text. Students should understand that in practice the judges are influenced by a number of factors: (1) precedent, (2) current social policies, (3) political and economic concerns, and (4) personal political, economic, and moral beliefs. Despite these influences, judges are conscious of the responsibility to take an objective view of the constitutional issues involved and not decide cases on the basis of their own personal feelings.

N. Concluding the Lesson

To conclude the lesson, have students respond to the questions in the "Reviewing and Using the Lesson" section on p. 112 of the text. Finally, have students return to the "Purpose of Lesson" on p. 107. Ask students to describe the extent to which they accomplished the objectives of the lesson.

Optional Activities
Reinforcement, Extended Learning, and Enrichment

1. Have students read a detailed account of *Marbury v. Madison* in a biography of John Marshall. They should report to the class the arguments presented to the Court which were rejected by Marshall.

2. Have students read a biography of Thomas Jefferson to learn about his reaction to the Supreme Court decision in *Marbury v. Madison*.

3. Have students research each of the following cases: *Fletcher v. Peck*, 6 Cranch 87 (1810); *Dartmouth College v. Woodward*, 4 Wheaton 518 (1819); and *Gibbons v. Ogden*, 9 Wheaton 1 (1824). Have students report to the class the decision in each case and the significance of the decision to contemporary events.

4. Have students research how the Supreme Court decides which cases to accept for review.

LESSON 22: How Is Power Divided between the Federal and State Governments?

Lesson Overview

This lesson describes the federal system of government created by the Constitution. Students learn that the Preamble to the Constitution makes it clear that, under our system, sovereignty belongs to the people and that the people delegate authority to both the federal and state governments. Students learn how this system of federalism differs from unitary and confederate systems. Students also learn that the supremacy clause of Article VI of the Constitution declares that in case of conflict, the laws made under the authority of the Constitution are superior to state law.

The case of *McCulloch v. Maryland* illustrates how the Supreme Court upheld the supremacy of the federal laws over state law, and, in so doing, extended the Court's power of judicial review over actions by state governments. The effect of *McCulloch v. Maryland* was to increase the powers of Congress. Students also learn that, by applying a broad interpretation to the commerce clause, Congress has gradually extended its regulatory authority. Finally, students learn how the United States' political and military role in the world, Supreme Court decisions, and federal attempts to influence state laws have contributed to the expanded role of our federal government today.

Lesson Objectives

At the conclusion of this lesson, students should be able to

1. describe the source of federal and state power

2. explain the differences between federal, unitary, and confederate forms of government

3. explain the importance of *McCulloch v. Maryland* and its main arguments

4. explain how the commerce clause in Article I has been used to expand the regulatory powers of Congress

5. explain the importance of *Gibbons v. Ogden* and its main arguments

6. describe a number of factors which have contributed to the expansion of the power of the federal government

Preparation/Teaching Materials

Student text, pp. 113–16

Optional. For each student in the class, prepare a copy of Student Handout – 22 "Unitary, Federal, and Confederate Systems" on p. 114 of this guide.

Teaching Procedures

A. Introducing the Lesson

Introduce the lesson by asking students why they think there are so many governments in the United States? Would it make more sense if we just had one central government for the entire country?

While students read the "Purpose of Lesson" on p. 113, post the "Terms to Know" on the board. Review with the class what students should be able to do at the completion of the lesson, as explained in the "Purpose of Lesson." Review the vocabulary items listed on the board and remind students to take special note of these terms as they study the material in the lesson.

B. Reading and Discussion

How was the federal system of government created by the Framers different from other governments of their time?

Have the class read "How was the federal system of government created by the Framers different from other governments of their time?" on p. 113 of the text. Review the definition of the term **sovereignty**. Check that students can define the term **federal system**. What is the relationship of sovereignty to the federal system of government?

C. Reading and Discussion

What kinds of governments existed before the federal system was established under the Constitution?

Have the class read "What kinds of governments existed before the federal system was established under the Constitution?" on p. 113–14 of the text. Check that students understand the terms **unitary system** and **confederate system** of government. Students should be able to explain how the Constitution combines elements of unitary and confederate systems into a federal system.

Direct attention to the "What do *you* think?" section on p. 114. You may want to use these questions to conduct a general class discussion on federalism.

Optional instructional activity. This exercise engages students in analyzing the structure of unitary, federal, and confederate systems of government. Distribute to each student a copy of the student handout #22, "Unitary, Federal, and Confederate Systems", on p. 114 of this guide. Have students work with a study partner to decide whether a unitary, federal, or confederate system would be most effective in establishing a system of public education in the nation. After students have completed their work, have them share their decisions with the class.

D. Reading and Discussion

How did the Supreme Court gain the power of judicial review over state government?

Have the class read "How did the Supreme Court gain the power of judicial review over state governments?" on p. 114 of the text. Students should understand the **supremacy clause**, which has been interpreted to mean that the Supreme Court can declare that state laws that violate federal laws should not be enforced.

E. Reading and Discussion

What was significant about the case of *McCulloch v. Maryland* (1819)?

Have the class read "What was significant about the case of *McCulloch v. Maryland* (1819)?" on pp. 114–15 of the text. Students should understand the details of the case and the two key issues involved:

■ Did Congress have the power to create a bank?

The Court ruled that Congress did have the authority to create a bank. This power was given to Congress by the "necessary and proper" clause of the Constitution

■ Could the state of Maryland tax a branch of the federal bank?

The authority of the federal government comes from the people rather than state governments. For this reason, the federal government, in fulfilling its responsibilities, is superior to the state governments. This was the purpose of the supremacy clause. The Court ruled that when a state law conflicts with a constitutional federal law, the federal law must be obeyed. Maryland's attempt to tax the federal bank was illegal because "the power to tax involves the power to destroy."

Students should understand that the Court ruling in *McCulloch v. Maryland* established the supremacy of the federal government within its sphere of authority.

Direct attention to the illustration on p. 115. Ask students to respond to the question in the caption: How did issues related to the creation of the Second Bank of the United States help define the authority of the federal government?

F. Reading and Discussion

How has the commerce power been used to expand federal authority?

Have the class read "How has the commerce power been used to expand federal authority?" on p. 115 of the text. During discussion, students should understand that the commerce clause gives Congress the power to regulate commerce among the states. Students should understand the details in the case *Gibbons v. Ogden*, 9 Wheaton 1 (1824), and that the Court ruled that navigation was part of commerce. Students should also be able to cite the significance of the decision in *National Labor Relations Board v. Jones & Laughlin Steel Corporation*, 301 U.S. 1 (1920).

G. Reading and Discussion

What power does the federal government have today?

Have the class read "What power does the federal government have today?" on pp. 115–16 of the text. Students should understand that most decisions about how much power is left to the states are made by Congress and not by the Supreme Court and that most laws that affect us directly are state laws. Students should understand that the federal government frequently attempts to influence state law by controlling federal funding.

Direct attention to the "What do *you* think?" section on p. 116. You may want to use these questions to conduct a general class discussion on federalism.

H. Concluding the Lesson

To conclude the lesson, have students respond to the questions in the "Reviewing and Using the Lesson" section on p. 116 of the text. Finally, have students return to the "Purpose of Lesson" on p. 113. Ask students to describe the extent to which they accomplished the objectives of the lesson.

This lesson concludes the study of Unit Three. If you had students develop personal objectives or a list of questions during the introduction of the unit, students should now review those objectives or questions and determine to what degree they achieved their goals. In addition, you may want to use the questionnaire, "Reflecting on Your Experience," on p. 28 of this guide to engage students in an evaluation of their participation in the lessons in this unit.

Optional Activities

Reinforcement, Extended Learning, and Enrichment

1. Select several students to consult with school administrators or a member of the school board and compile a list of education programs which affect your school.

2. This lesson states that most laws that affect you directly are state laws. Have students compile lists of federal and state laws that support or contradict this statement.

Unitary, Federal, and Confederate Systems

Imagine that a public education system does not exist in your state. Community leaders across the country have expressed the desirability and necessity of establishing public education to prepare young people to participate in the world of work, to receive higher education, and to participate in the democratic system of government. It would further be desirable if this education could be made available to all citizens without direct cost to the participants.

The problem, however, is that the community leaders cannot agree on several points. Which system of government would be better able to pay the high cost of the project? Which system would be best for determining the subjects that are to be taught? Which system would be best for determining who should do the teaching and what methods of instruction they should use? Which system would be best for selecting the books and materials to be used?

Given what you have learned about unitary, federal, and confederate systems of government, decide which system would provide the best methods for solving the problem. Before making your decision, develop a list of the advantages and disadvantages of using each system to solve the problem.

Unitary System		Federal System		Confederate System	
advantages	disadvantages	advantages	disadvantages	advantages	disadvantages

We have decided to solve the problem in the following way: _____

_____

_____

Unit Four: How Have the Protections of the Bill of Rights Been Developed and Expanded?

UNIT OVERVIEW. Chief Justice John Marshall called the Constitution a document "intended to endure for ages to come, and consequently, to be adapted to the various crises of human affairs." Unit Four examines how Americans have developed and expanded the protections in the Bill of Rights from the time of its ratification through the civil rights movement of the 1960s. The first lesson in the unit describes the constitutional issues that contributed to the Civil War and the crisis of union. Students learn how the institution of slavery and the Supreme Court decision in Dred Scott v. Sandford (1857) challenged the basic principles of government and ultimately threatened the Union itself. Students learn how the Civil War ended forever the idea of secession as a constitutional right and settled the issue of slavery.

The next lesson describes the Civil War Amendments and their effect on protecting the civil and political rights of African Americans. Students learn how Black Codes limited educational opportunities and how vigilante groups prevented African Americans from exercising their rights. Students learn how Congress attempted to enforce the rights included in the Fourteenth and Fifteenth Amendments through civil rights legislation. The U.S. Supreme Court and the executive, however, refused to enforce civil rights laws.

The lesson devoted to the Fourteenth Amendment focuses particular attention on the changed definition of citizenship, due process of law, and the equal protection clause. Students learn the differences between procedural and substantive due process and between equality of opportunity and equality of condition. Students also examine how the Supreme Court used the due process clause to selectively incorporate the Bill of Rights to protect the rights of individuals against actions by state governments. The next lesson describes how leaders in the civil rights movement applied the Constitution in the struggle to gain equality of opportunity for African Americans. Students learn how the struggle for equal rights engaged the legislative, executive, and judicial branches of the federal government.

The lesson on suffrage describes how the right to vote has expanded since the adoption of the Constitution. Students learn how the Constitution has been amended to secure voting rights for African American males, women, Native Americans, and young people aged 18 and older. Students also learn about Supreme Court cases and voting rights legislation that have resulted in nearly universal adult suffrage in the United States.

The final lesson in the unit describes the controversies over affirmative action and recent efforts to end unfair discrimination in American society. Students learn the purpose of affirmative action and the different programs available to women and members of racial and ethnic minority groups. Then students examine the issues raised by affirmative action programs.

UNIT OBJECTIVES. At the conclusion of this unit, students should be able to

1. explain why the Bill of Rights provided limited protection of individual rights prior to the Civil War

2. explain the purposes of the Civil War Amendments and civil rights legislation during Reconstruction and describe the effectiveness of these measures in protecting individual rights

3. explain what is meant by incorporation and describe the arguments over the incorporation of the Bill of Rights

4. describe the evolution from Reconstruction to the present of the due process of law and equal protection clauses of the Fourteenth Amendment

5. describe how Americans have used constitutional means to challenge laws that unfairly discriminate against women and members of racial and ethnic minority groups

6. explain the purposes of affirmative action programs and the tension between the ideas of equality of opportunity and equality of condition

7. describe the evolution of voting rights in the United States from the adoption of the Constitution to the present

8. evaluate, take, and defend positions related to the expansion of individual rights under the Constitution

INTRODUCING THE UNIT. Have the class read the "Purpose of Unit" on p. 117 of the text. Discuss the basic themes students can expect to learn about during their study of this unit and review the objectives of the unit. Ask students how they think a book about ideas, such as this text, might differ from traditional government texts. Why might they think it important to study about the development and growth of the protections in the Bill of Rights? Ask students to write four or five personal objectives they would like to accomplish during the study of this unit. You may want to ask them, instead, to write four or five basic questions they would like to explore during their study of these lessons. They should keep their personal objectives or questions in a journal or notebook for review at the conclusion of the unit. They may want to expand upon these personal objectives or questions as their study in the unit progresses.

Review the unit timeline. Encourage students to create a similar timeline in their journals or notebooks to track in more detail important events or developments described in each lesson.

LESSON 23: What Were the Constitutional Issues That Led to the Civil War?

<table>
<tr><td>

Lesson Overview

Economic differences among various sections of the country and the territorial expansion of the young nation intensified disagreements about the power of the national government and the relationship of the nation to the states. The different sectional interests of early nineteenth-century America might have been settled through political compromise, if it were not for the reappearance of the issue about which there could be no accommodation—the institution of slavery. In this lesson students examine how the continued existence of slavery became a symbol of the sectional rivalries between North and South and eventually forced Americans to examine and debate the nation's most fundamental principles. Students examine the U.S. Supreme Court's decision in the *Dred Scott* case and how it challenged Americans' beliefs in personal liberty and property rights. Students learn that the secessionist movement challenged the Framer's belief that they had created a perpetual Union, a national bond expressing the sovereign authority of the American people as a whole. Students also learn how the Emancipation Proclamation transformed the Civil War into not only a struggle to preserve the Union, but also a crusade for freedom. The Civil War ended forever the ideas of slavery in the United States and of secession as a constitutional right.

</td><td>

Lesson Objectives

At the conclusion of this lesson, students should be able to

1. explain how sectional differences and territorial expansion during pre-Civil War America encouraged different interpretations of the Constitution

2. explain how the institution of slavery forced Americans to examine and debate the nation's most fundamental principles

3. explain how the *Dred Scott* case intensified the conflict between the ideas of personal liberty and property rights

4. explain how the Civil War challenged the Framer's belief that they had created a perpetual union expressing the sovereign authority of the American people as a whole

5. explain the significance of the Emancipation Proclamation

Preparation/Teaching Materials

Student text, pp. 118–21

</td></tr>
</table>

Teaching Procedures

A. Introducing the Lesson

While students read the "Purpose of Lesson" on p. 118, post the "Terms to Know" on the board. Review with the class what students should be able to do at the completion of the lesson, as explained in the "Purpose of Lesson." Review the vocabulary items listed on the board and remind students to take special note of these terms as they study the material in the lesson.

B. Reading and Discussion

What problems were created by the growth of the United States after the Founding Era?

Have the class read "What problems were created by the growth of the United States after the Founding era?" on

p. 118 of the text. Students should understand that the period between 1789 and 1861 is characterized by economic growth and territorial expansion of the United States. Growth and expansion served, among other things, to highlight the sectional differences and controversies among various regions of the country. The regional diversity between northern and southern states increased differences of opinion about the role of the national government and the relationship between the national government and the states. These disagreements were intensified by the issue of slavery.

Direct attention to the map on p. 118. Ask students to respond to the question in the caption: How did the issue of the extension of slavery into the territories help bring about the Civil War?

C. Reading and Discussion

How did early nineteenth-century Americans disagree about the relationship between the nation and the states?

Have the class read "How did early nineteenth-century Americans disagree about the relationship between the nation and the states?" on pp. 118–19 of the text. Students should recall that regional differences existed during the writing and ratification of the Constitution, and continued in the new nation, over how to interpret the power the Constitution granted to the federal government. In time, these disagreements intensified. Early disagreements existed among the Framers about the institution of slavery. Students should recall that the institution of slavery was left intact by the compromises reached during the Philadelphia Convention. Slavery eventually disappeared in the Northern states, but continued in Southern states with increasingly profitable cotton production serving as a rationale for its existence. Slavery became a symbol of **sectionalism** and sectional rivalries between North and South.

D. Reading and Discussion

Why was the Dred Scott decision important?

Have the class read "Why was the Dred Scott decision important?" on p. 119 of the text. Students should understand the details of the case and the Court's ruling:

- African Americans, whether enslaved or free, were not citizens of the United States and could not enjoy the rights and protections of national citizenship under the Constitution.

- The federal government did not have the right to exclude slavery from the territories. Enslaved people were considered property and property rights were protected under the due process clause of the Fifth Amendment to the Constitution.

The effect of the Court decision in *Dred Scott* was to exacerbate the conflict between Northern and Southern states and it is considered one of the principle causes of the Civil War.

The election of 1860 prompted the Southern states to secede from the Union and form a new union, the Confederate States of America. Secessionists believed the Union to be a compact of sovereign states and, as such, they had a constitutional right to leave the Union to protect their most basic rights. President Lincoln and most Northerners believed that the Framers had created a **perpetual** Union.

Direct attention to the illustration on p. 119. Ask students to respond to the question in the caption: Why was the decision in the Dred Scott case a major defeat for antislavery forces?

Direct attention to the "What do *you* think?" section on pp. 119–20. You may want to have students work with a study partner to respond to the questions in this section. Have students share their responses with the class.

E. Reading and Discussion

How did the struggle to preserve the Union become a crusade for freedom?

Have the class read "How did the struggle to preserve the Union become a crusade for freedom?" on p. 120 of the text. Students should understand that, though personally opposed to slavery, President Lincoln believed his duty was the defense of the Constitution by refusing to recognize secession. As the struggle progressed, there was increased support in the North for ending slavery.

Direct attention to the illustration on p. 120. Ask students to respond to the question in the caption: What was President Lincoln's view of the principle of secession?

F. Reading and Discussion

Why did Lincoln issue the Emancipation Proclamation?

Have the class read "Why did Lincoln issue the Emancipation Proclamation?" on pp. 120–21 of the text. Students should be able to identify the Emancipation Proclamation as an executive order announcing that all slaves in states or parts of states still in rebellion on January 1, 1863, "shall be then, henceforward, and forever free." This made the Civil War not only a struggle for the preservation of the territorial Union, but also its founding principles. Victory ended forever the idea of secession as a constitutional right and settled the issue of slavery in the United States.

Direct attention to the illustration on p. 121. Ask students to respond to the question in the caption: What roles did free blacks and slaves play in the Civil War?

Direct attention to the "What do *you* think?" section on p. 121. You may want to use these questions to conduct a general class discussion.

Optional instructional activity. Ask students to imagine that they are presidential advisors. Have them draft a memo to President Lincoln about his proposed Emancipation Proclamation. What do they think of his plan to free slaves only in states or parts of states still in rebellion on January 1, 1863?

G. Concluding the Lesson

To conclude the lesson, have students respond to the questions in the "Reviewing and Using the Lesson" section on p. 121 of the text. Finally, have students return to the "Purpose of Lesson" on p. 118. Ask students to describe the extent to which they accomplished the objectives of the lesson.

Optional Activities

Reinforcement, Extended Learning, and Enrichment

1. Have students conduct additional research on the sectional differences between Northern and Southern states.

2. Have students conduct additional research on the *Dred Scott* case.

3. Have students research the role of free blacks in the anti-slavery movement and during the Civil War.

LESSON 24: What Amendments to the Constitution Were Added to Protect the Rights of African Americans?

Lesson Overview

Immediately following the Civil War, Congress passed laws designed to protect the rights of African Americans. When Congress tried vigorously to implement these laws, its efforts were strongly resisted by people who opposed racial equality. This lesson presents a brief historical overview of the Reconstruction period, describing how the Thirteenth, Fourteenth, and Fifteenth Amendments to the Constitution, and a series of civil rights laws, attempted to end political discrimination against African Americans. Students learn how the legislatures and courts in Southern states used the black codes to deny African Americans their rights and to prevent them from developing political power. When it became apparent that the Thirteenth Amendment was having little effect in protecting the rights of African Americans, Congress passed the Civil Rights Act of 1866. Little changed. As a result, Congress drafted the Fourteenth and Fifteenth Amendments giving African Americans the same political rights as other citizens. However, the Supreme Court and the president were unwilling to enforce these amendments and later the Court declared the Civil Rights Act of 1875 unconstitutional. Students also learn that the Fourteenth Amendment omitted granting women the right to vote.

Lesson Objectives

At the conclusion of this lesson, students should be able to

1. explain the purpose and substance of the Thirteenth, Fourteenth, and Fifteenth Amendments to the Constitution

2. explain why the Civil War Amendments and subsequent civil rights legislation were ineffective in protecting the rights of African Americans

3. describe how state legislatures and state courts used their authority to limit the rights of African Americans

4. explain how the Fourteenth Amendment omitted giving women the right to vote

Preparation/Teaching Materials

Student text, pp. 122–26

Teaching Procedures

A. Introducing the Lesson

To introduce the lesson, ask the class to think about what might motivate people to deny others their civil and political rights. What might be done to prevent such abuses from occurring in the future?

While students read the "Purpose of Lesson" on p. 122, post the "Terms to Know" on the board. Review with the class what students should be able to do at the completion of the lesson, as explained in the "Purpose of Lesson." Review the vocabulary items listed on the board and remind students to take special note of these terms as they study the material in the lesson.

B. Reading and Discussion

What was the Reconstruction period?

Have the class read "What was the Reconstruction period?" on p. 122 of the text. Students should understand that the key feature of this period was bringing back into the Union those states that had seceded during the Civil War. During the **Reconstruction** period there were numerous political battles over how best to protect the rights of African Americans.

C. Reading and Discussion

Why were the Civil War Amendments added to the Constitution?

Have the class read "Why were the Civil War Amendments added to the Constitution?" on p. 122 of the text. Students should understand the substance of the **Thirteenth**, **Fourteenth**, and **Fifteenth Amendments**. To help them do so you may want to post the following chart on the board:

Amendment	Purpose	Effect
Thirteenth		
Fourteenth		
Fifteenth		

As students read the remaining sections of this lesson, the different components of the chart can be completed. Students should understand that, during Reconstruction, Congress passed laws designed to protect the rights of African Americans, but enforcement of these laws was vigorously resisted by those opposed to racial equality, especially in Southern states. Eventually, enthusiasm for Reconstruction reforms waned.

D. Reading and Discussion

What was the effect of the Thirteenth Amendment?

Have the class read "What was the effect of the Thirteenth Amendment?" on pp. 122–23 of the text. Have students examine the Thirteenth Amendment to the Constitution (see the Reference Section in the student text). Students should understand that other than prohibiting involuntary servitude, the Thirteenth Amendment had little effect. No Southern state passed laws protecting the political, economic, or social rights of African Americans. Some states refused to ratify the amendment, others demanded payment for the loss of their slaves. Ask students to cite examples of resistance to implementing political, economic, and social protections for African Americans.

E. Reading and Discussion

Whose political power did the Black Codes protect?

Have the class read "Whose political power did the Black Codes protect?" on p. 123 of the text. Students should be able to identify the term **Black Codes**. Ask students to cite examples of how the Black Codes severely limited the rights of African Americans. Students should understand that the Black Codes were intended to prevent African Americans from developing political power.

Direct attention to the illustration on p. 123. Ask students to respond to the question in the caption: Why did some people want to prevent African Americans from getting an education?

F. Reading and Discussion

Why did Congress pass the Civil Rights Act of 1866?

Have the class read "Why did Congress pass the Civil Rights Act of 1866?" on pp. 123–24 of the text. Students should understand that the Civil Rights Act of 1866 was an attempt to help African Americans protect their rights; however, the law changed little because the president refused to enforce the law and the Supreme Court refused to hear claims based on the law. For this reason, Congress drafted the Fourteenth Amendment (explained in more detail in Lesson 25) and later the Fifteenth Amendment.

G. Reading and Discussion

How well did the Civil War Amendments protect the rights of African Americans?

Have the class read "How well did the Civil War Amendments protect the rights of African Americans?" on pp. 124–25 of the text. Students should understand that the Fifteenth Amendment was clearly intended to protect the right of African Americans to vote. Initially, the amendment had a positive effect; however, eventually the states destroyed the political gains of African Americans by enacting laws which included **poll taxes**, **literacy tests**, and **grandfather clauses** as requirements for voting.

Direct attention to the illustration on p. 124. Ask students to respond to the question in the caption: How did the Fifteenth Amendment protect the right to vote for African Americans?

Direct attention to the "What do *you* think?" section on p. 125. Have students work with a study partner to respond to the questions in this section. Have students share their responses with the class.

H. Reading and Discussion

Did the Bill of Rights, the Civil War Amendments, and the Civil Rights Act of 1875 accomplish their goals?

Have the class read "Did the Bill of Rights, the Civil War Amendments, and the Civil Rights Act of 1875 accomplish their goals?" on pp. 125–26 of the text. Students should understand that the Supreme Court ruled in the Slaughterhouse Cases of 1873 that the **privileges and immunities clause** of the Fourteenth Amendment did not apply to the states. Students should understand that the Civil Rights Act of 1875 gave the federal government the power to enforce the protections of citizens' rights. However, the executive branch refused to enforce the law, and the Supreme Court later declared it unconstitutional. Students should understand that the election of 1876 virtually ended Reconstruction. President Hayes refused to enforce the Fourteenth and Fifteenth Amendments. African Americans began to look to themselves and their own community institutions in the struggle to secure and protect their rights.

Direct attention to the illustration on p. 126. Ask students to respond to the question in the caption: How did Sojourner Truth and other community leaders struggle to win rights for African Americans?

Direct attention to the "What do *you* think?" section on p. 126. Have students work with a study partner to respond to the questions in this section. Have students share their responses with the class.

I. Critical Thinking Exercise

Examining Alternative Means of Preventing Discrimination

Have the class work in small groups of five students to complete the critical thinking exercise, "Examining Alternative Means of Preventing Discrimination," on p. 126 of the text. During the exercise, students propose actions that citizens might take to ensure that civil rights legislation is enforced. After groups have completed their work, have them share their ideas with the class.

J. Concluding the Lesson

To conclude the lesson, have students respond to the questions in the "Reviewing and Using the Lesson" section on p. 126 of the text. Finally, have students return to the "Purpose of Lesson" on p. 122. Ask students to describe the extent to which they accomplished the objectives of the lesson.

Optional Activities

Reinforcement, Extended Learning, and Enrichment

1. Have students research African Americans who struggled for equal rights. Have them write one-page biographies, each beginning with a relevant quotation such as the following by W.E.B. DuBois: "We claim for ourselves every single right that belongs to a freeborn American—political, civil, and social; and until we get these rights, we will never cease to protest and assail the ears of America." Use illustrations, quotations, and biographies to create a bulletin board. Have the class discuss and compare the views and strategies of different African Americans in terms of securing rights.

2. Have students conduct additional research on the political disagreements between the Republicans and Democrats during the Reconstruction period.

3. Have students conduct additional research on Jim Crow laws.

4. Have students research the Supreme Court decision in the Slaughterhouse Cases of 1873.

LESSON 25: How Did the Fourteenth Amendment Expand Constitutional Protections of Rights?

Lesson Overview

The Fourteenth Amendment guarantees the rights of citizens of the United States and prohibits the states from (1) abridging the privileges and immunities of citizens, (2) depriving any person of life, liberty, or property without due process of law, and (3) denying to any person the equal protection of the laws. In this lesson students examine the concepts of citizenship, due process of law, equal protection of the laws, and how the Fourteenth Amendment has been held by the U.S. Supreme Court to incorporate the Bill of Rights to protect against actions by state governments. Students learn that the purpose of the Fourteenth Amendment was to nullify the *Dred Scott* decision by confirming the status of national citizenship and making it clear that citizenship carries with it certain rights that no state government can take away. Students learn that the Fourteenth Amendment requires state governments to respect due process of law, and they learn to distinguish between procedural and substantive due process rights. Students also examine the concept of equality and learn the differences between equality of condition and equal protection of the law.

Finally, students learn that the Bill of Rights was originally intended to limit the powers of the federal government. The Fourteenth Amendment provided a basis for removing this limitation by specifically prohibiting the states from violating a person's right to life, liberty, and property without due process of law. Through a number of decisions, the Supreme Court has used the Fourteenth Amendment to selectively incorporate the protections in the Bill of Rights against the actions of state governments.

Lesson Objectives

At the conclusion of this lesson, students should be able to

1. explain the purpose and the three key provisions of the Fourteenth Amendment: privileges and immunities, due process of law, and equal protection of the laws

2. explain the difference between procedural and substantive due process

3. explain the difference between the ideas of equality of condition and equal protection of the laws

4. explain what is meant by "incorporation" and how the Supreme Court has used the Fourteenth Amendment to protect individual rights against the actions of state governments

5. describe the effect that incorporation has had on the federal system and the power of the states

Preparation/Teaching Materials

Student text, pp. 127–32

Optional. Invite a community resource person such as an attorney or political science professor to work with students in developing their understanding of the meaning of the Fourteenth Amendment.

Teaching Procedures

A. Introducing the Lesson

To introduce the lesson, direct attention to the illustration on p. 127 of the text. Ask students to respond to the question in the caption: Why is citizenship such an important status?

While students read the "Purpose of Lesson" on p. 127, post the "Terms to Know" on the board. Review with the class what students should be able to do at the completion of the lesson, as explained in the "Purpose of Lesson." Review the vocabulary items listed on the board and remind students to take special note of these terms as they study the material in the lesson.

B. Reading and Discussion

What parts of the Fourteenth Amendment remain important to us today?

Have the class read "What parts of the Fourteenth Amendment remain important to us today?" on p. 127 of the text. During the discussion, students should be able to cite the key provisions of Sections 1 and 5 of the Fourteenth Amendment.

C. Reading and Discussion

How does the Fourteenth Amendment change the definition of citizenship?

Have the class read "How does the Fourteenth Amendment change the definition of citizenship?" on p. 128 of the text. Students should understand that the

Fourteenth Amendment established that African Americans were citizens of the United States, nullifying the Supreme Court decision in the *Dred Scott* case. The Amendment also clarifies that national citizenship is paramount to state citizenship, and that U.S. citizens have certain rights that no state can take away.

D. Reading and Discussion

How does the Fourteenth Amendment extend the meaning of due process of law?

Have the class read "How does the Fourteenth Amendment extend the meaning of due process of law?" on p. 128 of the text. Ask students to recall the definition of **due process** which they studied in an earlier lesson. Why is due process such an important right? Students should understand that the Fifth Amendment prevents the federal government from depriving any person of life, liberty, or property without due process of law. The Fourteenth Amendment requires state governments to respect due process and gives the federal government the power to enforce this requirement.

Direct attention to the illustration on p. 128. Ask students to respond to the question in the caption: How are you protected by your right to due process?

Direct attention to the "What do *you* think?" section on p. 128. You may want to use these questions to conduct a general class discussion on due process of law.

E. Reading and Discussion

What is the difference between procedural and substantive due process of law?

Have the class read "What is the difference between procedural and substantive due process of law?" on pp. 128–29 of the text. During the discussion check that students can explain the differences between **procedural due process** and **substantive due process**.

Direct attention to the "What do *you* think?" section on p. 128. You may want to use these questions to conduct a general discussion on the application of procedural and substantive due process. Alternatively, you may want students to work individually, with a study partner, or in small groups to develop responses to the questions. If so, have students share their work with the class.

F. Reading and Discussion

How does the Fourteenth Amendment promote equal protection of the laws?

Have the class read "How does the Fourteenth Amendment promote equal protection of the laws?" on p. 129 of the text. Students should understand that the Fourteenth Amendment declares that no state may "deny to any person within its jurisdiction the equal protection of the laws." This provision establishes the principle of equality before the law, meaning that no individual or group is to receive special privileges nor be deprived of certain rights under the law. During the discussion check that students can explain the differences between **equal protection of the laws** and **equality of condition**.

Direct attention to the illustrations on p. 130. Ask students to respond to the question in the caption: Does equal protection of the law mean that all people have a right to equality of condition? Why? Why not?

Direct attention to the "What do *you* think?" section on p. 129. You may want to use these questions to conduct a general class discussion on the equal protection clause. Alternatively, you may want students to work with a study partner or in small groups to develop responses to the questions. If so, have students share their work with the class.

G. Reading and Discussion

How did incorporation make the protections of the Bill of Rights applicable to state governments?

Have the class read "How did incorporation make the Bill of Rights applicable to state governments?" on pp. 129–30 of the text. Students should understand that the Bill of Rights did not protect the rights of individuals from the actions of state or local governments. The Fourteenth Amendment provided the basis for removing this limitation by prohibiting the states from violating a person's right to life, liberty, and property without due process of law. Check that students can explain the term **incorporation**.

H. Reading and Discussion

How did the Fourteenth Amendment incorporate the Bill of Rights?

Have the class read "How did the Fourteenth Amendment incorporate the Bill of Rights?" on pp. 130–31 of the text. Students should understand that over time the Supreme Court, through its decisions, has selectively applied the provisions of the Bill of Rights to the states. The process of incorporation began in the 1920s when, in *Gitlow v. New York*, 268 U.S. 653 (1925), the Court ruled that the rights of free speech and press were protected by the Fourteenth Amendment. In a series of subsequent cases the Court incorporated all of the rights in the First Amendment, considering them **preferred freedoms** essential to a free society. In the 1930s the Court, in *Powell v. Alabama*, 287 U.S. 45

(1932), incorporated certain rights of criminal procedure as being essential to protecting liberty under the due process clause. However, in *Palko v. Connecticut*, 302 U.S. 319 (1937) the Court ruled that protection against double jeopardy was not essential to due process. Eventually, the Court adopted a **fair trial standard** for deciding which due process rights applied to state governments. In the 1960s the Court adopted selective incorporation of the criminal procedure guarantees in the Bill of Rights. The Court has also prohibited states from violating rights that do not specifically appear in the Bill of Rights, such as the right to marital privacy in the case of *Griswold v. Connecticut*, 381 U.S. 479 (1965).

Direct attention to the "What do *you* think?" section on pp. 131–32. You may want to use these questions to conduct a general class discussion on the equal protection clause. Alternatively, you may want students to work with a study partner or in small groups to develop responses to the questions. If so, have students share their work with the class.

I. Reading and Discussion

What are the results of the incorporation of rights?

Have the class read "What are the results of the incorporation of rights?" on p. 132 of the text. Students should understand that the Bill of Rights originally applied only to the actions of the federal government and was consequently ineffective in protecting the rights of individuals. The due process clause of the Fourteenth Amendment allowed the Supreme Court to apply the protections of the Bill of Rights to the actions of state and local governments. It is through this process of incorporation that the Bill of Rights has achieved its fundamental purpose—protecting the rights of American citizens.

J. Concluding the Lesson

To conclude the lesson, have students respond to the questions in the "Reviewing and Using the Lesson" section on p. 132 of the text. Finally, have students return to the "Purpose of Lesson" on p. 127. Ask students to describe the extent to which they accomplished the objectives of the lesson.

Optional Activities

Reinforcement, Extended Learning, and Enrichment

1. Have students research the struggle for rights for Native Americans and present their findings to the class. After the presentation, have individual students write poems or short stories focusing on this issue and the values and important interests that underlie it.

2. Hold a class debate on an amendment to ban discrimination on the basis of sex, age, and physical impairment or an amendment which would guarantee all citizens a job. Assign students positions to take during the debate. Each team should make a five-minute presentation justifying its position.

3. Have students choose one of the following contemporary issues concerning equal protections. They should write editorials justifying their positions on the issue selected.

   - Should public schools be allowed to exclude children with AIDS from attending regular classrooms?

   - Should the military be permitted to ban homosexuals?

   - Should a public high school be allowed to prohibit students from taking dates of the same sex to the prom?

   - Should state universities be permitted to suspend students who tell jokes, wear clothing, or decorate their dormitory rooms in ways offensive to women or to certain ethnic and racial groups?

LESSON 26: How Did the Civil Rights Movement Use the Constitution to Achieve Its Goals?

Lesson Overview

In this lesson students consider how the Fourteenth Amendment and other parts of the Constitution made it possible to secure and expand the rights of American citizens. Students examine the Supreme Court decisions in *Plessy v. Ferguson* (1896) and in *Brown v. Board of Education* (1954), contrasting interpretations of the equal protection clause during different periods of American history. Students learn the effects of the "separate but equal doctrine" and how the civil rights movement of the 1960s used both the protections in the Constitution and nonviolent direct action to end legal segregation. Students learn that ending legal segregation required the involvement of the legislative, executive, and judicial branches of the federal government, including the Civil Rights Act of 1964, Supreme Court decisions such as *Brown v. Board of Education*, and executive orders to use federal troops in enforcing the laws and the Court's decisions. During the critical thinking exercise in the lesson the class examines Rev. Martin Luther King, Jr.'s "Letter from Birmingham City Jail" (1963) to take and defend positions on the use of civil disobedience to challenge unjust laws in a constitutional democracy.

Lesson Objectives

At the conclusion of this lesson, students should be able to

1. explain how the Supreme Court's application of the equal protection clause has changed from the late nineteenth century to the present

2. explain the "separate but equal doctrine" established by the Supreme Court decision in the case of *Plessy v. Ferguson* and describe the consequences of the *Plessy* decision

3. explain the significance of the Supreme Court decision in *Brown v. Board of Education*

4. explain the role of the legislative, executive, and judicial branches of government in ending legal segregation

5. explain how the civil rights movement used nonviolent direct action to oppose legal segregation

6. describe how the civil rights movement is a good example of citizens using rights protected by the Constitution to secure other constitutional rights

Preparation/Teaching Materials

Student text pp. 133–39

Optional. Invite a community resource person, such as an attorney or local civil rights leader, to help students understand the decisions in the *Plessy* and *Brown* cases.

Teaching Procedures

A. Introducing the Lesson

While students read the "Purpose of Lesson" on p. 133, post the "Terms to Know" on the board. Review with the class what students should be able to do at the completion of the lesson, as explained in the "Purpose of Lesson." Review the vocabulary items listed on the board and remind students to take special note of these terms as they study the material in the lesson.

B. Reading and Discussion

What was the significance of the *Plessy v. Ferguson* decision?

Have the class read "What was the significance of the *Plessy v. Ferguson* decision?" on pp. 133–34 of the text. Students should understand the details in the Supreme Court case *Plessy v. Ferguson*, 163 U.S. 537 (1896).

They should be made aware that the Court decision in the case established the **separate but equal doctrine** and the legal basis for racial **segregation** in the United States. Discuss with the class Justice John Marshall Harlan's dissenting opinion in the case. What does he mean when he writes, "Our Constitution is color-blind"? What does he predict the consequences of the *Plessy* decision will be? Do students agree with his assessment of the majority decision in the case?

C. Reading and Discussion

What were the consequences of *Plessy v. Ferguson*?

Have the class read "What were the consequences of *Plessy v. Ferguson*?" on p. 134 of the text. Students should understand that the effect of the *Plessy* decision was to institutionalize racial discrimination and segregation, especially in southern states. Ask students to cite examples of state laws and local ordinances which separated the races and discriminated against African Americans. What means were used to evade the intent of the Fifteenth Amendment and deny African Americans political rights?

Direct attention to the illustrations on pp. 133 and 134. Ask students to respond to the questions in the captions: (1) How did "separate but equal" facilities deny African Americans equal protection of the law? (2) How did segregated facilities undermine the intent of the Fourteenth Amendment?

Direct attention to the "What do *you* think?" section on p. 134. You may want to use these questions to conduct a general class discussion on the *Plessy* case.

D. Reading and Discussion

What were the origins of the civil rights movement?

Have the class read "What were the origins of the civil rights movement?" on pp. 134–35 of the text. Even at the height of Jim Crow, many individuals and groups were able to chip away at the wall of discrimination. Students should understand the leading role the NAACP took in challenging discriminatory laws in the courts and legislatures. Students should understand the role of Rosa Parks and the boycott of the Montgomery bus system in starting the modern civil rights movement.

Direct attention to the illustration on p. 135. Ask students to respond to the question in the caption: How did Rosa Parks's refusal to give up her seat energize the civil rights movement?

E. Reading and Discussion

What was the significance of *Brown v. Board of Education*?

Have the class read "What was the significance of *Brown v. Board of Education*?" on pp. 135–36 of the text. Students should understand that the NAACP strategy was to use the legal system to challenge segregation in public education. Through a series of test cases aimed at institutions of higher education, NAACP lawyers were able to show that southern states were not living up to the conditions of "separate but equal" laid down in the *Plessy* decision. They were able to show that separate facilities were not equal in the programs or advantages offered to African Americans. Having laid this foundation in higher education, NAACP lawyers then sought a test case in the public secondary or elementary schools. In *Brown v. Board of Education of Topeka, Kansas*, 347 U.S. 483 (1954), NAACP lawyers were able to show evidence that segregated schools actually damaged the psychological development of African American children. Students

should understand the details of *Brown v. Board of Education* and the Supreme Court's decision in the case. In a second Brown decision in 1955 the Court considered remedies to the problem of implementing its 1954 decision. The Court ordered that public schools desegregate "with all deliberate speed" and authorized the lower courts to approve local desegregation plans. Ask students to explain the tactics used by southern states to resist the Court's desegregation order. Students should also be able to explain how the executive branch enforced the Court's decisions, using federal troops to enforce laws withholding federal funds from schools that did not integrate.

Direct attention to the illustrations on pp. 135 and 136. Ask students to respond to the questions in the captions: (1) What was the significance of Thurgood Marshall's victory in the *Brown v. Board of Education* case? (2) Why was it necessary to use federal troops to integrate schools in the South?

F. Reading and Discussion

How did the civil rights movement use the tactics of nonviolent direct action?

Have the class read "How did the civil rights movement use the tactics of nonviolent direct action?" on pp. 136–37 of the text. Students should be able to explain the terms **nonviolent direct action** and **civil disobedience**.

Direct attention to the illustration on p. 137. Ask students to respond to the question in the caption: How did nonviolent direct action help achieve the goals of the civil rights movement?

Direct attention to the "What do *you* think?" section on p. 137. You may want to use these questions to conduct a general class discussion. Alternatively, you may want students to work individually, with a study partner, or in small groups to develop responses to these questions. If so, have students share their work with the class.

G. Reading and Discussion

What were the origins of the Civil Rights Act of 1964?

Have the class read "What were the origins of the Civil Rights Act of 1964?" on pp. 137–38 of the text. Students should understand that the Civil Rights Act of 1964 was designed to end the enforcement of Jim Crow laws. Impetus for the legislation grew from sit-ins and protest marches led by Rev. Martin Luther King, Jr. and other civil rights leaders in the early 1960s. Constitutional authority for the legislation came from the Fourteenth Amendment and the commerce clause in Article I, Section 8 of the Constitution. The Civil Rights Act of

1964 outlawed discrimination in public accommodations such as hotels, restaurants, and theaters. It prohibited job discrimination by employers and labor unions and gave the government new authority to integrate the nation's public schools.

H. Critical Thinking Exercise

Examining Civil Disobedience in a Constitutional Democracy

Have the class work in small groups of five students to complete the critical thinking exercise, "Examining Civil Disobedience in a Constitutional Democracy," on p. 138 of the text. During the exercise students examine excerpts from Rev. Martin Luther King, Jr.'s "**Letter from Birmingham City Jail**" and evaluate the role of civil disobedience in a constitutional democracy. The full text of King's letter may be found in the Reference Section of the student text. Review the instructions for completing the exercise and the questions with the class. Allow adequate time for students to develop their responses. At the conclusion, have students share their responses with the class.

Direct attention to the illustration on p. 138. Ask students to respond to the question in the caption: What limits, if any, should be placed on protests that use civil disobedience?

I. Reading and Discussion

How did the civil rights movement use constitutional rights to achieve its objectives?

Have the class read "How did the civil rights movement use constitutional rights to achieve its objectives?" on p. 139 of the text. Students should understand that the achievements of the civil rights movement would not have been possible without the First Amendment rights to freedom of speech, press, petition, and assembly. The civil rights movement is a prime example of citizens using the rights in the Constitution to secure other constitutional rights.

J. Reading and Discussion

How did court decisions during the 1950s and 60s extend constitutional due process protections?

Have the class read "How did court decisions during the 1950s and 60s extend constitutional due process protections?" on p. 139 of the text. Students should understand that during the civil rights movement of the 1950s and 60s, the Supreme Court was particularly active in securing the rights of equality for racial minorities.

K. Concluding the Lesson

To conclude the lesson, have students respond to the questions in the "Reviewing and Using the Lesson" section on p. 139 of the text. Finally, have students return to the "Purpose of Lesson" on p. 133. Ask students to describe the extent to which they accomplished the objectives of the lesson.

Optional Activities

Reinforcement, Extended Learning, and Enrichment

1. Have students gather additional information about the cases *Plessy v. Ferguson*, 163 U.S. 537 (1896) and *Brown v. Board of Education of Topeka*, 347 U.S. 483 (1954) to share with the class.

2. Have students read biographies of Charles Houston and Thurgood Marshall. Have students explain the strategy they developed to challenge the separate but equal doctrine in the public schools.

3. Have students read a biography of Rev. Martin Luther King, Jr. and report on specific sit-ins and protest marches in which he participated.

4. Have students gather additional information on Rosa Parks, Linda Brown, and James Meredith. Have them present their information to the class in a talk-show format.

5. Have your class watch the PBS documentary *Eyes on the Prize*, available through your local public television station.

LESSON 27: How Has the Right to Vote Expanded Since the Adoption of the Constitution?

Lesson Overview

The right to vote has been a subject of controversy throughout our history. This lesson describes how suffrage has expanded steadily since 1789. The expansion has been so great, in fact, that further extension is no longer a serious issue. Rather, the focus in the United States is upon upgrading the quality and quantity of participation of those who already have the right to vote. It has been argued that not enough people who are eligible to vote do so; and not enough voters are informed or sufficiently skilled to make good decisions.

At its root, the conflict over the right to vote has been between those who believed in the principles of classical republicanism and those who favored a broader interpretation of representative democracy. It has had to do with the question of who can best protect natural rights and the common good. As each new group—white males without property, African Americans, American Indians, women, young adults—have fought for voting rights, they have had to make the case that they needed the vote in order to protect their basic rights. During the lesson students learn the constitutional amendments and Supreme Court decisions that have extended suffrage in the United States. During the critical thinking exercise the class examines why young Americans exercise their right to vote in such low numbers.

Lesson Objectives

At the conclusion of this lesson, students should be able to

1. provide an account of the history of the expansion of suffrage in the United States

2. explain ways in which suffrage was denied to various groups in the past

3. describe general voting requirements today

4. describe how the extension of the right to vote is related to some of the fundamental ideals and principles of our constitutional government

Preparation/Teaching Materials

Student text, pp. 140–45

Optional. Invite a community resource person such as a member of your local League of Women Voters to explain registration and voting procedures in your state.

Teaching Procedures

A. Introducing the Lesson

While students read the "Purpose of Lesson" on p. 140, post the "Terms to Know" on the board. Review with the class what students should be able to do at the completion of the lesson, as explained in the "Purpose of Lesson." Review the vocabulary items listed on the board and remind students to take special note of these terms as they study the material in the lesson.

B. Reading and Discussion

What is the difference between civil and political rights?

Have the class read "What is the difference between civil and political rights?" on p. 140 of the text. Students should be able to explain the differences between civil rights and political rights and to cite examples of each. They should also be able to explain why First Amendment freedoms of speech, press, petition, and assembly are examples of both civil and political rights. Ask students why they might think the right to vote is "a fundamental right."

C. Reading and Discussion

How has the right to vote become more inclusive in terms of economic status, gender, and age?

Have the class read "How has the right to vote become more inclusive in terms of economic status, gender, and age?" on pp. 140–43 of the text. Students should understand that the Constitution left to the states the power to decide who could vote. Students should be able to describe the expansion of voting rights for different groups in American society:

■ **Extending the right to vote to all white males.** Universal suffrage became a reality for white males in the decades between the Revolutionary War and the Civil War. Over time, states amended their election laws and eliminated property qualifications for white males.

■ **Extending the right to vote to African American males.** The **Fifteenth Amendment** guaranteed the right to vote for African American males. The **Twenty-Fourth Amendment** prohibited poll taxes as a means of denying the right to vote in federal elections. In 1965 Congress passed the **Voting Rights Act** authorizing the federal government to take over registration of voters in areas where state officials had regularly prevented African Americans from registering to vote. In 1966, in *Harper v. Virginia State Board of Elections*, 383 U.S. 663 (1966), the Supreme Court ruled that the use of poll taxes in state elections was a violation of the equal protection clause.

■ **Extending the right to vote to women.** In 1875 proponents of woman suffrage argued before the Supreme Court in *Minor v. Happersett*, 21 Wall (88 U.S.) 162 (1875), that the Fourteenth Amendment gave women the right to vote. The Court ruled that being a citizen does not automatically give a person the right to vote. Students should understand that in 1920, 130 years after the adoption of the Constitution, the **Nineteenth Amendment** gave women the right to vote. The struggle for woman suffrage was a long and difficult one. Students should be able to cite examples illustrating how women struggled in state legislatures and courts, on the streets, and in the Supreme Court before gaining the right to vote.

Direct attention to the illustrations on p. 142. Ask students to respond to the questions in the captions: (1) Why were women denied the right to vote until 1920? (2) What methods did Susan B. Anthony and other leaders of the woman suffrage movement use in their efforts to secure the vote for women?

■ **Extending the right to vote to Native Americans.** The Constitution mentions Indians twice in relation to taxation and regulation of commerce. Because of their special relationship to the federal government, Native Americans were not citizens of the United States. Following the Snyder Act of 1924, all Native Americans were made citizens of the United States.

■ **Extending the right to vote to eighteen-year-olds.** Students should know that the Supreme Court in *Oregon v. Mitchell*, 400 U.S. 112 (1970), established that the Congress could regulate the voting age in national elections but not in state elections. Students should know that the **Twenty-Sixth Amendment** granted voting rights to citizens eighteen years of age or older.

Direct attention to the illustration on p. 143. Ask students to respond to the question in the caption: What can be done to increase the number of eligible Americans who participate in elections?

Direct attention to the "What do *you* think?" section on pp. 143–44. You may want to use these questions to conduct a general class discussion on the necessity of voter participation in representative democracy.

D. Reading and Discussion
Is America more or less democratic today?

Have the class read "Is America more or less democratic today?" on p. 144 of the text. Students should understand that the United States has achieved nearly universal adult suffrage; however, there has been a steady decline in voter turnout in recent years. Ask students to explain some of the reasons for this decline.

Direct attention to the illustration on p. 144. Ask students to respond to the question in the caption: Are some Americans still denied the opportunity to vote? Explain.

E. Critical Thinking Exercise
Examining the Reasons Why Young Americans Do Not Vote

Have the class work in small groups of five students to complete the critical thinking exercise, "Examining the Reasons Why Young Americans Do Not Vote," on pp. 144–45 of the text. Read the instructions for completing the exercise and review the questions with the class. After students have completed their work, have them share their responses with the class.

F. Concluding the Lesson

To conclude the lesson, have students respond to the questions in the "Reviewing and Using the Lesson" section on p. 145 of the text. Finally, have students return to the "Purpose of Lesson" on p. 140. Ask students to describe the extent to which they accomplished the objectives of the lesson.

Optional Activities

Reinforcement, Extended Learning, and Enrichment

1. Have students create a collage advocating women's rights based on the statement by Frederick Douglass: "You cannot outlaw one part of the people without endangering the rights and liberties of all of the people."

2. Have students find additional information about Dorr's Rebellion.

3. Have students find additional information on the evolution of voting rights for Native Americans, including provisions of the Dawes Act of 1887 and Burke Act of 1906.

4. Have students find additional information about the Supreme Court case *Harper v. Virginia State Board of Elections*, 383 U.S. 663 (1966).

5. Have students find additional information about the Supreme Court case *Oregon v. Mitchell*, 400 U.S. 112 (1970).

6. Have students organize a voter registration drive in your school. They should contact the local chapter of the League of Women Voters, establish a date, and publicize the event.

LESSON 28: To What Extent Can the Law Correct Injustice and Other Problems in American Society?

Lesson Overview

This lesson describes one of the most controversial issues raised by the Fourteenth Amendment, that of affirmative action. Students learn of the history and rationale for affirmative action as well as some types of programs available. Students will confront the issues raised by preferential treatment programs, especially quotas, in a critical thinking exercise based on the Supreme Court case *Regents of the University of California v. Bakke* (1978). Students then consider the present guidelines used to determine what affirmative action programs are acceptable under the equal protection clause. Students also have an opportunity to evaluate these guidelines, consider their strengths and weaknesses, and make any suggestions for modification they think appropriate.

Lesson Objectives

At the conclusion of this lesson, students should be able to

1. explain the purposes of affirmative action programs, their relationship to the purposes of the Fourteenth Amendment, and the issues raised by affirmative action

2. evaluate, take, and defend positions on issues of affirmative action and on the present guidelines used to determine the constitutionality of affirmative action programs

Preparation/Teaching Materials

Student text, pp. 146–51

Optional. Invite a community resource person, such as a state legislator or local civil rights leader, to help the class understand the issues raised by affirmative action programs.

Teaching Procedures

A. Introducing the Lesson

While students read the "Purpose of Lesson" on p. 146, post the "Terms to Know" on the board. Review with the class what students should be able to do at the completion of the lesson, as explained in the "Purpose of Lesson." Review the vocabulary items listed on the board and remind students to take special note of these terms as they study the material in the lesson.

B. Critical Thinking Exercise

Examining the Role of Law in Solving Problems

Have the class work in small groups to complete the critical thinking exercise, "Examining the Role of Law in Solving Problems," on pp. 146–47 of the text. During the exercise students take and evaluate positions on whether Americans over-use the law and the legal system to settle disputes over constitutional questions. Review the instructions for completing the exercise and the questions with the class. At the conclusion, have students share their ideas with the class.

C. Reading and Discussion

What have been some recent efforts to end unfair discrimination in American society?

Have the class read "What have been some recent efforts to end unfair discrimination in American society?" on p. 147 of the text. Ask students to cite examples of efforts on the part of the Supreme Court and the Congress to end unfair discrimination. What are the issues the courts have wrestled with to determine whether unfair discrimination exists? Students should be able to explain how the Civil Rights Act of 1964 created the **Equal Employment Opportunities Commission** and outlawed job discrimination by private employers and labor unions. The **Equal Pay Act of 1972** prohibited compensation discrimination on the basis of gender. The **Education Act of 1972** outlawed gender discrimination in any education program receiving federal aid.

D. Reading and Discussion

Why do some people claim equality of opportunity is not enough to remedy past injustice?

Have the class read "Why do some people claim equality of opportunity is not enough to remedy past injustice?" on pp. 147–48 of the text. Some Americans argue that equality of opportunity does not address the wide differences in wealth, power, and education in our society. Have students discuss the following three examples:

- **Political influence**. Do students agree that, while all persons have an equal right to participate in the political process, some Americans have more influence than others?

- **Rights of the accused**. Do students agree that, while all persons accused of a crime have the right to a lawyer to defend them, some of the accused have better legal counsel than others?

Direct attention to the illustration on p. 147. Ask students to respond to the question in the caption: Does the government have an obligation to provide a defendant with the best possible legal counsel?

- **Right to an education**. Do students agree that, while every state offers all children a free public education, the quality of the education children actually receive varies widely?

Direct attention to the "What do *you* think?" section on p. 148. You may want to use the questions to conduct a general class discussion on the issue of equality of opportunity.

E. Reading and Discussion

Why were affirmative action programs started?

Have the class read "Why were affirmative action programs started?" on p. 148 of the text. Students should understand that many people believe that eliminating legal barriers to equal opportunity is not enough. The effects of past discrimination and continued prejudices against women and racial and ethnic minorities handicap the ability of people to take advantage of opportunities provided by the law. In the 1960s President Johnson urged Congress to create programs, **affirmative action**, that would go beyond removing legal barriers. These programs would increase opportunities in employment and education for members of groups discriminated against in the past. Affirmative action programs include the following:

- **Aggressive recruitment programs**. Business, industry, and government are to make sure that when opportunities in employment and education occur, women and members of minorities are encouraged to apply for them.

- **Remedial programs**. Educational programs are specially designed to help students who have particular educational and economic needs gain the basic skills to succeed in school and in the job market.

- **Preferential treatment programs**. These are programs designed to give women and members of minority groups who have experienced past discrimination preferred treatment in gaining jobs and access to higher education.

Direct attention to the illustrations on pp. 148 and 149. Ask students to respond to the questions in the captions: (1) Are affirmative action programs a justifiable means to correct the inequity of past discrimination? Explain. (2) In what ways have preferential treatment programs helped some groups gain access to jobs and careers that were previously closed to them?

You may want to use the following questions to conduct a general class discussion on affirmative action programs:

1. What examples can you cite of the effects of past discrimination on women and minorities?

2. Which of the three types of affirmative action programs (aggressive recruitment, remedial programs, preferential treatment) might students favor? Which might they oppose?

3. What important interests—such as cost, efficiency, the ability to compete in a worldwide economic marketplace, or rectification of past wrongs and injuries—should be considered when making public policy concerning equal opportunity issues?

4. What fundamental values, such as human dignity or equality, should be taken into consideration?

5. How much should the needs, talents, and abilities of particular individuals be considered when deciding who should receive benefits such as job training, job promotion, or scholarships to educational institutions?

6. In what ways might the use of quotas in job hiring and educational admissions programs correct past injustices? In what ways might the use of quotas promote injustice?

F. Reading and Discussion

What issues are raised by affirmative action programs?

Have the class read "What issues are raised by affirmative action programs?" on p. 149 of the text. Students should understand why affirmative action programs have been controversial.

- Supporters of such programs cite America's commitment to equality, to a society where there is equality of opportunity. They claim that equality of opportunity was not a reality in the past. Some action, therefore, is necessary to break down the legal and informal structures of discrimination and to remedy this past injustice.

- Critics appeal to the freedom of the individual—each person should be rewarded according to his or her own merits and not by favoritism, privilege, or membership in a specific group. Critics claim that preferential treatment programs create new forms of inequality. The use of quotas and **group entitlement** in education and employment has led to claims of unfairness from those who do not belong to groups receiving preferential treatment. Quotas, critics say, result in **reverse discrimination**. It is just as wrong to discriminate against people because of their gender, race, religion, or ethnic background as it is to discriminate in favor of people on the same basis. Critics remind us of our country's long struggle to establish individual rights as opposed to group rights.

Direct attention to the illustration on p. 146. Ask students to respond to the question in the caption: Should colleges guarantee that their student body is representative of the community?

G. Critical Thinking Exercise

Examining a Supreme Court Opinion on Affirmative Action

Have the class work in small groups of five students to complete the critical thinking exercise, "Examining a Supreme Court Opinion on Affirmative Action," on pp. 149–50 of the text. The exercise is based on the Supreme Court decision in *Regents of the University of California v. Bakke*, 438 U.S. 265 (1978). Review the instructions for completing the exercise and the questions with the class. Allow adequate time for students to complete their work, then have the groups share their responses with the class.

Optional instructional activity. To complete this case study, you may wish to have students simulate oral arguments before the Supreme Court. If so, have the class read only the facts of the case presented in the exercise and not the subsequent information about the Court's decision. Then have the class count off—one, two, three. The "ones" will represent Bakke. They should work together to prepare a three-to-five minute argument on behalf of Bakke. The "twos" should follow a similar procedure to represent the University of California. The "threes" will play the role of justices. They should prepare a list of questions to ask each side of the case during the presentation of arguments. If you have invited a community resource person to class, he or she may participate as a member of this group, or assist the other groups in their preparation. For detailed instructions on conducting this activity, please see "Pro Se Court" on p. 18 of this guide.

Additional information about this case you may want to share with the class to use during preparation of arguments:

Alan Bakke twice applied for admission to the medical school of the University of California at Davis. Despite strong "bench marks" (interviewers' summaries, overall grade point average, standardized test scores, and extracurricular activities), his application was rejected. The medical school at Davis had two admissions programs for its entering class of 100 students, the regular and the special admissions program. The special admissions program set aside 16 seats in each class for various minority groups (African Americans, Hispanics, Asians, and Native Americans) who did not compete for the other 84 openings and were not required to meet the grade point average of non-minority applicants. Bakke claimed that he was discriminated against because of his race. He brought suit claiming that the University "quota" system violated the California Constitution, the equal protection clause of the Fourteenth Amendment to the U.S. Constitution, and Title VI of the Civil Rights Act of 1964. The Supreme Court of California upheld Bakke and the University appealed to the United States Supreme Court.

After completing the simulation, debrief the activity by having students reevaluate their initial views about the case, using the questions posed in the exercise as a guide. Having heard the arguments of other students, have they changed their minds in any way? If they had been on the Court, how would they have decided this case and why? Have the class read the remainder of the exercise which contains the Supreme Court decision. How close does the reasoning in the majority and minority opinions reflect the opinions raised by the class?

H. Reading and Discussion

What guidelines has the Supreme Court used in dealing with issues of affirmative action?

Have the class read "What guidelines has the Supreme Court used in dealing with issues of affirmative action?" on pp. 150–51 of the text. Students should understand that preferential treatment programs raise difficult issues for the Court. In cases subsequent to *Bakke*, Court decisions have produced the following general guidelines: (1) affirmative action programs should be temporary arrangements; (2) programs should be targeted to remedy the consequences of past discrimination in a specific situation; and (3) the chance of unfair consequences for non-minority individuals should be minimized.

Direct attention to the "What do *you* think?" section on p. 151. You may want to have students work individually, with a study partner, or in small groups to develop responses to the questions. At the conclusion, have students share their ideas with the class.

I. Concluding the Lesson

To conclude the lesson, have students respond to the questions in the "Reviewing and Using the Lesson" section on p. 151 of the text. Finally, have students return to the "Purpose of Lesson" on p. 146. Ask students to describe the extent to which they accomplished the objectives of the lesson.

This lesson concludes the study of Unit Four. If you had students develop personal objectives or a list of questions during the introduction of the unit, students should now review those objectives or questions and determine to what degree they achieved their goals. In addition, you may want to use the questionnaire, "Reflecting on Your Experience," on p. 28 of this guide to engage students in an evaluation of their participation in the lessons in this unit.

Optional Activities
Reinforcement, Extended Learning, and Enrichment

1. Have students research and present oral arguments in the case of *Ward's Cove Packing Co. v. Atonio*, 490 U.S. 642 (1989). Arguments should focus on the central issue of who should bear the burden of proof when a worker complains that a company discriminates in its hiring or promotion practices.

2. Have students devise a survey about affirmative action, asking questions similar to those raised in this lesson. After surveying the school community, have students collate, analyze, and publish their results in the school or local newspaper.

3. Have students write a newspaper editorial expressing their views about (1) Professor Shelby Steele's statement that efforts to combat racial discrimination through quotas, affirmative action, racially weighted tests, and other techniques have psychologically handicapped minorities by making them dependent on racial preference programs rather than on their own efforts; or (2) Urban League President John Jacob's statement that racial discrimination is so entrenched at all levels of U.S. society that only affirmative action and similar programs can overcome it.

4. Have students write letters to their member of Congress suggesting fair ways to eliminate business practices which impede the advancement of women and minorities.

5. Have students collect newspaper and magazine articles on issues of affirmative action in your state or community. They may use these articles to create a bulletin board.

Unit Five: What Rights Does the Bill of Rights Protect?

UNIT OVERVIEW. The Bill of Rights protects freedom of religion, freedom of expression, the right to privacy, and numerous procedural rights of the criminally accused. In the first lesson students examine freedom of religion. They learn the differences between the establishment and the free exercise clauses of the First Amendment. Students learn the historical and contemporary significance of these rights and examine the problem of balancing freedom of religion against other important values and interests of society.

The next two lessons in the unit describe freedom of expression. Students learn the importance of freedom of expression to the individual and to society. Students learn standards of constitutional law that aid the courts in deciding under what circumstances freedom of speech and press may be limited. Students then study the freedoms of petition, assembly, and association. They learn the historical and contemporary significance of these rights and what limitations may be placed on the exercise of the right to assembly. Students learn how the right to association, though not specifically mentioned in the First Amendment, is related to other rights in the Constitution.

The lesson on procedural due process rights describes the importance and historical significance of protecting citizens accused of crimes from unfair actions by members of government. Students learn the rights included in the Fourth, Fifth, Sixth, and Eighth Amendments and examine some issues involving their application and interpretation.

The lesson on the Fourth and Fifth Amendments focuses on probable cause, unreasonable searches and seizures, warrants, and self-incrimination. Students learn that these protections limit the methods that law enforcement officials may use in investigating crimes. Students examine the history of the Fourth Amendment and the controversies about its application and interpretation.

The Fifth through Eighth Amendments protect the criminally accused after arrest. The lesson describes the limitations that the grand jury, the right to counsel, and the double jeopardy protection impose on government officials and court proceedings. Students learn how the Eighth Amendment limits the actions of both the courts and the Congress. Students examine the controversies about the application and interpretation of procedural rights and how the courts have tried to balance individual rights against the interests and welfare of society.

UNIT OBJECTIVES. At the conclusion of this unit, students should be able to

1. explain the purposes and importance of the rights protected in the Bill of Rights

2. describe the differences between the establishment and free exercise clauses and explain the issue involved in limiting free exercise of religious beliefs

3. explain the importance to the individual and society of the right of free expression

4. explain considerations used when placing limits on the freedoms of expression, including speech and assembly

5. explain the history, purpose, and importance of procedural due process rights included in the Fourth, Fifth, Sixth, and Eighth Amendments

6. describe the controversies over application and interpretation of procedural due process rights, including the exclusionary rule, the right to counsel, and capital punishment

7. evaluate, take, and defend positions on issues raised by freedom of religion, freedom of expression, and procedural due process rights

INTRODUCING THE UNIT. Have the class read the "Purpose of Unit" on p. 153 of the text. Discuss the basic themes students can expect to learn about during their study of this unit and review the objectives of the unit. Ask students how they think a book about ideas, such as this text, might differ from traditional government texts. Why might they think it important to study about the Bill of Rights? Ask students to write four or five personal objectives they would like to accomplish during the study of this unit. You may want to ask them, instead, to write four or five basic questions they would like to explore during their study of these lessons. They should keep their personal objectives or questions in a journal or notebook for review at the conclusion of the unit. They may want to expand upon these personal objectives or questions as their study in the unit progresses.

Review the unit timeline. Encourage students to create a similar timeline in their journals or notebooks to track in more detail important events or developments described in each lesson.

LESSON 29: Why Does the First Amendment Limit the Government's Power over Religion?

Lesson Overview

This lesson introduces the religion clauses of the First Amendment and explains the distinction between the establishment and free exercise clauses. Students examine the sources of the Founders' beliefs about the need to separate church and state. The establishment clause says that "Congress shall make no law respecting an establishment of religion." Students consider different interpretations of this clause and the controversies that have arisen over its meaning. They examine a number of cases involving the establishment of religion, evaluate the values and interests involved, and decide what position they would take in resolving these issues. Students learn there are two parts to the idea of freedom of religion: the freedom to believe and the freedom to practice one's beliefs. The first is absolute; the second is not. The right to practice one's beliefs may conflict with other important values and interests of society. Students examine the issues involved in setting limitations on religious practices and take a position on a particular case involving a conflict between the establishment and free exercise clauses.

Lesson Objectives

At the conclusion of this lesson, students should be able to

1. describe the history of the growth of religious freedom in America and explain the importance of freedom of religion

2. describe the differences between the establishment and free exercise clauses of the First Amendment

3. explain the different interpretations of the establishment clause

4. explain conflicts that may exist between the establishment and free exercise clauses

5. explain the issues and considerations involved in limiting the free exercise of religious beliefs

6. evaluate, take, and defend positions on issues regarding the establishment and free exercise clauses

Preparation/Teaching Materials

Student text, pp. 154–59

Optional. Invite a community resource person such as a lawyer or judge, to help students examine the issues raised in this lesson.

Optional. For each student in the class, prepare a copy of Student Handout – 29, *Wisconsin v. Yoder* on p. 144 of this guide.

Teaching Procedures

A. Introducing the Lesson

To introduce the lesson, ask students to offer examples of actions by government that they would consider to be "establishment of religion" which they may have read about or know from their own experience.

While students read the "Purpose of Lesson" on p. 154, post the "Terms to Know" on the board. Review with the class what students should be able to do at the completion of the lesson, as explained in the "Purpose of Lesson." Review the vocabulary items listed on the board and remind students to take special note of these terms as they study the material in the lesson.

B. Reading and Discussion

What is the historical background of religious freedom?

Have the class read "What is the historical background of religious freedom?" on pp. 154–55 of the text. During discussion students should understand the term **established church** and be able to cite examples of other nations that have had, or still have today, an established church. Students should be able to explain the effects of the **Great Awakening** in drawing colonial Americans away from established religions and into new religious groups, promoting the idea that all Protestant groups were equal. Students should understand that the large number of religious groups made it unlikely that one particular church could dominate or claim special privileges; however, Catholics and Jews were not supported by the government and often were the targets of discrimination. Students should understand that eighteenth-century Americans generally thought that religion was important in developing the character needed to maintain a free society. By the time the Constitution was written, most Americans thought that freedom of belief was an essential right that strengthened both church and state. During the discussion, ask students to recall the view of classical republicans about established religion and government involvement with religious and moral education. Also have students note examples of both religious tolerance and intolerance during the colonial period. You may wish to augment the students' understanding of why the Founders felt that religious freedom needed to be protected. If so, share the following colonial era examples of religious intolerance with the class.

- When a Dutch ship bound for Brazil ran off course, Peter Stuyvesant, governor of New Amsterdam, issued an edict preventing the Jews on board from settling in his city. He said that he did not want them to "infect the colony.... If we give them Liberty," he explained, "we cannot deny their brethren the Papists."

- Mary Dyer was sentenced to hang when she refused to renounce her Quaker beliefs. As the noose was placed around her neck she shouted over the drumroll: "My life availeth me not in comparison to the liberty of the truth."

- In 1662 Magistrate Richard Waldron ordered that two women who "speak and write blasphemous opinions...[be] dragged through dirt and snow...and whipped."

- Jane Walford successfully sued a neighbor who, in 1656, accused her of being a witch. She was awarded £5 and court costs.

- Five-year-old Cassandra Southwick was sold into slavery in the West Indies after her Quaker parents died in prison. The Portsmouth sea captain who was paid to transport her, refused to do so and adopted her into his own family.

- A neighbor of Goody Cole accused her of hexing his boat and making it sink in a storm. Another neighbor accused her of poisoning his cows and having dinner with elves in pointed hats. In 1692, she was sentenced to life imprisonment. Upon her death, a stake was to be driven into her heart and her body thrown into a roadside ditch.

- Edward Burrough secretly published and distributed a pamphlet denouncing religious intolerance. It was titled "New Englande a Degenerate Plant." He wrote that Puritans, "having forgot their former Sufferings...have faire ourstrip their persecutors."

Direct attention to the illustration on p. 154. Ask students to respond to the question in the caption: How did colonial experience shape the Founders' views on religious freedom?

C. Reading and Discussion

Why did the Founders believe in the separation of church and state?

Have the class read "Why did the Founders believe in the separation of church and state?" on p. 155 of the text. Students should understand that early Americans believed that separation of church and state was necessary to (1) protect religion from being corrupted by the state and (2) to protect government from the corruption caused by religious conflict. During discussion, ask students to cite the views of Roger Williams, Thomas Jefferson, and James Madison.

Direct attention to the "What do *you* think?" section on p. 155. You may want to use these questions to conduct a general class discussion on religious freedom.

D. Reading and Discussion

How was religious freedom protected in the Constitution?

Have the class read "How was religious freedom protected in the Constitution?" on p. 155 of the text. Students should recall that Article VI of the Constitution bans religious tests for holding public office in the federal government. However, some states maintained religious tests until as recently as 1961 when the Supreme Court held Maryland's religious test unconstitutional.

E. Reading and Discussion

How does the Bill of Rights prohibit state establishment of religion?

Have the class read "How does the Bill of Rights prohibit state establishment of religion?" on p. 155 of the text. Students should know that the First Amendment says "Congress shall make no law respecting an establishment of religion...." The First Amendment prevents the federal government from declaring an established church. Once the Fourteenth Amendment incorporated the First, the establishment clause was understood to prevent state establishment of religion as well.

F. Reading and Discussion

How have the courts interpreted the establishment clause?

Have the class read "How have the courts interpreted the establishment clause?" on p. 156 of the text. Students should note the following disagreements about the establishment clause:

- **Broad interpretation**. The First Amendment prevents the government from providing any aid for any religion. No tax money can be used to support any religious activity. The government may provide religious groups the same services everyone else receives, such as fire and police protection, and the government may make it easier for people to practice their beliefs, e.g., schools may excuse students during religious holidays.

- **Narrow interpretation**. The First Amendment does not prohibit government from supporting religion. The government is prohibited from giving one religious group preferential treatment.

- **Literal interpretation**. The First Amendment only prohibits the establishment of an official government religion. The government may participate in particular religious practices, such as Christmas celebrations.

After discussing the three types of interpretation, pose a few situations which raise establishment clause issues. Call on members of the class to state how people taking a particular interpretation, broad, narrow, or literal, might feel about the following situations:

- "In God We Trust" on coins
- public school study of religious works such as the Bible, Bhagavad Gita, Koran, and I Ching in terms of world literature
- the singing of hymns in public school choruses
- christmas programs during public school assemblies
- prayers during public school graduation ceremonies
- a federal appropriation which allots funds for parochial schools to buy textbooks in order "to promote better education"
- the president's annual lighting of a national Christmas tree and the first lady's hosting of a White House Easter egg hunt

G. Critical Thinking Exercise

Taking and Defending a Position on the Establishment Clause

Divide the class into four groups to complete the critical thinking exercise, "Taking and Defending a Position on the Establishment Clause," on p. 157 of the text. Assign each group one of the four cases in the exercise. You may want to divide the class into eight groups and assign two groups to each case. Review the instructions for completing the exercise and the questions with the class. After the groups have had time to analyze their assigned case, have them explain their decisions and reasoning to the rest of the class. Have the groups describe what the positions of all three interpretive schools might be.

During the discussion, compare and contrast the cases by asking questions. For example, is the fact that New York state required teachers to begin school with a prayer significantly different, in terms of deciding constitutionality, from New York City's voluntary program which allowed schools to decide whether to release students for off-campus religious instruction?

You may want to share with the class excerpts from the Supreme Court decisions in the cases in this exercise. Caution students that the majority opinion in a case is the interpretation of the Court and is not necessarily a "right" answer. It is also important to examine the dissenting opinion(s) to obtain a better understanding of the reasoning of the Court. The following are the opinions of the Court listed in the order in which they appear in the exercise:

- *Lemon v. Kurtzman*, 403 U.S. 602 (1971). A majority of the justices invalidated the statute.

  Majority opinion. Chief Justice Burger, writing for the majority, held that the state statute fostered an excessive entanglement between church and state. "In order to determine whether the government entanglement with religion is excessive, we must examine the character and purposes of the institutions which are benefitted." The church schools involved in the program are located close to a parish building containing identifying religious symbols, there are religiously oriented extracurricular activities, and two-thirds of the teachers are of religious orders. The substantial religious character of these schools gives rise to an entangling church-state relationship which the establishment clause is designed to avoid. (The decision established the three-part "Lemon" test.)

  Dissenting opinion. Justice White, dissenting in part, wrote "I cannot hold that the First Amendment forbids an agreement between the school and the State that the state funds would be used only to teach secular subjects. We should not forget that the Pennsylvania statute does not compel church schools to accept state funds."

- *Zorach v. Clauson*, 343 U.S. 306 (1952). A majority of the justices upheld the program.

  Majority opinion: We are a religious people whose institutions presuppose a Supreme Being.... When the state encourages religious instruction or cooperates with religious authorities by adjusting the schedule of public events to sectarian needs, it follows the best of our traditions. For it then respects the religious nature of our people and accommodates the public service to their spiritual needs. To hold that it may not would be to find in the Constitution a requirement that the government show a callous indifference to religious groups.

Dissenting opinion: If public education were taking so much of the pupils' time as to injure the public or the students' welfare by encroaching upon their religious opportunities, simply shortening everyone's school day would facilitate voluntary and optional attendance at church classes. But that suggestion is rejected upon the ground that if they are made free, many students would not go to church. Here schooling... serves as a temporary jail for a pupil who will not go to church. It takes more subtlety of mind than [we] possess to deny that this is governmental constraint in support of religion.... [As for] the Court's suggestion that opposition to this plan can only be anti-religious, atheistic, or agnostic...[our] evangelistic brethren confuse an objection to compulsion with an objection to religion.

■ *Engle v. Vitale*, 370 U.S. 421 (1962). Even though students who chose not to participate could leave the room or remain silent, the Supreme Court struck down the requirement that public school students begin the school day by reciting a prayer.

Majority opinion. It is no part of the business of government to compose official prayers for any groups of the American people to recite as a part of a religious program carried on by government. [This kind of union of government and religion] tends to destroy government and to degrade religion.

Dissenting opinion. This nondenominational prayer "did not amount to a formal establishment of an official religion" and therefore did not violate the First Amendment any more than the daily invocation to God before the Supreme Court sessions, prayers in Congress, the third stanza of our national anthem, the phrase "one nation under God" in the pledge of allegiance, or "In God We Trust" on coins.

■ *Lynch v. Donnelly*, 465 U.S. 668 (1984). The Court ruled that the publicly funded display which included traditional winter solstice symbols, a nondenominational holiday greeting, and Christian symbols did not violate the Constitution.

Majority opinion. There is an unbroken history of official acknowledgment by all three branches of government of the role of religion in American life from at least 1789.... When viewed in the proper context of the Christmas holiday season, it is apparent that...there is insufficient evidence to establish that the [display] is a purposeful or surreptitious effort to express some kind of subtle governmental advocacy of a particular religious message.... The creche in the display depicts the historical origins of this traditional event long recognized as a national holiday. [These] are legitimate secular purposes.

Dissenting opinion. [It is a] plain fact [that the display] amounts to an impermissible governmental endorsement of a particular faith.... The effect on minority religious groups, as well as on those who may reject all religion, is to convey the message that their views are not similarly worthy of public recognition, nor entitled to public support.

H. Reading and Discussion
What rights are protected by the free exercise clause?

Have the class read "What rights are protected by the free exercise clause?" on p. 157 of the text. Students should understand that the free exercise clause is intended to make sure that people who want to practice their religion will be able to do so. The free exercise clause includes the freedom to believe, which the Supreme Court has said is an absolute right, and the freedom to practice those religious beliefs. Under certain conditions, however, the right to practice one's beliefs may be limited to protect other important values and interests of society.

I. Reading and Discussion
What are the conflicts between the free exercise and establishment clauses?

Have the class read "What are the conflicts between the free exercise and establishment clauses?" on p. 157 of the text. Discuss with the class each of the situations illustrating conflicts between the establishment and free exercise clauses and the questions they raise.

J. Reading and Discussion
Is it possible to balance the rights of "free exercise" against other interests of society?

Have the class read "Is it possible to balance the rights of 'free exercise' against other interests of society?" on pp. 157–58 of the text. Students should be able to cite examples of other interests of society that may conflict with a person's right to free exercise, such as health and safety. Students should understand the term **compelling state interest**.

Direct attention to the illustrations on p. 156 and 158. Ask students to respond to the questions in the captions: (1) Does prayer in public schools violate the establishment clause? Does a moment of silence violate the free exercise clause? (2) Should public school officials be allowed to require inoculations against communicable diseases for students whose parents argue against them on religious grounds?

Direct attention to the "What do you think?" section on p. 158. You may want to use these questions to conduct a general class discussion on the establishment and free exercise clauses.

Optional instructional activity. This exercise is a moot court presentation of the historic case, *Wisconsin v. Yoder*, 406 U.S. 205 (1972), involving the Amish challenge to compulsory school attendance on the claim that the law interfered with their freedom of religion. Divide the class into five groups: (1) justices of the court, (2) arguments for Wisconsin, (3) rebuttal arguments for Wisconsin, (4) arguments for Yoder, and (5) rebuttal arguments for Yoder. Distribute to each student a copy of student handout – 29 on p. 144 of this guide. If you have invited a community resource person to the classroom, he or she can assist students during preparation of the arguments and during the debriefing discussion at the conclusion of the activity. For detailed instructions on conducting a moot court, please see p. 19 of this guide.

At the conclusion of the activity lead a discussion focusing on the students' reasoning in the case. You may wish to poll them to determine if they favor the Amish point of view or if they believe Wisconsin's case is more persuasive. After the discussion, you may wish to inform the class that the Supreme Court of the State of Wisconsin found in favor of the Amish, reversing the trial court. The case was appealed to the United States Supreme Court which upheld the decision of the state court. Chief Justice Warren E. Burger, writing for the majority, said:

> ... There is no doubt as to the power of a State, having a high responsibility for education of its citizens, to impose reasonable regulations for the control and duration of basic education. Providing public schools ranks at the very apex of the function of a State.

> ... In order for Wisconsin to compel school attendance beyond the eighth grade against a claim that such attendance interferes with the practice of a legitimate religious belief, it must appear either that the State does not deny the free exercise of religious belief by its requirement, or that there is a state interest of sufficient magnitude to override the interest claiming protection under the Free Exercise [of religion] Clause....

> ... The conclusion is inescapable that secondary schooling, by exposing Amish children to worldly influences in terms of attitudes, goals, and values contrary to beliefs, and by substantially interfering with the religious development of the Amish child and his integration into the way of life of the Amish faith community at the crucial adolescent stage of development, contravenes the basic religious tenets and practice of the Amish faith, both as to the parent and the child.

K. Critical Thinking Exercise
Evaluating the Free Exercise Clause

Have the class work in small groups of five students to complete the critical thinking exercise, "Evaluating the Free Exercise Clause," on p. 158 of the text. During the exercise, students evaluate and decide whether ritual animal sacrifice is a protected practice under the free exercise clause. The Supreme Court case referred to is *Church of the Lukumi Babalu Aye, Inc. and Ernesto Pichardo v. City of Hialeah*, 113 S. Ct. 2217 (1993).

The Santeria religion, a fusion of traditional African religion with elements of Roman Catholicism, practices animal sacrifice as a principal form of devotion. The primary purpose of such sacrifices, which occur during various rituals or ceremonies, is to make an offering to spirits, but the sacrificed animals are cooked and eaten except after certain rituals. In April 1987, a church practicing Santeria announced plans to open a house of worship in Hialeah, Florida. This announcement prompted the Hiaheah city council to hold an emergency public meeting on June 9, 1987.

In September 1987, the council adopted (1) an ordinance prohibiting the possession, sacrifice, or slaughter of an animal with the intent to use such animal for food purposes; and (2) an ordinance prohibiting the sacrifice of animals, and defining sacrifice as the unnecessary killing of an animal in a public or private ritual or ceremony not for the primary purpose of food consumption. Claiming among other things, that the city had violated the church's rights under the free exercise of religion clause of the Constitution's First Amendment, the church and its president filed an action for declaratory, injunctive, and monetary relief in the United States District Court for the Southern District of Florida.

The District Court ruled for the city on the free exercise claim, expressing the view that (1) although the ordinances were not religiously neutral, their effect on the church's religious conduct was incidental to the ordinances' secular purpose and effect; (2) the ordinances were justified by the city's compelling interests in preventing health risks, preventing emotional injury to children, protecting animals from cruel and unnecessary killing.

The United States Court of Appeals for the Eleventh Circuit affirmed. The United States Supreme Court, in a unanimous decision reversed. The opinion of the court, held that the ordinances (1) were not neutral, in that they had as their object the suppression of religion; (2) were not of general applicability, in that they pursued the city's governmental interests only against conduct motivated by religious belief; (3) were not drawn in narrow terms to accomplish governmental interests; (4) did not advance compelling governmental interests; and (5) were void as contrary to the principles of the free exercise of religion clause.

Optional instructional exercise. You may want to have the class participate in a pro se court to evaluate and decide the issues raised by this case. If so, please see p. 18 of this guide for detailed instructions on structuring a pro se court in your classroom.

L. Concluding the Lesson

To conclude the lesson, have students respond to the questions in the "Reviewing and Using the Lesson" section on p. 159 of the text. Finally, have students return to the "Purpose of Lesson" on p. 154. Ask students to describe the extent to which they accomplished the objectives of the lesson.

Optional Activities

Reinforcement, Extended Learning, and Enrichment

1. Have students report on the religious ideas of Roger Williams, Ann Hutchinson, and Thomas Hooker.

2. Have students report on contemporary freedom of religious expression issues in newspapers and newsmagazincs.

3. Have students do research on cases of religious issues in the public schools. Some establishment cases are *Engel v. Vitae*, 370 U.S. 421 (1962); *Abington School District v. Schempp*, 374 U.S. 203 (1963); *Lemon v. Kurtzman*, 403 U.S. 602 (1971); *Stone v. Graham*, 449 U.S. 39 (1980); *Mueller v. Allen*, 463 U.S. 388 (1983); *Wallace v. Jaffree*, 105 S.Ct. 2479 (985); and *Lee v. Weisman*, 112 S. Ct. 2649 (1992).

4. Have students write reviews of plays, films, and novels which raise issues of religious establishment and exercise. Suggestions might include *1984, The Crucible, Ten Sovereigns for Sister Sarah*, and *Friendly Persuasion*.

5. Have students write short stories about individuals who have struggled for religious freedom. The stories can be fiction or based on historical persons presented in this lesson.

Wisconsin v. Yoder 406 U.S. 205 (1972)

*T*he State of Wisconsin requires parents to send their children to public or private schools until they reach the age of 16. The purpose of the law is to provide all children with educational opportunities. Any parent who is convicted of violating this law can be fined or imprisoned.

Jonas Yoder was a member of an Old Order Amish community in Wisconsin. The members of this community believe that they must raise their children according to the principles of the Old Order Amish religion. After completion of the eighth grade (usually by age 14), Amish teenagers are expected to continue their education by working with their parents. Through experience, Amish teenagers acquire the specific skills needed to perform the adult roles of Amish farmers or housewives. They also acquire Amish attitudes favoring manual labor and self-reliance. At the same time, the Amish teenager has opportunities to deepen his or her religious faith, so that he or she can be prepared to accept the religious obligations of adult members of the Amish community. In this way, Amish life is maintained and strengthened.

The Amish believe that their children cannot be prepared for adult Amish life by attending high school. They feel that the teenage members of the Amish community would be drawn away from their traditional religious beliefs and occupations by exposure to science, machines, and modern lifestyles that high school students receive.

The State of Wisconsin believes that high school attendance until the age of 16 is important for all children and that the Amish should not be treated differently from other residents of Wisconsin. In addition, since there are several hundred religious sects, granting exceptions to compulsory education would threaten the existence of the public school system. The public schools bring together children from the neighborhood or the community. It is here that all creeds, colors, and religious groups meet on an equal footing and learn to live together. It is in the public schools that children learn the values and skills that allow them to participate fully in American life. Also, argued the state of Wisconsin, suppose that some of the Amish children decide to leave their religious community and venture out into the world at large? Wouldn't they be ill-prepared for life in American society?

Jonas Yoder refused to allow his 15-year-old son to attend high school. In 1968, Mr. Yoder and several other Amish parents who had refused to send their children to school were arrested, tried, and convicted of breaking the state law. They asked the Wisconsin Supreme Court to reverse their convictions.

LESSON 30: How Does the First Amendment Protect Freedom of Expression?

Lesson Overview

The Founders considered the protections of free speech, press, assembly, and petition fundamental to political freedom. This lesson develops the concepts of freedom of speech and press found in the First Amendment to the Constitution. Students learn why freedom of expression is important to both the individual and society and they examine the historical significance of the First Amendment. Students learn that in spite of the fact that the prohibition against governmental intrusions on freedom of expression is stated in absolute terms in the First Amendment, the Supreme Court has held certain limits to be constitutional. Students then consider the difficult questions of when freedom of expression should be limited and under what conditions. In examining these issues, students consider different approaches scholars and judges have taken. Finally, students explore an issue of free speech that has particular relevance in their own lives, that of speech codes on college and university campuses.

Lesson Objectives

At the conclusion of this lesson, students should be able to

1. explain the importance of freedom of expression to both the individual and society

2. explain the historical significance of freedom of expression

3. explain considerations useful in deciding when to place limits on freedom of speech and press

4. evaluate proposed standards for determining the proper scope and limits of freedom of expression, and take and defend positions on those standards

5. evaluate, take, and defend positions on issues involving the right to freedom of expression

Preparation/Teaching Materials

Student text, pp. 160–64

Teaching Procedures

A. Introducing the Lesson

Introduce the lesson by asking students to cite rules at your school that concern freedom of expression. These could include rules concerning appropriate speech and conduct, as well as dress codes and other such rules. What are their views concerning the limits these rules place on expression? Are these limits justified?

While students read the "Purpose of Lesson" on p. 160, post the "Terms to Know" on the board. Review with the class what students should be able to do at the completion of the lesson, as explained in the "Purpose of Lesson." Review the vocabulary items listed on the board and remind students to take special note of these terms as they study the material in the lesson.

B. Reading and Discussion

Why is protecting the right to freedom of expression important?

Have the class read "Why is protecting the right to freedom of expression important?" on p. 160 of the text. You may want to have the class examine the First Amendment to determine what protections are included (see Reference Section in student text). Students should understand that the First Amendment was written because the Founders believed that the freedom to express personal opinions is essential in a representative democracy. Post the five arguments which favor freedom of expression on the board, and ask students to explain and cite examples to support each:

- **promotes individual growth and human dignity**
- **is important for the advancement of knowledge**
- **is a necessary part of our representative government**
- **is vital to bringing about peaceful social change**
- **is essential for the protection of individual rights**

Given these benefits and their importance to a free society, ask students when, if ever, the right to freedom of expression might be limited and why.

C. Reading and Discussion

How was freedom of expression protected in early America?

Have the class read "How was freedom of expression protected in early America?" on p. 161 of the text. Students should understand that in seventeenth-century Britain citizens had won the right to speak and publish without prior censorship by the government. However, they could still be prosecuted for **seditious libel**, a crime against the government. The Constitution makes no mention of freedom of the press and there is no indication that the Framers intended to prevent prosecution for seditious libel. The First Amendment was designed to quiet fears that Congress might interfere with the press, as confirmed by the **Sedition Act** of 1798. Many people opposed limitations on freedom of expression, and by the election of 1800 it was considered an essential part of representative democracy.

D. Reading and Discussion

How did the trial of John Peter Zenger help establish freedom of the press?

Have the class read "How did the trial of John Peter Zenger help establish freedom of the press?" on p. 161 of the student text. Students should understand that the importance of the Zenger trial was that it established a precedent for protecting the right to disseminate truthful accusations against and criticism about the government.

You may wish to share the following information about the Zenger trial with your class:

In 1710, John Peter Zenger, a German immigrant, was hired as a printer's apprentice by William Bradford, who had once been tried and convicted for printing Quaker broadsides. In 1733, Zenger and his wife Anna Catherine founded their own printing house. They were soon contracted by the Popular Party to print the first political opposition newspaper in America, The *New York Weekly Journal*. Because of articles which ridiculed the government, the press was ordered shut down in 1734 and Zenger was arrested. He was imprisoned for eight months because he refused to reveal the names of the editors and writers. Meanwhile Anna defied government authority by continuing to print, consulting with her husband through a small hole in the jail door.

In August of 1735, Zenger was tried. He and his lawyer, Andrew Hamilton, decided that their defense would be the truth; in other words, if what was printed were true, he should not be held for libel. This was an extraordinary new concept, for British law was "the greater the truth, the greater the libel." When the royal judge dismissed the argument and forbade the entry of evidence to prove the truth of what had been printed about the government, Hamilton appealed directly to the jury. He claimed that Zenger had a right and duty as a free human being to make others aware of the abuse of power by the government. His argument was based on a classical republican sense of civic duty, natural law, and the traditional common law rights of Englishmen. Today, it is still one of the most eloquent statements of the importance of freedom of expression in limiting government power and holding public officials accountable for their actions.

> *[It] is a right which all free men claim, that they are entitled to complain when they are hurt.*

> *They have a right publicly to demonstrate against the abuses of power in the strongest terms, to put their neighbors upon their guard against the craft or open violence of men of authority and to assert with courage the sense they have of the blessings of liberty, the value they put upon it, and their resolution at all hazards to preserve it as one of the greatest blessings that Heaven can bestow…. Power may justly be compared to a great river—while kept within its bounds it is both beautiful and useful. But when it overflows its banks… it bears down all before it and brings destruction and desolation…. If then this is the nature of power, let us at least do our duty and like wise men who value freedom use our utmost care to support liberty, the bulwark against lawless power…. I cannot but think it my and every honest man's duty that while we pay all due obedience to those in authority, we ought at the same time to be upon our guard against power…. The questions before the court and you, gentlemen of the jury is not… the cause of one poor printer, nor New York alone…. No! It is the cause of liberty. By an impartial and incorrupt verdict, you will have laid a noble foundation for securing for ourselves, our posterity, and our neighbors that to which Nature and the laws of our country have given use by right—the liberty of both exposing and opposing power… by speaking and writing the truth!*

The jury set Zenger free. Hamilton was honored by local citizens who raised money to purchase a "Seal of Freedom" with which to award him. Zenger continued to print until his death in 1746. His wife then continued their work as did his son, John Zenger, Jr.

Have students offer other historical examples of suppression of freedom of expression. What values and interests were involved in each example?

E. Reading and Discussion

When has freedom of expression been suppressed?

Have the class read "When has freedom of expression been suppressed?" on p. 161 of the text. Students should be able to observe, as many have argued, that suppression of freedom of expression tends to occur at times when the government feels most threatened.

Direct attention to the illustration on p. 161. Ask students to respond to the question in the caption: How might government persecution of dissidents, which occurred during the McCarthy era, endanger a free society?

F. Critical Thinking Exercise

Evaluating and Developing Positions on the Scope and Limits of Freedom of Expression

Have the class work in small groups of five students to complete the critical thinking exercise, "Evaluating and Developing Positions on the Scope and Limits of Freedom of Expression," on p. 162 of the text. During the exercise, students evaluate and develop positions on whether freedom of expression for groups that advocate anti-democratic ideas may be limited. Review the instructions for completing the exercise and the questions. Allow adequate time for students to evaluate and develop their positions. At the conclusion, have students share their positions and their reasoning with the class. During preparation, you may wish to suggest some concrete examples for students to discuss, such as the following:

- white supremacists distributing leaflets expressing their beliefs outside a market in an African American neighborhood
- performance artists whose show in a city auditorium contains obscenities
- the selling of records and videos of a rap group which encourages violence towards the police
- chanting by anti-abortion activists outside an abortion clinic

During class discussion, have students share the important interests and values which would be promoted or endangered by each position, as well as justifications for their own personal views. Can the class reach some type of consensus on the scope and limits of free expression? On which aspects do they agree or disagree?

Optional instructional activity. You may want to conduct a class debate on the issues raised in this critical thinking exercise. If so, divide the class into five groups: (1) panel of moderators, (2) affirmative arguments, (3) rebuttal arguments in the affirmative, (4) opposition arguments, (5) rebuttal arguments in opposition. Post the following resolution on the board: *Resolved: that the freedom of expression of groups that advocate anti-democratic ideas may be limited.* For detailed instructions on conducting a class debate, please see p. 22 of this guide. During preparation for the debate, you may want students to examine such court cases as *Tinker v. Des Moines Independent Community School District*, 393 U.S. 503 (1969); *Clark v. Community for Creative Non-Violence*, (1984); *Texas v. Johnson*, 491 U.S. 397 (1989); *Schenk v. United States*, 249 U.S. 47 (1919); *Dennis v. United States*, 341 U.S. 494 (1951); *Gitlow v. New York*, 268 U.S. 652 (1925). After the presentations, discuss the strengths and weaknesses of the arguments

presented and how those arguments might have reflected the ideas of natural rights, constitutional government, and republicanism.

G. Reading and Discussion

What are commonly accepted limitations on freedom of expression?

Have the class read "What are commonly accepted limitations on freedom of expression?" on p. 162 of the text. Students should note that freedom of expression may conflict with other important values and interests of society, such as health, safety, the right to a fair trial, and national security. Ask students to cite other examples. Students should understand that limitations on freedom of expression are referred to as **time, place, and manner restrictions**, governing when, where, and how one may speak and not the content of that speech. These restrictions are considered reasonable as long as they are applied without regard to content and do not make it overly difficult to express one's ideas.

H. Reading and Discussion

What considerations has the Supreme Court used to limit freedom of expression?

Have the class read "What considerations has the Supreme Court used to limit freedom of expression?" on pp. 162-63 of the text. The Supreme Court has upheld "time, place, and manner" restrictions as long as they are **neutral** and applied fairly. The Court has taken the position that no matter how dangerous or obnoxious the ideas, people should be allowed to express their views. Sometimes the Court will allow limits on the **content** of the expression if it could endanger the public safety or national security.

Direct attention to the illustration on p. 163. Ask students to respond to the question in the caption: How would you define speech that presents a clear and present danger to society?

I. Reading and Discussion

Does the First Amendment protect all forms of expression?

Have the class read "Does the First Amendment protect all forms of expression?" on p. 163 of the text. Students should understand the **clear and present danger** standard applied by the courts. Using this standard the courts have said that expression can be limited when it endangers national security, incites violence, or is libelous, perjurious, or obscene. Commercial speech may be regulated to prevent fraud and false advertising or when it endangers public health. The courts have generally upheld the right of the press to cover trials. Students should understand that some judges and scholars argue that the Framers did not intend to protect all kinds of speech, that free expression is based on the idea that the free exchange of political ideas is essential to democracy.

Direct attention to the "What do *you* think?" section on p. 163. You may want to use these questions to conduct a general class discussion on freedom of expression.

J. Critical Thinking Exercise

Taking and Defending Positions on an Issue of Freedom of Expression

Have the class work in small groups of five students to complete the critical thinking exercise, "Taking and Defending Positions on an Issue of Freedom of Expression," on pp. 163–64 of the text.

During the exercise, students examine the issue of "speech codes" on college and university campuses. To introduce the activity, you may want to engage students in a discussion of hate speech that includes graffiti, epithets, articles in student newspapers, and racial, ethnic, and gender jokes. Review the instructions for completing the exercise and the questions with the class. Allow adequate time for students to develop their positions. At the conclusion, have students share their work with the class. Then, you may want to have the class develop a proposed policy on hate speech for your school and share their ideas with your school principal.

Direct attention to the illustration on p. 164. Ask students to respond to the question in the caption: What limitations, if any, should be placed on speakers on colleges campuses?

K. Concluding the Lesson

To conclude the lesson, have students respond to the questions in the "Reviewing and Using the Lesson" section on p. 164 of the text. Finally, have students return to the "Purpose of Lesson" on p. 160. Ask students to describe the extent to which they accomplished the objectives of the lesson.

Optional Activities
Reinforcement, Extended Learning, and Enrichment

1. Have students sponsor a school forum on the importance of the right to artistic expression in a free society. They may invite local authors, artists, musicians, poets, and actors to participate. Topics to discuss might include censorship, government restrictions on artists who receive federal funds, obscenity laws, and recent court cases concerning limits on expression.

2. Have students research the issue of censorship in public school libraries. A panel of visitors such as school board members, attorneys, and librarians could address the question: Should school libraries carry books containing adult language, or ideas and language offensive to certain groups, even if the books have educational value?

3. Have students research some of the following landmark cases: *Schenck v. United States*, 249 U.S. 47 (1919); *Gitlow v. New York*, 268 U.S. 652 (1925); *Dennis v. United States*, 341 U.S. 494 (1951); *Roth v. United States*, 354 U.S. 476 (1957); *Miller v. California*, 413 U.S. 15 (1973); *FCC v. Pacifica Foundation*, 438 U.S. 726 (1978).

4. Have students prepare a presentation on the "fairness doctrine" and "public interest" standards regulating political debate on radio and television.

5. Have students prepare a presentation discussing regulation of commercial speech. They may wish to contact someone in an advertising agency, on a newspaper, or at a television or radio station.

6. Have students write a newspaper editorial taking a position on a question posed by political theorist Alexander Meiklejohn in his work *Political Freedom*: "Shall we give a hearing to those who hate and despise freedom, to those who, if they had the power, would destroy our institutions?"

LESSON 31: How Does the First Amendment Protect Freedom of Assembly, Petition, and Association?

Lesson Overview

This lesson continues the discussion of the right to freedom of expression. It deals with the rights of assembly and petition. Also included in this lesson is the right of association, which is not mentioned in the Constitution but has been recognized as a basic right. Students examine the significance of the right of assembly and petition and their importance to the Founders. Students learn how the Supreme Court has recognized the right of association. Students consider what limitations the courts have placed on these rights and the issues raised by such limitations. Finally, students examine a recent case involving the fundamental rights of religion, speech, and association.

Lesson Objectives

At the conclusion of this lesson, students should be able to

1. explain the purpose and importance of the rights of assembly, petition, and association

2. describe the historical background of these rights and their importance to the Founders

3. explain issues involved in placing limits on these rights

4. evaluate, take, and defend positions on standards to use in limiting freedom of assembly

5. evaluate, take, and defend positions on a contemporary case involving First Amendment rights

Preparation/Teaching Material

Student text, pp. 165–69

Optional. Invite a community resource person such as an attorney or judge to work with the class during the critical thinking exercise in the lesson.

Teaching Procedures

A. Introducing the Lesson

To introduce the lesson, ask students whether they have ever exercised the rights of petition, assembly, or association. Ask them to cite examples of their usage of these rights. Have there ever been any limits placed on their exercise of these rights. Are such limitations fair? Why or why not? What benefits come to the community and to themselves because of these rights?

While students read the "Purpose of Lesson" on p. 165, post the "Terms to Know" on the board. Review with the class what students should be able to do at the completion of the lesson, as explained in the "Purpose of Lesson." Review the vocabulary items listed on the board and remind students to take special note of these terms as they study the material in the lesson.

B. Reading and Discussion

What is the importance of the rights to assembly, petition, and association?

Have the class read "What is the importance of the rights to assembly, petition, and association?" on p. 165 of the text. Students should be able to define the rights of assembly, petition, and association. They should be able to explain that these rights are important to the protection of our political rights.

C. Reading and Discussion

Why were the rights of assembly and petition important to the Founders?

Have the class read "Why were the rights of assembly and petition important to the Founders?" on p. 165 of the text. Students should understand that assembly and petition were part of English common law and that the right to petition was part of the Magna Carta. The American colonists used the right of petition to communicate with the British Parliament.

D. Reading and Discussion

How have the rights of assembly and petition been used?

Have the class read "How have the rights of assembly and petition been used?" on pp. 165–66 of the text. Students should be able to explain that the right to petition was used during (1) the Revolutionary War when soldiers or their widows petitioned Congress for pensions and back pay; (2) the early nineteenth century as a means for the enslaved and disenfranchised to communicate with public officials; (3) the Great Depression when veterans petitioned for their military bonuses; and (4) the civil rights movement. Ask students to explain how government placed limitations on the exercise of these rights. Given the Founders' motivation in drafting the First Amendment, might they have approved of the way the rights of assembly and petition were limited in later years? How would students justify or oppose the **gag rule** or the dispersion of the **Bonus Army**? Do they agree or disagree with Rev. King's statement about the importance of these protections? What important interests, e.g., public safety and economic costs, should be considered when determining the scope and limits of these rights? What fundamental values, e.g., individual liberty and human dignity, should be considered?

Direct attention to the "What do *you* think?" section on p. 166. You may want to use these questions to conduct a general class discussion on the right of association.

Direct attention to the illustration on p. 166. Ask students to respond to the question in the caption: How has the right to petition been used by Americans to influence their elected representatives?

E. Reading and Discussion

What limitations may be placed on the right of assembly?

Have the class read "What limitations may be placed on the right of assembly?" on p. 167 of the text. Students should understand that government is responsible for making sure that demonstrations are "peaceable" and do not endanger community safety or unreasonably inconvenience the public.

Direct attention to the illustration on p. 167. Ask students to respond to the question in the caption: Why is the right to assemble fundamental to a democratic society?

F. Critical Thinking Exercise

Developing Standards to Use in Limiting Freedom of Assembly

Have the class work in small groups of five students to complete the critical thinking exercise, "Developing Standards to Use in Limiting Freedom of Assembly," on p. 167 of the text. Review the instructions for completing the exercise and the questions with the class. After groups have responded to the questions, have them develop a set of guidelines or considerations for making decisions on limiting the freedom of assembly. Have the groups share their considerations with the class. During the discussion, students should note that the freedom to voluntarily associate with others is essential, not only to promote political interests to counter the strength of centralized power, but also to achieve one's individual potential. Ask questions to lead students to see that it is through our personal and private associations—political parties, professional organizations, social clubs, labor

unions, or religious organizations—that we create meaningful lives.

G. Reading and Discussion

What limits has the Supreme Court placed on freedom of assembly?

Have the class read "What limits has the Supreme Court placed on freedom of assembly?" on p. 168 of the text. The Court has said that any government regulation must (1) be designed to protect a legitimate government interest and not intended to suppress the freedom of expression and (2) be applied in a non-discriminatory manner. The right of assembly extends to **public forums** such as streets, sidewalks, and parks. Free access to public property is especially important to people who cannot afford costly communications such as advertising in newspapers and television.

H. Reading and Discussion

How is the right of association protected?

Have the class read "How is the right of association protected?" on pp. 168–69 of the text. Students should understand that the right of association is not specifically mentioned in the Constitution. It is implied by the other rights in the First Amendment. The first time the Court upheld this right was in the case *NAACP v. Alabama*, 357 U.S 449 (1958). The state of Alabama brought legal action to expel the NAACP for organizing a bus boycott and aiding students seeking to desegregate the state university. The trial court attempted to obtain the NAACP's membership list. The NAACP refused, fearing that its members might then be subject to economic reprisals, harassment, and violence. The NAACP was charged with contempt and they appealed to the Supreme Court. The Court found that the membership list was so related to the member's right to pursue their lawful interests privately, and to associate freely, as to be constitutionally protected. Forced disclosure would severely limit the NAACP's First Amendment right of association and Alabama had not shown a need for the list which was great enough to justify the limitation.

In *Barenblatt v. United States*, 360 U.S. 109 (1959), the Court upheld the conviction for contempt of Congress of a witness who had refused to testify before the House Committee on Un-American Activities about his beliefs and membership in a communist club at the University of Michigan. The Court defined the government's interest as national self-preservation.

Students also should understand that the Supreme Court has ruled that the government cannot interfere in a person's choices about with whom to associate in private life, but the government may force private organizations not to discriminate on the basis of race, gender, or ethnic background. This issue creates a tension between the ideal of eliminating unfair discrimination and the right of each individual to live his or her own life as free as possible from government interference.

Direct attention to the illustration on p. 168. Ask students to respond to the question in the caption: Do people have a right to join in private associations which exclude others on the basis of gender, race, religion, or ethnicity?

I. Critical Thinking Exercise
Taking and Defending a Position on a First Amendment Issue

Have the class work in small groups to complete the critical thinking exercise, "Taking and Defending a Position on a First Amendment Issue," on p. 169 of the text. During the exercise the class participates in a moot court activity. Students take and defend positions on a case arising from the Equal Access Act that prohibits public schools that receive federal funding from discriminating against student clubs because of their religious or philosophical orientation. Review the instructions for completing the exercise and the questions with the class. Divide the class into five groups: (1) justices of the court, (2) arguments for the board of education, (3) rebuttal arguments for the board of education, (4) arguments for Mergens, and (5) rebuttal arguments for Mergens. Allow adequate time for students to respond to the questions in the exercise and to prepare their arguments. Students playing the role of justices should prepare questions to ask during the presentations. If you have invited a community resource person to the classroom, he or she may help students prepare their arguments and then serve on the panel of justices during the presentations. For detailed instructions on conducting a moot court, please see p. 19 of this guide.

Following the presentation of arguments, the justices should announce their decisions and explain their reasoning. Students should evaluate the strengths and weaknesses of the arguments presented and the decision of the justices. Your community resource person should participate in this discussion.

You may want to share the Court decision in the case, *Board of Education of the Westside Community Schools v. Mergens*, 496 U.S. 226 (1990). Counsel for the school board argued that allowing access to a religious club violated the establishment clause. If Westside recognized the Christian Club, it would appear to be endorsing that religion over others. Mergen's counsel argued that equal access is not the same as endorsement. A Jewish Club or Hindu Club could also have been formed if there was student interest and they would not have violated the First Amendment. In the majority opinion, the Court wrote, "We think that secondary school students are mature enough and are likely to understand that a school does not endorse or support speech that it merely permits on a non-discriminatory basis.... The proposition that schools do not endorse everything they fail to censor is not complicated.... The broad spectrum of officially recognized student clubs at Westside and the fact that Westside students are free to initiate and organize additional students' clubs counteract any possible message of official endorsement of preference for religion or a particular belief. In the dissenting opinion, Justice Stevens wrote, "Can Congress really have intended to issue an order to every public high school in the nation stating, in substance, that if you sponsor a chess club, a scuba diving club, or a French club—without formal classes in those subjects—you must also open the doors to every religious, political or social organization, no matter how controversial or distasteful its views may be? I think not."

J. Concluding the Lesson

To conclude the lesson, have students respond to the questions in the "Reviewing and Using the Lesson" section on p. 169 of the text. Finally, have students return to the "Purpose of Lesson" on p. 165. Ask students to describe the extent to which they accomplished the objectives of the lesson.

Optional Activities
Reinforcement, Extended Learning, and Enrichment

1. Have students research the congressional hearings of the McCarthy era. Have them examine the Hollywood Ten or other groups who have been blacklisted and discriminated against on the basis of association. Have students stage a simulated congressional hearing to dramatize the constitutional questions involved.

2. Have students select a medium of their choice—music, art, drama, writing, or video—in which to express their views about the importance and interrelationship of First Amendment rights in a free society. Have students share their work with the class.

LESSON 32: What Is the Importance of Procedural Due Process?

Lesson Overview

The purpose of this lesson is to help students understand the importance of the protections provided by procedural due process. Students learn why the Founders believed procedural due process was essential to protect the rule of law and constitutional government. Students begin the lesson by reviewing the difference between procedural and substantive due process of law and they learn the lessons of history when due process rights are not respected. Students examine violations of rights that have occurred and think about what protections can prevent such injustices in the future. Students learn the importance of procedural due process rights in an adversary legal system. During the lesson, students identify the key due process rights protected by the Fourth, Fifth, Sixth, and Eighth Amendments.

Lesson Objectives

At the conclusion of this lesson, students should be able to

1. describe the differences between procedural and substantive due process of law

2. explain the procedural due process rights included in the Constitution and Bill of Rights

3. explain the history and importance of procedural due process rights

4. describe the differences between an adversary and inquisitorial system

5. identify violations of due process rights in a particular case

Preparation/Teaching Materials

Student text, pp. 170–74

Teaching Procedures

A. Introducing the Lesson

To introduce this lesson, ask students what might be fair or unfair about each of the situations listed below. In what way might the situation be related to procedural due process rights?

■ A student is accused of smoking in the rest room and suspended without a hearing.

■ The city council publicizes notice of a hearing to discuss a proposed recycling policy.

■ All first-time drunk driving offenders receive the same punishment set by state legislators.

While students read the "Purpose of Lesson" on p. 170, post the "Terms to Know" on the board. Review with the class what students should be able to do at the completion of the lesson, as explained in the "Purpose of Lesson." Review the vocabulary items listed on the board and remind students to take special note of these terms as they study the material in the lesson.

B. Reading and Discussion

What is the difference between procedural and substantive due process of law?

Have the class read "What is the difference between procedural and substantive due process of law?" on

p. 170 of the text. Review with the class the definitions of substantive and procedural due process learned in Lesson 25. Ask students to cite examples of constitutional protections of due process rights.

Direct attention to the illustration on p. 170. Ask students to respond to the question in the caption: How does the right to a trial by jury provide a check on the power of the state?

C. Reading and Discussion

What is the historical background of procedural due process

Have the class read "What is the historical background of procedural due process?" on pp. 170–71 of the text. Students should recall that trial by jury was guaranteed in the Magna Carta. The practice of taking an **oath** and the crime of **perjury** grew out of the Court of the Star Chamber. The right against self-incrimination grew out of a need to curb the excesses of the Star Chamber and the use of torture as a means to compel people to confess to crimes. The practice of torture also led to protection against cruel and unusual punishments. Common law prevented judges from issuing **general warrants** and **writs of assistance**.

D. Reading and Discussion
Why are procedural rights important in an adversary legal system?

Have the class read "Why are procedural rights important in an adversary legal system?" on pp. 171–72 of the text. Students should be able to explain the differences between an **adversary system** and an **inquisitorial system**. Procedural rights are important because our adversary system requires that neither side in a case have an unfair advantage.

An important procedural right not in the Constitution is the requirement that in criminal proceedings the government must prove its case **beyond a reasonable doubt**. The government must prove the defendant guilty. The defendant is not required to offer proof of his or her innocence. The ideas of "innocent until proven guilty" is the foundation of all other due process rights. Ask students what they think might be some advantages of the adversary system. What might be some disadvantages?

E. Reading and Discussion
What guarantees of due process appear in the Bill of Rights?

Have the class read "What guarantees of due process appear in the Bill of Rights?" on p. 172 of the text. After students have finished their reading, have them examine the Fourth, Fifth, Sixth, and Eighth Amendments (see Reference Section in student text). Ask students to enumerate the due process rights in these amendments.

Direct students to the "What do *you* think?" section on p. 172. Have them work with a study partner to develop responses to the questions. Then have students share their responses with the class. Alternatively, you may want to use these questions to conduct a general class discussion on due process guarantees in the Bill of Rights.

F. Reading and Discussion
What is the importance of the protection provided by procedural due process?

Have the class read "What is the importance of protection provided by procedural due process?" on p. 172 of the text. Ask students why they think it is important for every citizen to understand and support due process rights.

Direct attention to the illustration on p. 172. Ask students to respond to the question in the caption: Why is it important for the courts to try to balance the rights of a person accused of a crime against the rights of the rest of the community?

G. Critical Thinking Exercise
Identifying Violations of Due Process

Have the class work in small groups to complete the critical thinking exercise, "Identifying Violations of Due Process," on p. 173 of the text. Review the instructions for completing the exercise and the questions with the class. Allow adequate time for students to complete the exercise, then have them share their responses with the class. During the discussion, ask students what they think might have happened to Smith if other individuals had not taken the responsibility to pursue justice. What responsibility do your students think they have in terms of due process issues?

Direct attention to the "What do *you* think?" section on p. 173. You may want to use these questions to conduct a general class discussion on issues related to due process rights.

H. Reading and Discussion
How does the rule of law protect the rights of individuals?

Have the class read "How does the rule of law protect the rights of individuals?" on p. 174 of the text. During the discussion stress the importance of procedural due process in protecting the rights of life, liberty, and property from abuse by the government. Ask students to explain the relationship of due process rights to the natural rights philosophy and to constitutional government. Discuss the Frederick Douglass quotation: "There is hope for a people when their laws are righteous, whether for the moment they conform to them or not." What reforms or changes do your students think need to be made in order for our society to realize more fully the ideals upon which due process is based?

I. Concluding the Lesson

To conclude the lesson, post the phrases "keystone of liberty" and "heart of the law" on the board. Ask students why due process might have been described by these phrases. Ask students if their life, liberty, or property were threatened by the government, what rights would they most want to see protected?

To conclude the lesson, have students respond to the questions in the "Reviewing and Using the Lesson" section on p. 174 of the text. Finally, have students return to the "Purpose of Lesson" on p. 170. Ask students to describe the extent to which they accomplished the objectives of the lesson.

Optional Activities

Reinforcement, Extended Learning, and Enrichment

1. Arrange for the class to visit and observe a local court hearing. Have an attorney accompany the class to explain court procedures and respond to questions. If possible, arrange for the judge to speak with the class.

2. Assign *Gideon's Trumpet* by Anthony Lewis, a vivid account of the facts in the case *Gideon v. Wainwright*, 372 U.S. 335 (1961). You may want students to view the film of the same title, which is based on Lewis's book. It is readily available in most video rental stores.

4. Assign a report on *Mapp v. Ohio*, 367 U.S. 643 (1961) or other cases centering on procedural due process issues.

5. Have students describe a situation which raises a question of procedural due process affecting young people. For example, it might be a story about students who were dismissed without a hearing from a school sports team. The students were reported to have been drinking at a party, thus breaking their team contract which prohibited smoking and drinking by team players.

6. Have students write short stories concerning situations which raise noncriminal procedural due process issues. Examples are a local zoning battle or a secret government meeting to make decisions about use of public lands.

7. Have students research current rulings and legislation concerning habeas corpus. Have them then debate whether these rights should be limited further.

LESSON 33: How Do the Fourth and Fifth Amendments Protect Us Against Unreasonable Law Enforcement Procedures?

Lesson Overview

The Fourth Amendment protects against unreasonable searches and seizures. The Supreme Court also has interpreted the Fourth Amendment to protect the right to privacy. During the lesson students examine the purposes and importance of the Fourth Amendment as well as the historical reasons for its passage. Students then consider issues related to enforcement of the provisions in the Fourth Amendment. They examine different approaches that have been suggested to ensure that law enforcement officials do not abuse their powers. This lesson also describes the Fifth Amendment protection against self-incrimination. Students examine two self-incrimination cases and consider the limitations the courts have placed on this right. Students learn that the debate over the protections in the Fourth and Fifth Amendments involves the struggle to find a balance between individual rights and the need to protect society. At the conclusion of the lesson, you may want to have students interview members of the community such as lawyers, judges, or police officers about their views on enforcing the Fourth Amendment.

Lesson Objectives

At the conclusion of this lesson, students should be able to

1. explain the purpose and history of the Fourth Amendment to the Constitution

2. explain issues raised in interpreting and applying Fourth Amendment protections against warrantless searches

3. explain the importance of the Fifth Amendment provision against self-incrimination

4. explain common limitations on the right against self-incrimination

5. evaluate, take, and defend positions on cases involving the right against self-incrimination

Preparation/Teaching Materials

Student text, pp. 175–81

Optional. For each student in the class, prepare a copy of Student Handout – 33 on the exclusionary rule on p. 159 of this guide.

Optional. Invite a community resource person such as an attorney or judge to work with the class on the critical thinking exercise.

Teaching Procedures

A. Introducing the Lesson

To introduce the lesson, ask students to cite examples of issues of privacy they know or have read about. How important is the right to privacy in the daily lives of citizens?

While students read the "Purpose of Lesson" on p. 175, post the "Terms to Know" on the board. Review with the class what students should be able to do at the completion of the lesson, as explained in the "Purpose of Lesson." Review the vocabulary items listed on the board and remind students to take special note of these terms as they study the material in the lesson.

B. Reading and Discussion

What is the purpose of the Fourth Amendment?

Have the class read "What is the purpose of the Fourth Amendment?" on pp. 175–76 of the text. Have students read the amendment in the text. Ask them to identify the key provisions in the amendment. Students should

understand that although not specifically mentioned, the Court has interpreted the Fourth Amendment to protect the **right to privacy** from invasion by the government. Ask students to describe how a right to privacy might be implied from the Fourth Amendment. Students should understand that the right to privacy is important to maintaining other rights such as freedom of belief, expression, and property. Ask students to explain how the Fourth Amendment might be related to other important rights in the Constitution and Bill of Rights. Students should understand that the right to privacy has become increasingly important in the face of technological advancements in surveillance techniques. Ask students to cite examples of technological advancements that might raise Fourth Amendment issues. Have students read the quotation from Justice Robert Jackson on p. 176 to underscore the importance of protecting citizens from unreasonable searches and seizures. Ask students whether they agree with Justice Jackson's observation. Students should understand the term **probable cause**. Discuss the literal and broad interpretation of the Fourth Amendment. Ask students whether they think a broader interpretation is justified.

Direct attention to the illustration on p. 175. Ask students to respond to the question in the caption: How do search warrants protect every person's right to be secure?

C. Reading and Discussion

What is the history of the Fourth Amendment?

Have the class read "What is the history of the Fourth Amendment?" on pp. 176–77 of the text. Students should understand the terms **general warrants** and **writs of assistance**. Ask students to cite examples from history of violations of people's protection against unreasonable searches and seizures.

Direct attention to the illustrations on pp. 176 and 177. Ask students to respond to the questions in the captions: (1) How is the right to privacy different today from what it was when the Framers wrote the Constitution? (2) What is the importance of the right to be secure in one's home from unreasonable searches and seizures?

D. Reading and Discussion

What controversies are raised in the interpretation and application of the Fourth Amendment?

Have the class read "What controversies are raised in the interpretation and application of the Fourth Amendment?" on pp. 177–78 of the text. Students should understand the three questions which arise from the Fourth Amendment:

■ **When is a warrant not required?** There are times when law enforcement cannot wait for the court to issue a warrant, such as when a robbery is in progress. Under emergency circumstances, it is necessary for police officers to be able to arrest a person or search property without a warrant. Later, the officer must convince a judge that he or she had probable cause to implement the arrest or conduct the search.

■ **What is probable cause?** At the moment of the arrest, law enforcement must have reliable knowledge that the suspect either has already committed a crime or is doing so at the time of arrest.

■ **How can the Fourth Amendment be enforced?** How can society prevent law enforcement from arbitrarily and unfairly searching a person and his or her property? From arresting a person without good reason for doing so?

Additional information follows the critical thinking exercise—Section E. In discussing issues concerning warrants and probable cause, ask students whether they agree with the applications and limitations of these rights as described in the text.

Direct attention to the illustration on p. 178. Ask students to respond to the question in the caption: What are some situations when police officers should be able to make an arrest without a warrant?

E. Critical Thinking Exercise

Evaluating, Taking, and Defending a Position on Probable Cause

Have students work with a study partner to complete the critical thinking exercise, "Evaluating, Taking, and Defending a Position on Probable Cause," on p. 178 of the text. During the exercise students evaluate a number of situations involving search and seizure and probable cause to determine whether they might be violations of the Fourth Amendment. After students have completed their work, ask them to share their responses with the class.

F. Reading and Discussion

What are means of enforcing the Fourth Amendment?

Have the class read "What are means of enforcing the Fourth Amendment?" on pp. 178–79 of the text. Students should understand that law enforcement should have enough power to protect us from criminals. Review the powers listed in the text. Ask students under what circumstances they think law enforcement officials should be allowed to engage in each of the actions listed. What might happen if these powers were not limited? List on the board each of the policies currently in use to prevent the abuse of power by police officers: (1) **departmental discipline**, (2) **civilian review boards**, (3) **civil suits**, and (4) **exclusionary rule**. Have students make a list of the strengths and weaknesses of each policy. Can they reach consensus about which policy or policies they would support?

Direct attention to the "What do *you* think?" section on p. 179. You may want to use these questions to conduct a general class discussion on issues related to the Fourth Amendment.

G. Reading and Discussion

What is the significance of the exclusionary rule?

Have the class read "What is the significance of the exclusionary rule?" on p. 179 of the text. Students should be able to identify the **exclusionary rule** and explain that, while created and used to limit the powers of the federal government, it was first applied to criminal prosecutions at the state and local level by the Supreme Court decision in *Mapp v. Ohio*, 367 U.S. 643 (1961).

Direct attention to the "What do *you* think?" section on p. 179. You may want to use these questions to conduct a general class discussion on issues related to enforcing the procedural due rights guaranteed in the Fourth Amendment.

Optional instructional material. You may want to make a copy for each student of Student Handout – 33, "Enforcing the Fourth Amendment," found on p. 159 of this guide. The material can be used to expand the discussion of the exclusionary rule. You may also want to use the material to conduct a simulated legislative hearing on proposed modifications to the exclusionary rule. If so, please see p. 14 of this guide for detailed instructions on conducting a simulated congressional hearing.

H. Reading and Discussion

What is the purpose of the Fifth Amendment provision against self-incrimination?

Have the class read "What is the purpose of the Fifth Amendment provision against self-incrimination?" on p. 179 of the text. Before beginning the discussion of the Fifth Amendment, you may want students to examine the amendment (see Reference Section in student text) and identify the other rights it protects: (1) requiring an indictment by a grand jury for capital crimes, (2) prohibiting double jeopardy, (3) guaranteeing due process of law, and (4) guaranteeing just compensation. During the discussion students should be able to identify the **right against self-incrimination**. Its primary purpose is to prohibit the government from threatening, mistreating, or torturing people to obtain evidence against them. Refusing to testify by "taking the Fifth" is controversial because many people see it as a right that benefits only the guilty. It is, however, essential to upholding the principle that a person is presumed innocent until proven guilty beyond a reasonable doubt. This clause protects both the accused and witnesses from abuses by law enforcement and the legal system.

I. Critical Thinking Exercise

Examining Issues of Self-Incrimination

To complete the critical thinking exercise, "Examining Issues of Self-Incrimination" on p. 179 of the text, divide the class into six groups. Assign three groups to work with the case of *Commonwealth v. Dillon*, 4 U.S. 116 (1791), one group to play the role of justices and the others to represent the Commonwealth and Dillon. Assign the other three groups to work with the case of *Arizona v. Fulminante*, 499 U.S. 279 (1991), again one group to play the role of justices and the others to represent Fulminante and Arizona. Review the

instructions for completing the exercise and review the questions with the class. Allow adequate time for students to complete their preparations. For detailed instructions on conducting a moot court, please see p. 15 of this guide. If you have invited a community resource person to the class, he or she can help students develop their positions in the cases and help evaluate the presentations. At the conclusion of the exercise, have the justices announce their decisions and their reasoning.

J. Reading and Discussion

What happened to Dillon and Fulminante?

Have the class read "What happened to Dillon and Fulminante?" on pp. 180–81 of the text. Students should understand that issues regarding the right against self-incrimination have been debated for centuries.

K. Reading and Discussion

How have protections against self-incrimination developed?

Have the class read "How have protections against self-incrimination developed?" on p. 181 of the text. Students should understand that the protection against self-incrimination was originally limited to legal proceedings. The Supreme Court ruled in *Miranda v. Arizona*, 384 U.S. 436 (1966), that law enforcement must warn suspects that they may remain silent and that they have a right to have an attorney present when being questioned. The "Miranda warning" does not, however, preclude voluntary statements from the accused.

L. Reading and Discussion

What are common limitations on the right against self-incrimination?

Have the class read "What are common limitations on the right against self-incrimination?" on p. 181 of the text. Students should understand the following limitations on the right against self-incrimination:

■ It protects individuals, not organizations. It is a personal protection, and does not extend to friends or family members.

■ Under certain circumstances a person may be compelled to testify if the court offers **immunity**. Refusal may bring a charge of **contempt of court**.

Direct attention to the "What do *you* think?" section on p. 181. You may want to use these questions to conduct a general class discussion on the right against self-incrimination.

M. Concluding the Lesson

To conclude the lesson, have students respond to the questions in the "Reviewing and Using the Lesson" section on p. 181 of the text. Finally, have students return to the "Purpose of Lesson" on p. 175. Ask students to describe the extent to which they accomplished the objectives of the lesson.

Optional Activities

Reinforcement, Extended Learning, and Enrichment

1. During oral arguments in *Stone v. Powell*, 428 U.S. 465 (1976), the following exchange occurred between Chief Justice Warren Burger and the counsel for the defendant:

   Chief Justice: "Do you believe that a murderer going scott-free is the right price to pay for a mistake by a magistrate?"

   Counsel: "The real question is whether a man is to be imprisoned if his trial was lacking in constitutional fairness."

   Have students write a newspaper editorial or create an editorial cartoon taking a position on the above quotations.

2. Have students research the McCarthy, Watergate, or Iran-Contra hearings in terms of the self-incrimination clause of the Fifth Amendment.

3. Have students research the cases, *Miranda v. Arizona*, 384 U.S. 436 (1966); and *Mapp v. Ohio*, 367 U.S. 643 (1961).

4. Although the Supreme Court created the exclusionary rule, Congress has since debated it and included modifications of it in various criminal justice bills, such as the Law Enforcement Act of 1988. The executive branch has also taken positions on the exclusionary rule. Have students research legislative and judicial changes to the exclusionary rule. Have students write to the White House requesting information on the current administration's position on exclusionary rule issues.

Enforcing the Fourth Amendment

Policies such as those you have been discussing are used in numerous places throughout the United States to encourage law enforcement officers to obey the law. Perhaps the most controversial of these policies is the **exclusionary rule**. This rule excludes evidence obtained by law enforcement officers who violated those rights protected by the Constitution. The rule is most often used to exclude evidence gained from illegal searches and seizures. It also is used to exclude evidence obtained in violation of the Fifth Amendment right against self-incrimination and the Sixth Amendment right to counsel, which we will examine in the next lesson.

Even though the term exclusionary rule is a recent one, the idea itself was part of the English common law. Confessions that were obtained by force or torture could not be used in court. The intent of this policy was to prevent law enforcement officers from forcing people to confess. The results of such action were worthless in court.

The exclusionary rule is not contained in the Constitution and it is not required by the Constitution. It has been created by judges to discourage law enforcement officers from breaking the law. Throughout history, there have been many examples of officers violating individual rights.

The exclusionary rule has been used since 1914 to limit the powers of federal law enforcement agencies such as the FBI. It was not until 1961 that the Supreme Court ruled that the exclusionary rule must be used in criminal prosecutions at state and local levels (*Mapp v. Ohio*). Since that time there has been continual controversy about its use. Some of the main arguments of those taking opposing positions on this issue are briefly explained below.

1. **Arguments for the exclusionary rule.** Supporters of the exclusionary rule give the following arguments in its defense:

   - **It discourages officials from violating the law.** People argue that the rule is a practical way of discouraging law enforcement officers from violating constitutional rights to gain evidence. If officers know ahead of time that evidence gained illegally cannot be used in court, they are less likely to break the law.

   - **It makes sure that courts obey the law.** If judges were to allow illegally gained evidence in court, they would become accomplices in breaking the law and violating the Constitution.

   - **It rarely results in criminals being set free.** Although there are no comprehensive studies of how many criminals are set free by the exclusionary rule, the number is far lower than most people believe. California has the strictest exclusionary rule in the nation. A study by the National Institute for Justice showed that less than one percent of persons accused of serious crimes in California are not prosecuted because of the rule. Three-fourths of that small percentage were people accused of nonviolent drug-related crimes. In the case of the violent crimes of murder, rape, and robbery, only one out of every 2,500 persons accused was set free because of the rule.

     Studies in other states show similar results. At the federal level, less than one-half of one percent of persons accused of serious crimes are released as a result of the exclusionary rule. If the exclusionary rule was abolished, the conviction rate in serious crimes would increase by an even smaller percentage.

   - **It makes the point that government is not above the law**. It provides a means of enforcing rules that limit the power of government, thus making it clear that everyone is expected to obey the law. This is the basis for the rule of law—no one is above the law.

2. **Arguments against the exclusionary rule**. Opponents of the exclusionary rule make the following arguments:

- **It is not reasonable to exclude reliable evidence of a crime**. The evidence gained in an illegal search is as reliable as if it had been gained legally. It is unreasonable to ignore evidence simply to make police obey the law.

- **There are better ways to make officers obey the law**. In Great Britain, officers are encouraged to obey the law by making them subject to civil or criminal trials when they violate the law. This practice should be used in the United States because it does not require prohibiting the use of illegally obtained evidence in court.

- **The rule encourages police lawlessness**. The rule encourages officers to lie or falsify reports on searches in order to get around the exclusionary rule.

- **The rule breeds disrespect for the courts.** The public cannot be expected to respect a system that frees criminals just because the evidence against them was gained illegally.

- **Thousands of criminals do go free**. Although the percentages are small, so many people are arrested that thousands of guilty people are released each year as a result of the rule.

- **The rule does not protect innocent people**. The worst cases of violations of individual rights are those against innocent people the officers do not intend to arrest in the first place. In such situations the officers may purposely search and seize people illegally and then release them. They may do this to (1) control crimes such as illegal gambling and prostitution, (2) confiscate illegal weapons or stolen property, (3) deter crime, or (4) satisfy public opinion calling for aggressive police action against crime.

The exclusionary rule remains a controversial weapon for the defense of constitutional rights. Although its use has been challenged, no other method of defending Fourth Amendment rights has yet attracted widespread support. Until such a method is discovered, the courts will probably continue to exclude illegally obtained evidence.

LESSON 34: How Do the Fifth through Eighth Amendments Protect Our Rights within the Judicial System?

Lesson Overview

The Fifth and Sixth Amendments contain a number of procedural due process rights to ensure that a person receives a fair trial. The Eighth Amendment protects the rights of people who have been arrested and are being held for trial by prohibiting excessive bail and protects persons who have been convicted of crimes from cruel and unusual punishment. During this lesson, students will briefly review the importance and history of these rights. Students learn about the right to counsel and its role in the American judicial system and then they examine controversies over its application. Students learn the meaning of "cruel and unusual punishment" as it applies to capital punishment. They look at the history of the death penalty and consider the issues involved in allowing capital punishment. Students should understand that even if the Supreme Court rules the death penalty is constitutional, this does not mean that state legislatures have to impose it. There is a distinction between the legality of the death penalty and the political choice to use it.

Lesson Objectives

At the conclusion of this lesson, students should be able to

1. identify the rights protected by the Fifth, Sixth, and Eighth Amendments to the Constitution

2. explain the history and purpose of these rights

3. describe the issues involved in allowing capital punishment

4. evaluate, take, and defend positions on the use of capital punishment

Preparation/Teaching Materials

Student text, pp. 182–87

Optional. For each student in the class, prepare a copy of Student Handout – 34, "Arguments For and Against Capital Punishment" on p. 165 of this guide.

Teaching Procedures

A. Introducing the Lesson

While students read the "Purpose of Lesson" on p. 182, post the "Terms to Know" on the board. Review with the class what students should be able to do at the completion of the lesson, as explained in the "Purpose of Lesson." Review the vocabulary items listed on the board and remind students to take special note of these terms as they study the material in the lesson.

B. Reading and Discussion

How do provisions of the Fifth Amendment protect an individual's rights after arrest?

Have the class read "How do provisions of the Fifth Amendment protect an individual's rights after arrest?" on p. 182 of the text. During the discussion check that students understand the terms **indicted** and **acquitted**. Students should understand the difference between a **grand jury** and a trial jury and what safeguard a grand jury indictment is intended to provide. Students should understand the purpose of the **double jeopardy** provision in the Fifth Amendment.

C. Reading and Discussion

What limitations does the Sixth Amendment place on the government?

Have the class read "What limitations does the Sixth Amendment place on the government?" on pp. 182–83 of the student text. Students should understand that Sixth Amendment provisions are intended to provide a fair hearing in court for persons accused of crimes. Students should be able to explain each of the following provisions in the Sixth Amendment: (1) **speedy trial**, (2) **public trial**, (3) **impartial jury**, (4) **location of the trial**, (5) **information on the charges**, (6) **confronting witnesses**, (7) **favorable witnesses**, and (8) **assistance of counsel**. Ask students what they think would happen if they did not have these rights. Are there any circumstances when they might want to waive these rights? How might these rights protect you from the majority of the community if it were hostile to you? Discuss with the class why, taken as a whole, these protections provide an important means for (a) limiting government power, (b) preserving individual rights, and (c) promoting a just society. Upon what ideas of the classical republicans and natural rights philosophers are these rights based? What historical traditions laid the foundation for the Sixth Amendment? Which grievances listed in the Declaration of Independence illustrate violations of these rights?

D. Reading and Discussion
What is the importance of the right to counsel?

Have the class read "What is the importance of the right to counsel?" on p. 183 of the text. Review with the class the definitions of **adversary** and **inquisitorial system**. Students should be able to explain how the adversary system operates and define the terms **prosecuting attorney** and **defense attorney**. Students should understand that the Court and the Congress have extended the right to counsel to guarantee (1) that every person accused of a **felony** may have a lawyer, and (2) that those who cannot afford to hire a lawyer will have one appointed by the court. These rights also apply to other stages in the criminal justice process. Ask students whether they think the adversarial or inquisitorial system would be more just to those accused of criminal acts. Why? Should the right to counsel ever be limited? If so, under what circumstances? How did limits placed on the right to counsel in the past impede justice? What other interests and values might have been threatened as well? You may want students to find additional information concerning the landmark Supreme Court case *Gideon v. Wainwright*, 372 U.S. 335 (1963).

Direct attention to the illustration on p. 183. Ask students to respond to the question in the caption: Why is the right to counsel so important?

E. Critical Thinking Exercise
Examining Current Controversies over the Right to Counsel

Have students work with a study partner to complete the critical thinking exercise, "Examining Current Controversies about the Right to Counsel," on p. 183 of the text. During the exercise students examine and take positions on the issue of providing court appointed counsel for the accused person who cannot afford to hire his or her own attorney. Review the instructions for completing the exercise with the class. After students have completed the exercise, have them share their work with the class. Ask students whether they think it desirable to establish standards of effective counsel. If so, what standards might they set? In sharing and comparing their views, have students note competing interests and values which would be promoted or undermined by the different positions presented in the exercise.

F. Reading and Discussion
How are the rights of the Sixth Amendment enforced?

Have the class read "How are the rights of the Sixth Amendment enforced?" on p. 184 of the text. Students

should understand the importance of the right to appeal a decision to a higher court. Each state government and the federal government have a system of appellate courts, with the U.S. Supreme Court being the court of last resort. If, after reviewing the trial record, an appellate court decides the trial has been unfair, it can overturn the lower court's verdict. If that happens, the prosecution can usually choose whether to try the case again.

G. Reading and Discussion
What limitations does the Eighth Amendment place on the government?

Note: Before proceeding to this section, you may want to inform students that they will not be studying the Seventh Amendment. The Seventh Amendment preserves the right to a trial by jury in most civil cases. Although it specifically mentions cases of common law, it has never been interpreted to exclude other types of civil cases. Like the rest of the Bill of Rights, it was designed only to limit the power of the federal government. This Amendment has never been incorporated or applied to the states.

Have the class read "What limitations does the Eighth Amendment place on the government?" on p. 184 of the text. Students should understand that the Eighth Amendment protects individuals accused of crimes but awaiting trial as well as individuals who have been tried and convicted. Students should be able to explain how the protection against "excessive bail" limits the judiciary as well as how protection against "excessive fines" and "cruel and unusual punishment" limits the legislature. Ask students to explain in what way the Eighth Amendment is based on the presumption of innocence. What limits have been placed on the right to be free on bail pending trial? Are such limitations justified? In what way might excessive fines violate individual rights and promote injustice? Upon what fundamental values is the right to be free from cruel and unusual punishment based? What types of punishments might fall into the category of "cruel and unusual"?

H. Critical Thinking Exercise
Examining Early Positions on Punishment

Have students work with a study partner to complete the critical thinking exercise, "Examining Early Positions on Punishment," on p. 184 of the text. During the exercise students consider Montesquieu's and Jefferson's statements about the nature and function of punishment. Review the instructions for completing the exercise and the questions with the class. After students have completed their work, have them share their ideas with the class. In justifying their positions on the issue, have students explain what important interests and fundamental values they considered in reaching their opinions.

I. Reading and Discussion

What are the purposes of the Eighth Amendment rights?

Have the class read "What are the purposes of the Eighth Amendment rights?" on pp. 184–85 of the text. Students should understand that the right to **bail** allows suspects to be free while preparing their defense and avoids unfairly punishing suspects by holding them in jail before they are found guilty or innocent. Ask students to explain each of the problems that arise in implementing the right to bail: (1) **unfair treatment of the poor**, (2) **punishment of innocent poor**, and (3) **increased chances of conviction and more severe sentences**. What remedies might resolve some of these problems? Students should be able to explain that the protection against **excessive fines** forces courts to levy fines that are reasonable with respect to the crime committed. They should be able to explain that the protection against **cruel and unusual punishment** reflects a fundamental belief in the dignity of all human beings.

J. Reading and Discussion

What is the history of capital punishment in the United States?

Have the class read "What is the history of capital punishment in the United States?" on p. 185 of the text. During the discussion, students should be able to explain the term **unguided discretion**.

K. Reading and Discussion

What is the basis of opposition to the death penalty?

Have the class read "What is the basis of opposition to the death penalty?" on p. 186 of the text. Students should understand that there are a number of factors upon which people base their opinions about the death penalty, including (1) the role of juries, (2) race, (3) deterrence, and (4) expense.

L. Reading and Discussion

What issues are involved in allowing capital punishment?

Have the class read "What issues are involved in allowing capital punishment?" on p. 186 of the text. Ask

students to cite factors which have created moral and political opposition to the death penalty. Students should be able to explain the Supreme Court decision in *Furman v. Georgia*, 408 U.S. 238 (1972). Students should be able to explain the term **guided discretion**.

Direct attention to the illustration on p. 186. Ask students to respond to the question in the caption: What are the major arguments for and against the death penalty?

Optional instructional activity. You may want to conduct a simulated legislative committee hearing on the use of the death penalty in your state. If your state has death penalty statutes, the committee should conduct hearings to determine whether to draft a bill to abolish capital punishment in the state. If your state does not have capital punishment, the committee should be considering a bill to institute it in the state. Divide the class into the following groups: (1) legislative committee, (2) families of victims of violent crimes, (3) citizens committee for safer neighborhoods, (4) citizens for human rights, and (5) citizens against the death penalty. Distribute to each student a copy of the material "Arguments For and Against Capital Punishment" on p. 165 of this guide for use during preparation. For detailed instructions on conducting a legislative committee hearing, please see p. 14 of this guide.

M. Reading and Discussion

What is the relationship of procedural justice and a republican form of government?

Have the class read "What is the relationship of procedural justice and a republican form of government?" on pp. 186–87 of the text. Ask students to summarize what they consider to be the most important point in the reading.

N. Concluding the Lesson

To conclude the lesson, have students respond to the questions in the "Reviewing and Using the Lesson" section on p. 187 of the text. Finally, have students return to the "Purpose of Lesson" on p. 182. Ask students to describe the extent to which they accomplished the objectives of the lesson.

This lesson concludes the study of Unit Five. If you had students develop personal objectives or a list of questions during the introduction of the unit, students should now review those objectives or questions and determine to what degree they achieved their goals. In addition, you may want to use the questionnaire, "Reflecting on Your Experience," on p. 28 of this guide to engage students in an evaluation of their participation in the lessons.

Optional Activities

Reinforcement, Extended Learning, and Enrichment

1. Have students reenact oral arguments in the case of *Stanford v. Kentucky* 492 U.S. 361 (1989), then have students write one-page opinions justifying how they would have decided the case. Have them address the issue of whether the cruel and unusual punishment clause especially applies to those who were juveniles when they committed these crimes.

2. Have students create posters to publicize the importance of procedural due process to a free society.

3. Have students prepare and conduct a survey of the school community on the constitutionality and desirability of the death penalty. Students should design questions that elicit why those surveyed believe as they do. Students should tabulate and report the results in your school or community newspaper.

4. Have students interview probation officers, public defenders, judges, state legislators, or victim advocates about what reforms of the bail system, if any, they would suggest, as well as their views about the following statement: "The presumption of innocence, secured after centuries of struggle, would lose its meaning [if those accused of committing a crime could not be released on bail prior to trial]." See *Stack v. Boyle*, 342 U.S. 1 (1951).

5. Have students find and present additional information on the landmark Supreme Court case *Gideon v. Wainright*, 372 U.S. 335 (1963).

6. Have students find and present additional information on the case *Furman v. Georgia*, 408 U.S. 238 (1972).

7. During the study of this lesson, have students collect newspaper articles on Sixth and Eighth Amendment issues in your community or state. Have students share these articles with the class.

Arguments For and Against Capital Punishment

Arguments favoring the death penalty:

- **It acts as a deterrent**. The death penalty deters crime no matter what the findings of social science studies appear to reveal. The findings are inconclusive and contradicted by common sense and the observations of many people in the criminal justice system whose daily lives place them close enough to the problem to enable them to observe the effects of the penalty.

- **It is supported by public opinion**. A majority of the American public supports the death penalty. This position is also reflected by a majority in Congress and the state legislatures. Thus, the penalty does not violate contemporary standards of decency, fair play, and respect for human beings.

- **It serves as retribution**. It is not unworthy to exact retribution from persons guilty of horrible crimes.

- **It considers victims' rights and feelings**. The family and friends of murder victims are victims themselves. They often call for and deserve to have the death penalty imposed on those who have wronged them and their loved ones.

- **The cost can be reduced**. It is true that, given the numerous appeals allowed under the right to habeas corpus, the death penalty at present can result in a higher cost to the public than life imprisonment. However, by limiting the number of habeas corpus appeals a prisoner can make, the cost can be significantly reduced. The Supreme Court has already started to reduce the number of habeas corpus appeals.

- **Dangerous criminals are set free**. The system presently operates in such a way that murderers serving long or life sentences can sometimes be paroled if they meet certain standards. This parole system makes mistakes. All too often dangerous persons are set free. Sometimes they seek revenge on those responsible for their conviction. People should not have to live in fear of a murderer's release. Also, the general public usually is endangered by the presence of murderers.

Arguments against the death penalty:

- **It doesn't deter crime**. The main argument for the death penalty is that it deters crime. Neither social science studies nor opinions of the Supreme Court support this claim. Although social science studies may have shortcomings, the evidence they reveal is the only rational basis available for developing an informed position on this issue. All other bases for claiming that evidence supports deterrence are personal and not objective.

- **A reasonable person would be deterred from crime by the threat of imprisonment or loss of life**. However, killing another person is not a reasonable act. Usually, murder is committed in a heightened emotional state when a person's reason is impaired or it is planned logically in a way to escape detection. In the first instance, punishment is not considered by the murderer. In the second instance, the murderer expects to escape punishment. In neither instance would the threat of death act as a deterrent.

- **Statistics show that states with death penalties do not have lower murder rates than states that do**. In a 1986 study by the Federal Bureau of Justice Statistics, it was found that of the ten states with the highest murder rates, eight had the death penalty. In the ten states with the lowest murder rates, seven did not have the death penalty.

- **The death penalty violates equal protection of the laws.** The way the death penalty is applied results in unfair discrimination against black people. It is used far more often when the killer is black and the victim is white. It is applied inconsistently to blacks and whites, and it is used far more often against poor people than rich people.

- **Innocent people have been executed.** Although the numbers are not large, innocent people have been executed. In 1986 a study showed that of 16,505 persons arrested for murder, 139 were sentenced to death and later found innocent. Of this number, 23 were actually executed. A humane society cannot tolerate the execution of innocent people. Such accidents can be avoided by prohibiting the death penalty and providing for life imprisonment.

- **The cost of administering the death penalty is higher than keeping people in prison for life.** A study conducted in Florida revealed that the cost of executing a prisoner, including the cost of trial and appeals, was $3.2 million. The cost of keeping that same prisoner in prison for life would have been $516,000. Obviously, it would cost taxpayers less to prohibit the death penalty.

- **Other civilized nations have abolished the death penalty.** The United States is one of the few industrialized democracies in the world that still retains the death penalty. The fact that other nations have abolished the penalty sets a standard that the United States should follow.

- **Contemporary moral standards should prevent the death penalty.** The United States has advanced to the point where the imposition of the death penalty violates standards of morality and justice that should be upheld. It is a barbarous act more characteristic of less developed and repressive societies and should not be used by a civilized nation.

Evaluating the arguments:

1. What appear to be the strengths and weaknesses of each of the arguments presented by each side?

2. What are the moral positions taken by each side? What values and interests are involved in each position?

3. Should the question of the death penalty be handled by the courts as a constitutional issue or by the state legislatures or Congress? Explain your position.

4. What position would you take on the constitutionality of the death penalty? Explain your position.

5. What position would you take on the desirability of the death penalty, regardless of its constitutionality? Upon what interests and values is your position based?

6. What steps could you take to influence decisions about the death penalty?

Unit Six: What Are the Roles of the Citizen in American Democracy?

UNIT OVERVIEW. Justice Louis Brandeis called citizenship the "most important office" in the land. Ultimately, self-government depends foremost not upon presidents, members of Congress, or justices, but upon each of us as citizens. This unit focuses attention on the meaning of citizenship, the rights and responsibilities of citizens, contemporary developments affecting our citizenship, contemporary constitutional issues, and the influence of the American experience on other nations.

In the first lesson, students learn how one acquires citizenship in the United States and the differences between citizens and resident aliens. Students examine the relationship between contemporary citizenship and the ideals of classical republicanism. They also explore how the American ideal of citizenship has adapted itself to an increasingly diverse society.

In the next lesson students explore the rights and responsibilities of citizenship and the ways in which citizens fulfill their civic responsibilities. Students learn the characteristics of effective citizenship and the importance of citizen participation in a representative democracy.

Next students explore how increasing diversity, technological advancements, and globalization of world economies may influence means of citizen participation as well as the nature of citizenship itself. Students also explore a number of constitutional rights issues being raised by changes in American society.

Students learn how the American experience in constitutional democracy has influenced government and the development of constitutions in other nations. Then students analyze the differences between the Constitution and Bill of Rights and the Universal Declaration of Human Rights.

The final lesson in the unit includes a series of critical thinking exercises that involve students in applying the fundamental principles of natural rights, representative democracy, and constitutional government to a variety of issues involved in balancing the interests of society with the interests of the individual citizen.

UNIT OBJECTIVES. At the conclusion of this unit, students should be able to

1. explain the term "citizenship," explain the differences between citizens and resident aliens, and explain how one acquires citizenship in the United States

2. describe the obligations of citizenship in a constitutional democracy and ways that citizens exercise their rights and fulfill their responsibilities

3. describe contemporary trends and developments and the impact they might have on the nature of citizenship in the third century of government under the Constitution and Bill of Rights

4. explain the complex constitutional rights issues raised by changes in American society

5. describe the influence of the American experience in constitutional democracy on governments and constitutionalism in other countries

6. explain the major differences between the Universal Declaration of Human Rights and the U.S. Constitution and Bill of Rights

7. evaluate, take, and defend positions on issues related to citizenship in contemporary America and on the impact of contemporary developments on citizenship in the next century

INTRODUCING THE UNIT. Have the class read the "Purpose of Unit" on p. 189 of the text. Discuss the basic themes students can expect to learn about during their study of this unit and review the objectives of the unit. Ask students how they think a book about ideas, such as this text, might differ from traditional government texts. Why might they think it important to understand the rights and responsibilities of citizenship? Why is it important to understand contemporary events and developments that may have an impact on the nature of citizenship in the future? Ask students to write four or five personal objectives they would like to accomplish during the study of this unit. You may want to ask them, instead, to write four or five basic questions they would like to explore during their study of these lessons. They should keep their personal objectives or questions in a journal or notebook for review at the conclusion of the unit. They may want to expand upon these personal objectives or questions as their study in the unit progresses.

Review the unit timeline. Encourage students to create a similar timeline in their journals or notebooks to track in more detail important events or developments described in each lesson.

LESSON 35: What Does It Mean to Be a Citizen?

Lesson Overview

In this lesson students examine the legacy of American citizenship and its relationship to the natural rights philosophy, republicanism, and constitutional democracy. Students learn how persons acquire citizenship in the United States and the differences between the rights of citizens and resident aliens. Students learn that one of the great challenges of the American experiment in republican government has been forming a common bond out of the diversity of self-interests in American society. The critical thinking exercise in the lesson engages the class in determining ways to increase citizen participation in the public affairs of the nation.

Lesson Objectives

At the conclusion of this lesson, students should be able to

1. explain the relationship between good citizenship and self-interest in a representative democracy

2. describe the differences between citizens and resident aliens and explain how one acquires citizenship in the United States

3. explain how the ideal of citizenship has adapted itself to an increasingly diverse society

4. evaluate, take, and defend positions on the relationship between citizenship and classical republicanism

Preparation/Teaching Materials

Student text pp. 190–94

Teaching Procedures

A. Introducing the Lesson

To introduce the lesson, discuss the quotation in the unit introduction by Justice Louis Brandeis who characterized citizenship as the "most important office" in the land. What did Justice Brandeis mean? Do students agree or disagree that citizens hold the most important office in the nation?

While students read the "Purpose of Lesson" on p. 190, post the "Terms to Know" on the board. Review with the class what students should be able to do at the completion of the lesson, as explained in the "Purpose of Lesson." Review the vocabulary items listed on the board and remind students to take special note of these terms as they study the material in the lesson.

B. Reading and Discussion

How have Americans thought of citizenship?

Have the class read "How have Americans thought of citizenship?" on p. 190 of the text. Review with the class the fundamental ideas of the natural rights philosophy and classical republicanism. Students should recall that the Founders believed that civic virtue should be promoted by religion and education. The Founders believed that religion promoted virtuous behavior, enabling people to control their passions, and produced upright, responsible citizens. They also recognized that education was essential to good citizenship. Citizens should be schooled in the ideals and principles upon which government is based.

C. Reading and Discussion

How did Tocqueville connect good citizenship with self-interest in the American democracy?

Have the class read "How did Tocqueville connect good citizenship with self-interest in American democracy?" on pp. 190–91 of the text. Students should discuss the importance of the tradition of local self-government as a school where the habits of citizenship are developed. Students should also discuss the importance of voluntary association in promoting the common good. Students should understand the term **enlightened self-interest**.

Direct attention to the illustration on p. 191. Ask students to respond to the question in the caption: How does the tradition of local self-government embody Tocqueville's concept of "spirit of association"?

Direct attention to the "What do *you* think?" section on p. 192. You may want to use these questions to conduct a general class discussion on the relationship between self-interest and the common good.

D. Reading and Discussion

Who is a citizen?

Have the class read "Who is a citizen?" on p. 192 of the text. Students should understand the terms **resident**

alien and **naturalized citizen**. They should understand that aliens living in the United States are guaranteed most of the rights possessed by citizens. Resident aliens, however, may not vote or hold public office. This is the main distinction between citizens and aliens.

E. Critical Thinking Exercise

Evaluating, Taking, and Defending a Position on Extending the Right to Vote for School Board Members to Resident Aliens

Have the class work in small groups of five students to complete the critical thinking exercise, "Evaluating, Taking, and Defending a Position on Extending the Right to Vote for School Board Members to Resident Aliens," on p. 192 of the text. During the exercise students take and defend positions on a proposal that resident aliens be allowed to vote in local school board elections. Review the instructions for completing the exercise and the questions with the class. After students have completed their work, have them share their ideas with the class.

F. Reading and Discussion

How has the American ideal of citizenship adapted itself to an increasingly diverse society?

Have the class read "How has the American ideal of citizenship adapted itself to an increasingly diverse society?" on pp. 192–93 of the text. Students should understand that for the Founders, good citizenship meant responsible conduct and acceptance of the nation's political principles. Throughout much of our history, American citizenship has also meant political freedom and equality of opportunity. The diversity of the American population places a heavy responsibility on these ideals of citizenship. It is largely these ideals that hold us together as a nation. The need to balance unity with diversity remains a challenge.

Direct attention to the illustration on p. 192. Ask students to respond to the question in the caption: How has the diversity of new citizens enriched America?

G. Critical Thinking Exercise

Evaluating the Relationship between the Ideals of Classical Republicanism and Contemporary American Citizenship

Have the class work in small groups to complete the critical thinking exercise, "Evaluating the Relationship between the Ideals of Classical Republicanism and Contemporary American Citizenship," on pp. 193–94 of the text. The exercise involves the class in determining ways to involve more citizens in the public affairs of the nation. Review the instructions for completing the exercise and the questions with the class. After students have completed their work, have them share their ideas with the class.

Conclude the exercise by having students examine the illustration on p. 194. Ask them to respond to the question in the caption: How can America be a "nation of nations" and still have a common civic culture?

H. Concluding the Lesson

To conclude the lesson, have students respond to the questions in the "Reviewing and Using the Lesson" section on p. 194 of the text. Finally, have students return to the "Purpose of Lesson" on p. 190. Ask students to describe the extent to which they accomplished the objectives of the lesson.

Optional Activities

Reinforcement, Extended Learning, and Enrichment

1. Have students create a cartoon illustrating a situation in which citizens ought to practice civic virtue.

2. Have students write letters to the Athenian statesman Pericles, explaining why they agree or disagree with his statement that "We...do not call a man who takes no part in public life quiet or unambitious; we call such a man useless."

LESSON 36: How Do We Use Our Citizenship?

Lesson Overview

In this lesson, students examine the characteristics of effective citizenship in a constitutional democracy. The lesson describes the differences between citizenship in a constitutional democracy and citizenship in a totalitarian state. Students learn that citizens of a constitutional democracy should have a reasoned loyalty and commitment to obeying the law rather than unquestioning deference to authority. Students learn the difference between civil rights and political rights and how each of these rights suggests a corresponding obligation. Finally, the lesson describes the qualities citizens need to develop in order to become effective citizens in a constitutional democracy, such as civic values and principles, civic skills, and civic dispositions. During the critical thinking exercise, the class explores the difficulties in determining the common good in a nation with a large diversity of self-interests.

Lesson Objectives

At the conclusion of this lesson, students should be able to

1. explain how citizenship in a constitutional democracy differs from citizenship in a totalitarian state

2. describe the rights and responsibilities of citizenship in a constitutional democracy

3. describe the importance of effective citizen participation in a constitutional democracy

4. describe the qualities citizens should develop to become effective citizens in a constitutional democracy

5. explain how citizens can exercise their rights and responsibilities in a constitutional democracy

6. evaluate, take, and defend positions on effective ways in which citizens can fulfill their responsibilities

Preparation/Teaching Material

Student text, pp. 195–99

Teaching Procedures

A. Introducing the Lesson

To introduce the lesson, ask students to cite examples of ways in which Americans use their citizenship. While students read the "Purpose of Lesson" on p. 195, post the "Terms to Know" on the board. Review with the class what students should be able to do at the completion of the lesson, as explained in the "Purpose of Lesson." Review the vocabulary items listed on the board and remind students to take special note of these terms as they study the material in the lesson.

B. Reading and Discussion

How do citizens in a constitutional democracy differ from those in a dictatorship or totalitarian state?

Have the class read "How do citizens in a constitutional democracy differ from those in a dictatorship or totalitarian state?" on p. 195 of the text. Students should understand that in a constitutional democracy citizens are expected to be critical and participating members of the community. Students should understand that even in a constitutional democracy there is disagreement about the

rights and responsibilities of citizens. Some emphasize the importance of obedience to the law. Others favor active participation, which might even include a duty to disobey laws believed to be unjust.

Direct attention to the "What do *you* think?" section on p. 196. You may want to use these questions to conduct a general class discussion on the role of civil disobedience in a constitutional democracy.

C. Reading and Discussion

What types of rights and responsibilities do citizens have?

Have the class read "What types of rights and responsibilities do citizens have?" on p. 196 of the text. During the discussion students should be able to describe the difference between **civil rights** and **political rights** and to cite examples of each. Students should understand that every right implies corresponding obligations, such as respecting the rights of other citizens to exercise those same rights, obeying the law, paying taxes, serving on juries, and voting in elections. Some argue that citizens have a moral obligation to defend the nation or to assist in other emergencies.

Direct attention to the illustration on p. 196. Ask students to respond to the question in the caption: Does U.S. citizenship carry with it an obligation to perform national service? Explain.

Direct attention to the "What do *you* think?" section on p. 196. You may want to use these questions to conduct a general class discussion on respecting and defending the rights of other citizens.

D. Reading and Discussion
Why should we try to be effective citizens?

Have the class read "Why should we try to be effective citizens?" on p. 196 of the text. Students should understand that the natural rights philosophy emphasizes the need for citizens to monitor how well the elected government is doing its job and complying with its contractual obligations to its individuals. Classical republicanism emphasizes the obligation of citizens to serve the common good of the community and to place the common good above self-interest. Both of these concepts are part of the American tradition of citizenship.

E. Critical Thinking Exercise
Reconciling the Common Good and Individual Self-Interest

Have the class work in small groups to complete the critical thinking exercise, "Reconciling the Common Good and Individual Self-Interest," on p. 197 of the text. During the exercise the class examines the difficulties in determining the common good in a nation with a large diversity of self-interests. Review the instructions for completing the exercise with the class and review the questions. After students have completed their work, have them share their responses with the class.

F. Reading and Discussion
What do we need to understand to become effective citizens in a constitutional democracy?

Have the class read "What do we need to understand to become effective citizens in a constitutional democracy?" on p. 197 of the text. Students should understand that effective citizenship in a constitutional democracy requires that citizens possess certain beliefs, commitments, and skills. Among these are

■ **civic values**—belief in the ideals expressed or implied in the nation's founding documents, including the Declaration of Independence and the Preamble to the Constitution. Among these values are life, liberty, and the pursuit of happiness; the dignity of the individual; justice; and equality.

■ **civic principles**—belief in those principles of government that enable society to realize its civic values. Among these principles are the rule of law, popular sovereignty, and freedom of expression.

■ **civic skills**—the abilities an individual needs to help realize civic values and make civic principles work. Among these are knowledge of the government's history and how it operates, analytical and problem solving skills, and communication skills.

■ **civic dispositions**—qualities of behavior that sustain civic culture in a free society. Among these are tolerance, fairness, respect for the opinions of others, commitment to the truth, and **civility**.

Direct attention to the "What do *you* think?" section on p. 197. You may want students to work with a study partner or in small groups to develop responses to these questions. After students have completed their work, have them share their responses with the class.

G. Reading and Discussion
What do we mean by empowerment?

Have the class read "What do we mean by empowerment?" on pp. 197–98 of the text. Students should be able to define the term **empowerment**. During the discussion, ask students to describe how possessing civic values, principles, skills, and dispositions contributes to our empowerment as citizens.

Direct attention to the illustration on p. 198. Ask students to respond to the question in the caption: How does participation in public affairs "empower" citizens?

H. Reading and Discussion
How do we learn to become effective citizens?

Have the class read "How do we learn to become effective citizens?" on p. 198 of the text. Students should understand that schooling and experience are the best ways to acquire the knowledge and skills necessary to function as an effective citizen in a constitutional democracy. The process begins in childhood and should be practiced at home, in the classroom and school, and in the community.

I. Reading and discussion
How do we exercise our rights and responsibilities as citizens?

Have the class read "How do we exercise our rights and responsibilities as citizens?" on pp. 198–99 of the text. Students should understand the terms **social action** and **political action** and be able to cite examples of each. Citizens must decide for themselves how a problem might be most effectively solved.

Direct attention to the illustration on p. 199. Ask students to respond to the question in the caption: Does "citizenship" obligate a person to participate in social and political actions? Why?

J. Critical Thinking Exercise

Examining the Responsibilities of Citizenship and Deciding on How They Can Be Fulfilled

Have the class work in small groups to complete the critical thinking exercise, "Examining the Responsibilities of Citizenship and Deciding on How They Can Be Fulfilled," on p. 199 of the text. During the exercise the class determines ways in which citizens can become involved in finding solutions to the problems of youth violence. Review the instructions for completing the exercise and the question with the class. After students have completed their work, have them share their ideas with the class.

K. Concluding the Lesson

To conclude the lesson, have students respond to the questions in the "Reviewing and Using the Lesson" section on p. 199 of the text. Finally, have students return to the "Purpose of Lesson" on p. 195. Ask students to describe the extent to which they accomplished the objectives of the lesson.

Optional Activities

Reinforcement, Extended Learning, and Enrichment

1. Have students select several rights we enjoy as American citizens. For each right have them indicate one or more corresponding responsibilities.

2. Have students write a one or two paragraph essay describing the purpose of political participation.

3. Have the class conduct a survey of your school to gather information on how students participated in the last school election. Did they vote, sign a nominating petition, contribute time to a candidate's campaign, make posters, talk to other students about the candidate they supported, wear a campaign button, or make a speech on behalf of a candidate? Publish the results in your school newspaper.

4. Have students read chapters 1 and 2 of George Orwell's *Animal Farm*. Ask students to identify who attended the meeting and why. What were the goals of the meeting? What were the benefits and costs of participating in the meeting? What other forms of participation did the animals engage in as a result of the meeting? What benefits and costs resulted from their participation? Did anyone behave contrary to the goals of the group? Why?

LESSON 37: How May Citizenship Change in the Nation's Third Century?

Lesson Overview

This lesson turns away from the historical development of citizenship and looks to the future. In the lesson students examine the potential impact upon American citizenship created by increasing diversity in society, modern technology, and growing interdependence with the rest of the world. Students learn that the American ideal of *E Pluribus Unum* has helped to balance the benefits of diversity with the unifying influence of a common civic culture. In a far more diverse and complex society, Americans face the challenge of sustaining that balance. Students learn that technological advancements in telecommunications have expanded the possibilities for participatory citizenship. Increasingly sophisticated computer technologies are forcing Americans to reexamine the most basic principles and institutions of our constitutional democracy. Students learn that one consequence of the communications revolution has been an increased interaction and interdependence with the rest of the world. Economic competition, the environment, and the movement of people around the world require an awareness of political associations larger in scope than the nation-state. During the critical thinking exercise, students assess the consequences of a "teledemocracy," or electronic city-state.

Lesson Objectives

At the conclusion of this lesson, students should be able to

1. describe developments currently taking place in the world that have the potential to have an impact on the future of American citizenship, such as increased diversity, technological progress, and closer international relationships

2. explain some of the advantages and disadvantages of the impact of increased diversity in society on the political system

3. describe the potential impact of increasingly sophisticated technology on representative democracy

4. evaluate, take, and defend positions on whether a "teledemocracy" would be beneficial for the nation

Preparation/Teaching Materials

Student text, pp. 200–203

Teaching Procedures

A. Introducing the Lesson

Ask students to play the role of futurists by imagining the United States thirty or forty years from now. What predictions might they make about American citizenship? What developments might change the way Americans think about natural rights, republican government, and constitutional democracy. What might our institutions of government be like and how might they protect individual rights?

While students read the "Purpose of Lesson" on p. 200, post the "Terms to Know" on the board. Review with the class what students should be able to do at the completion of the lesson, as explained in the "Purpose of Lesson." Review the vocabulary items listed on the board and remind students to take special note of these terms as they study the material in the lesson.

B. Reading and Discussion

What are some developments now taking place in the world that will likely affect the future of American citizenship?

Have the class read "What are some developments now taking place in the world that will likely affect the future of American citizenship?" on p. 200 of the text. Have students identify the three developments likely to have an impact on the future of American citizenship: (1) increasing diversity in American society; (2) modern technology, especially computers and telecommunications; and (3) growing interdependence with the rest of the world. Ask students to predict what impact these developments might have on American citizenship.

C. Reading and Discussion

How is diversity in American society creating new challenges for the ideal of American citizenship?

Have the class read "How is diversity in American society creating new challenges for the ideal of American citizenship?" on pp. 200–201 of the text. Ask students to identify the term *E Pluribus Unum*. How does it characterize the ideals of American society? What examples can they cite to illustrate how Americans have balanced diversity with our common civic culture? How is this related to the concerns of the Founders and Framers who shaped American representative democracy? Ask students to cite examples of how immigration to the United States has changed the faces of "We the People."

Direct attention to the illustration on p. 200. Ask students to respond to the questions in the caption: What strengths can immigrants bring to a society? What problems can arise as a result of large-scale immigration?

D. Reading and Discussion

What consequences will the change toward a more diverse society have for us as citizens?

Have the class read "What consequences will the change toward a more diverse society have for us as citizens?" on p. 201 of the text. Students should understand that there is disagreement about the answer to this question. Some believe that recent immigration is no different from immigration in earlier periods of American history. The mix of people has strengthened the American economy, culture, and institutions, and reaffirmed our commitment to the principles and ideals of our political system. Ask students to cite examples of other periods of increased immigration to the United States. Others worry that there are limits to how much diversity the country can absorb. If we lose the common bonds that unite us, increasingly complex self-interests may prevail over the common good. Ask students what challenges for the future they see in balancing the *Pluribus* with the *Unum* in our society.

Direct attention to the "What do *you* think?" section on p. 201. You may want to use these questions to conduct a general class discussion of the impact of diversity on the political system. Alternatively, you may want to have students work with a study partner or in small groups. If so, have students share their responses with the class.

E. Reading and Discussion

How is citizenship being changed by modern technology?

Have the class read "How is citizenship being changed by modern technology?" on p. 201 of the text. Students should understand that current and future technological advances have created opportunities for ordinary citizens to participate in the affairs of government to a much greater extent. Students should understand the terms **teledemocracy** and **electronic city-state**. Ask students how they think these developments might have an impact on the principles of representative democracy. What potential challenges do they represent for a constitutional democracy?

Direct attention to the illustration on p. 201. Ask students to respond to the question in the caption: Does modern technology help or hinder American citizenship?

F. Critical Thinking Exercise

Role-Playing James Madison In the Third Century of Government under the Constitution

Have the class work in small groups of five students to complete the critical thinking exercise, "Role-Playing James Madison in the Third Century of Government under the Constitution," on p. 202 of the text. During the exercise students take and defend positions on issues raised by creating a teledemocracy and an electronic city-state. Read the instructions for completing the exercise and review the questions with the class. Allow adequate time for students to complete the exercise and then have them share their responses with the class.

Optional instructional activity. Follow-up this exercise by involving the class in a legislative debate on an imaginary bill before Congress. The bill provides funding to subsidize the purchase of personal computers by persons or families wanting electronic access to their elected representatives and to the government's data files. Divide the class into four groups: (1) legislators opposed to the bill, (2) legislators who favor the bill, (3) legislators who favor access to representatives but not to data files, and (4) legislators who might be persuaded to vote either way. For detailed instructions on conducting a legislative debate, please see p. 16 of this guide.

G. Reading and Discussion

How is internationalism affecting American citizenship?

Have the class read "How is internationalism affecting American citizenship?" on p. 202 of the text. Students should understand that one of the consequences of the communications revolution has been increased interaction and interdependence among the nations of the world. Students should understand the term **global village**. The effect of the global village has been to increase the movement of people, goods, and information around the world. The movement of people seeking greater economic opportunities is likely to increase. Such migrations are challenging the traditional concept of the nation-state. Ask students how migration of people among the nations of the world might influence traditional patterns of allegiance and loyalty.

Direct attention to the illustration on p. 202. Ask students to respond to the question in the caption: In what ways does the internationalization of business affect tradition and culture?

Direct attention to the "What do *you* think?" section on p. 203. You may want to use these questions to conduct a general class discussion on the impact of technology and globalization on our traditional notions of citizenship.

H. Concluding the Lesson

To conclude the lesson, have students respond to the questions in the "Reviewing and Using the Lesson" section on p. 203 of the text. Finally, have students return to the "Purpose of Lesson" on p. 200. Ask students to describe the extent to which they accomplished the objectives of the lesson.

Optional Activities

Reinforcement, Extended Learning, and Enrichment

1. Have students find information on the government's increased use of technology to gather and store data related to a variety of activities by citizens.

2. Have students find newspaper and magazine articles about the information superhighway and the issues this technology raises concerning freedom of expression.

3. Have students find information about globalization of the economy and its impact on property rights, especially intellectual property.

LESSON 38: What Can American Citizens Learn about Constitutionalism from Other Countries?

Lesson Overview

This lesson develops an international perspective on the growth of constitutional democracy and the influence of the American experience on other nations of the world. The lesson examines the impact of the Declaration of Independence and the U.S. Constitution and Bill of Rights on other people and their governments. The lesson focuses on emerging democracies and the increasing importance of human rights in international affairs. Students learn that our founding documents influenced the French Revolution of 1789, the Polish Constitution of 1791, and independence movements in Latin America in the early nineteenth century. Since World War II, the American experience has influenced government in Germany, Japan, and the emerging democracies of Eastern Europe. Students learn that in addition to the documents themselves, the most important influences have included constitution-making by convention, popular ratification, *The Federalist*, an independent judiciary, and federalism. Students compare the differences between the U.S. Bill of Rights and other national guarantees of rights. During the critical thinking exercise in the lesson, students examine and evaluate the Universal Declaration of Human Rights.

Lesson Objectives

At the conclusion of this lesson, students should be able to

1. describe the influence American ideas about government and individual rights have had on other nations of the world

2. describe how constitutional democracy in other nations differs from constitutional democracy in the United States

3. describe the differences between the Bill of Rights and the Universal Declaration of Human Rights and between negative and positive rights

4. evaluate, take, and defend positions on what rights, if any, in the Universal Declaration of Human Rights should be established in the United States

Preparation/Teaching Material

Student text, pp. 204–208

Optional. Invite a community resource person such as a foreign consul or a human rights advocate, to participate in the lesson with the class.

Teaching Procedures

A. Introducing the Lesson

To introduce the lesson, direct attention to the illustration on p. 204 of the text. Ask students to respond to the question in the caption: Did the principles and values of American constitutional democracy influence world events in the 1980s and 90s? If so, how?

While students read the "Purpose of Lesson" on p. 204, post the "Terms to Know" on the board. Review with the class what students should be able to do at the completion of the lesson, as explained in the "Purpose of Lesson." Review the vocabulary items listed on the board and remind students to take special note of these terms as they study the material in the lesson.

B. Reading and Discussion

What has been the influence of American ideals about government and human rights on the rest of the world?

Have the class read "What has been the influence of American ideals about government and human rights on

the rest of the world?" on pp. 204–205 of the text. During the discussion, ask students to cite historical and contemporary examples of how the Declaration of Independence and the U.S. Constitution and Bill of Rights have influenced other revolutionary movements and governments around the world.

Direct attention to the illustration on p. 205. Ask students to respond to the question in the caption: How might constitutionalism change in the post Cold War period?

C. Reading and Discussion

What elements of American constitutionalism have been most widely adopted by other countries?

Have the class read "What elements of American constitutionalism have been most widely adopted by other countries?" on p. 205 of the text. Students should understand that the U.S. Constitution established a precedent for written constitutions and that today nearly all countries possess a written constitution. The process for creating the U.S. Constitution also established the precedents of (1) using conventions to draft the document and (2) to submit it to the populace for ratification. The principles elaborated upon in *The Federalist* have been adopted in constitutions around the world. The most admired feature of the American model, next to the Bill of Rights, is the **independent judiciary** which acts as a watchdog of the Constitution. The concept of **federalism** has been influential also, especially in the creation of a European union.

Direct attention to the "What do *you* think?" section on p. 205. You may want to use these questions to conduct a general class discussion about the responsibilities of Americans to promote representative democracy, constitutional government, and human rights in other nations.

D. Reading and Discussion

How have other constitutional democracies differed from the American model?

Have the class read "How have other constitutional democracies differed from the American model?" on pp. 205–206 of the text. Students should understand that other nations have their own political traditions and not all of our ideals can be easily transplanted elsewhere. Ask students to explain why other nations have not readily adopted our models for the presidency and separation of powers.

E. Reading and Discussion

How does parliamentary government differ from a constitutional system based on separation of powers?

Have the class read "How does parliamentary government differ from a constitutional system based on separation of powers?" on p. 206 of the text. Students should understand the terms **parliamentary government** and **prime minister**. During the discussion, ask students to describe the structure of a parliamentary government and to contrast it with a system based on separation of powers.

Direct attention to the illustration on p. 206. Ask students to respond to the question in the caption: What advantages might be enjoyed under the British constitution as compared with the U.S. Constitution?

F. Reading and Discussion

What has been the influence of the U.S. Bill of Rights on constitutional government elsewhere?

Have the class read "What has been the influence of the U.S. Bill of Rights on constitutional government elsewhere?" on pp. 206–207 of the text. Students should understand that before the twentieth century, individual rights in countries around the world were largely viewed as an internal political matter. Following the atrocities committed before and during World War II, the issue of human rights became much more important. Ask students to identify President Roosevelt's **Four Freedoms**: (1) freedom of speech and expression, (2) freedom of worship, (3) freedom from want, and (4) freedom from fear. Ask students how they think freedom from want and freedom from fear differ from the freedoms enumerated in the Constitution and Bill of Rights. In what way do these ideas relate to the debate, which the class studied in an earlier lesson, about equality of opportunity and equality of condition? Ask students to define the term **human rights**. Students also should understand that the **European Convention on Human Rights** established a European court to which the citizens of Western Europe could appeal when they believed their rights had been violated. Students should understand that the protection of rights has become an important diplomatic issue among nations, as in our relations in recent years with the Republic of South Africa. Ask students to cite examples of other nations where human rights have been, or currently are, an international issue. Do they think economic and diplomatic sanctions are an effective means of forcing nations to observe common standards of human rights? Why or why not?

Direct attention to the illustration on p. 207. Ask students to respond to the question in the caption: In what ways are Roosevelt's Four Freedoms essential to maintaining basic human rights for people everywhere?

G. Reading and Discussion

How do other national guarantees of rights differ from the U.S. Bill of Rights?

Have the class read "How do other national guarantees of rights differ from the U.S. Bill of Rights?" on pp. 207–208 of the text. During the discussion students should be able to define the terms **social rights** and **economic rights** and cite examples to explain how these rights differ from civil and political rights. Students should understand that other national guarantees of rights reflect the values and priorities of the cultures that created them. Have students examine the Universal Declaration of Human Rights (see Reference Section in student text) to find examples of civil, political, social, and economic rights.

H. Reading and Discussion

What is the difference between negative and positive rights?

Have the class read "What is the difference between negative and positive rights?" on p. 208 of the text. Students should be able to explain that **negative rights** are restraints on the power of government and prevent a government from taking away rights that citizens already possess. On the other hand, **positive rights** require a government to actively secure benefits for its citizens such as economic security, health care, or a clean environment. Have students cite examples of negative and positive rights from the Universal Declaration of Human Rights.

I. Critical Thinking Exercise
Examining the Universal Declaration of Human Rights

A copy of the Universal Declaration of Human Rights may be found in the Reference Section of the student text. Before beginning this exercise have the class read the Preamble to the Declaration. What are the purposes of the Declaration? What is meant by the Declaration's phrase "a common standard of achievement"? Might compliance with this standard undermine the concepts of national identity and sovereignty? Why or why not? Should countries be bound by some common law? Is there some type of commonality of human experience which justifies the concept of human rights? What moral obligation, if any, do individuals have to promote and protect human rights? What responsibility, if any, do citizens in a free society have to help those living in societies where citizens are not free to achieve their rights? If you think that the Universal Declaration of Human Rights should be enforced, how might that be done?

After the discussion, have the class work in small groups of five students to complete the critical thinking exercise, "Examining the Universal Declaration of Human Rights," on p. 208 of the text. Review the instructions for completing the exercise and the questions with the class. After students have completed their work have them share their responses with the class.

J. Concluding the Lesson

To conclude the lesson, have students respond to the questions in the "Reviewing and Using the Lesson" section on p. 208 of the student text. Finally, have students return to the "Purpose of Lesson" on p. 204. Ask students to describe the extent to which they accomplished the objectives of the lesson.

Optional Activities
Reinforcement, Extended Learning, and Enrichment

1. Students may want to become personally involved in the struggle for worldwide human rights by participating in letter-writing campaigns designed to influence public policy about human rights issues. To do so, they should contact the local office of the nonsectarian, bipartisan organization Amnesty International. A representative will send packets of information and perhaps visit with interested students.

2. Have students conduct telephone or personal interviews with journalists, congressional staffers, international law professors, or a member of Amnesty International about what role America should play in the advancement of human rights issues internationally.

3. Have students create a multimedia report highlighting the role artists have played in advocating and promoting human rights and making others aware of violations of these rights.

4. Have students find information on the history and struggle for human rights in Central and South American nations, in China, and in Eastern Europe.

5. Have students find information on the constitutions of Germany and Japan after World War II.

LESSON 39: What Are Some Constitutional Issues Facing United States Citizens in the Nation's Third Century?

Lesson Overview

In this lesson students consider some constitutional rights issues being raised by changes in American society—group rights and the right to life and death, for example. They also consider those rights which are referred to in the Ninth Amendment as unenumerated rights, including such protections as the right to privacy which is implied by other constitutional provisions but not included in the Constitution or Bill of Rights. Students consider the problem of how to identify unenumerated rights and examine the arguments in favor of and against using the ideas of natural rights to identify unenumerated rights. Students consider the problem of whether to limit the discretionary power of the Supreme Court in favor of the legislative process when determining which rights are to be protected.

Lesson Objectives

At the conclusion of this lesson, students should be able to

1. explain how changes in the complexity of American society create new constitutional issues

2. describe constitutional issues currently being raised in American society

3. describe unenumerated rights and the controversies raised by the Ninth Amendment and explain how conflicts over unenumerated rights might be settled

Preparation/Teaching Material

Student text, pp. 209–212

Optional. Invite a community resource person such as a state or federal judge, to discuss the issue of unenumerated rights with the class.

Teaching Procedures

A. Introducing the Lesson

To introduce the lesson, ask students to cite examples of proposed changes or amendments to the Constitution. What would such amendments accomplish? Why do they think the Constitution has been amended so few times in 200 years?

While students read the "Purpose of Lesson" on p. 209, post the "Terms to Know" on the board. Review with the class what students should be able to do at the completion of the lesson. Review the vocabulary items listed on the board.

B. Reading and Discussion

Why has the Constitution been changed so infrequently?

Have the class read "Why has the Constitution been changed so infrequently?" on p. 209 of the text. Students should understand that numerous constitutional amendments have been proposed, but only 27 have been adopted. The U.S. Constitution remains one of the world's oldest and shortest written constitutions. The oldest written constitution in the world still in effect today is the Massachusetts state constitution which was

adopted in 1780. During the discussion, you may want to have students examine Article V of the Constitution (see Reference Section in student text) to develop their understanding of the process by which amendments become part of the Constitution.

C. Reading and Discussion

What are some constitutional rights issues being raised by changes in American society?

Have the class read "What are some constitutional rights issues being raised by changes in American society?" on pp. 209–210 of the text. Students should understand that these are complex and difficult issues to resolve. Students should be able to explain the questions raised by each of the following issues:

- **Group rights**. How far should constitutional guarantees go in providing favored treatment for **historically excluded groups**? To what extent should government accommodate linguistic minorities?

- **Right to life and death**. What is the legal and ethical meaning of life? Is there a distinction between **life** and **existence**? When does life begin, when does it end? Do individuals have a right to end their own lives or to have someone assist in doing so?

- **Right to privacy**. In a computer age, what is the extent of the Fourth Amendment's protections? Who should have access to government data files and for what purpose? What constitutional limitations should apply to the private sector, for example to corporations?

- **Rights of the individual and providing for the common good**. How will we balance the rights of the individual to property and pursuit of happiness with the responsibility to provide such things as clean air and preservation of natural habitats?

- **Rights of citizens and rights of resident aliens**. If immigration continues, what new issues are likely to arise regarding the rights of citizens and resident aliens?

Direct attention to the illustrations on p. 210. Ask students to respond to the question in the caption: How can government agencies best mediate the conflict between legitimate individual rights and the common good?

D. Reading and Discussion
What are unenumerated rights?

Have the class read "What are unenumerated rights?" on pp. 210–11 of the text. Students should understand the term **unenumerated rights**. They should understand that the objective of the Ninth Amendment was to protect rights that were not enumerated in the Constitution or Bill of Rights. The Ninth Amendment embodies the principle that there are fundamental rights we take for granted, not just those rights that are specified in particular documents. Ask students to cite examples of rights we take for granted, but which are nonetheless protected.

Direct attention to the "What do *you* think?" section on p. 211. You may want to use these questions to conduct a general discussion on protecting unenumerated rights.

E. Reading and Discussion
Who should have the power to identify unenumerated rights?

Have the class read "Who should have the power to identify unenumerated rights?" on pp. 211–12 of the text. Students should understand that there are differences of opinion on how this question should be answered. At issue is the basic principle of constitutional government. Should the Supreme Court use its power of judicial review to determine which unenumerated rights are to be protected? If so, what standards should the justices use? Critics cite the Supreme Court decision in *Griswold v. Connecticut*, 381 U.S. 479 (1965), as an example of giving the Court too much power. Students should understand that the Court used the idea of "penumbras, formed by emanations" from other enumerated rights to justify the protection of a right to marital privacy. There will continue to be disagreement on the role judges should play in a constitutional democracy. Some believe in the philosophy of **judicial restraint**, limiting the discretionary power of judges and emphasizing use of the political process to pass laws that protect rights. Others argue for **judicial activism**, emphasizing that the courts, as watchdogs of the Constitution, have and should play a special role in the definition and protection of individual rights.

F. Concluding the Lesson

To conclude the lesson, have students respond to the questions in the "Reviewing and Using the Lesson" section on p. 212 of the text. Finally, have students return to the "Purpose of the Lesson" on p. 209. Ask students to describe the extent to which they accomplished the objectives of the lesson.

Optional Activities
Reinforcement, Extended Learning, and Enrichment

1. Have students conduct a class debate on the role the Supreme Court should play in expanding rights. You may want to invite a district, state, or federal judge to discuss the issues with your class.

2. Have students write a short position paper stating whether they agree with Justice Black that the way the Court has interpreted claims for unenumerated rights has too often allowed justices to "trespass, all too freely, on the legislative domain of the States as well as the Federal Government."

3. Have students survey the school community asking what unenumerated rights individuals think they have. Have students publish the results in the school newspaper.

LESSON 40: What Is Meant by Returning to Fundamental Principles?

Lesson Overview

This is the concluding lesson in the study of *We the People... The Citizen and the Constitution*. The format of this lesson differs from others in the text. The lesson involves students in a number of critical thinking exercises. Each exercise presents a series of quotations representing many great ideas and principles that have shaped our constitutional heritage, some contradictory but of equal merit to the others. In each exercise, students apply principles and ideas to a contemporary issue and then take a position and defend their judgments.

Lesson Objectives

At the conclusion of this lesson, students should be able to

1. explain in what ways the American experience in self-government can be called an "adventure in ideas"

2. evaluate, take, and defend positions on a number of issues related to the fundamental principles and values of government and individual rights in American society

Preparation/Teaching Materials

Student text, pp. 213–18

Optional. Invite a community resource person such as a political science professor, a judge, or an attorney, to work with the class in completing the critical thinking exercises in the lesson.

Teaching Procedures

A. Introducing the Lesson

To introduce the lesson, direct attention to the illustration on p. 213. Ask students to respond to the question in the caption: Do you have an obligation as a citizen and a human being to exercise your moral authority when injustice occurs?

Have the class read the "Purpose of Lesson" on p. 213 of the text. Discuss with students why they think it might be important in a representative democracy to discuss and debate ideas and issues related to the principles that have shaped our constitutional heritage.

B. Reading and Discussion

Why are fundamental principles important?

Have the class read "Why are fundamental principles important?" on p. 213 of the text. Students should understand that our nation was not created by common culture, geography, or centuries of tradition. Our nation was created by ideas. "In the long run," John Maynard Keynes observed, "it is ideas and not men who rule the world."

C. Reading and Discussion

What did the Founders mean by returning to first principles?

Have the class read "What did the Founders mean by returning to first principles?" on p. 214 of the text.

Discuss with the class the importance in a republican democracy of reminding each new generation of citizens why we have government and the principles upon which that government is based.

D. Critical Thinking Exercises

During each of the six critical thinking exercises in this lesson, students examine a contemporary situation and determine which fundamental principles apply to the issues raised in the exercise. Students then take and defend a position on how to resolve the situation on the basis of the fundamental principles involved. The following briefly describes the situation in each exercise:

- **Liberty v. Order**. This exercise focuses on the issue of crime in our cities and police "sweeps" of apartments to search for illegal weapons. City officials propose a policy requiring tenants in public housing projects to waive their Fourth Amendment rights as a condition of their leases.

- **Rights of the Accused**. This exercise focuses on the problem of illegal drugs in the United States. Congress passed a law authorizing authorities to confiscate the property of individuals suspected of trafficking in drugs. Some claim the law is unconstitutional.

- **Unity v. Diversity**. This exercise focuses on the issue of an official language and the burden of educators in multilingual classrooms. The question raised is whether a common language is essential to the survival of American democracy.

- **Individual Rights v. the Sovereignty of the People**. This exercise raises the question of whether Americans can revise or abolish the Bill of Rights. The situation involves the Supreme Court's decision upholding the burning of an American flag as an act of free speech. The Court's decision prompted demands for a constitutional amendment prohibiting the desecration of "Old Glory."

- **The Dangers and Benefits of Energetic Government**. This exercise focuses on the issue of "energetic" government. The question raised is whether the government should provide a national health care plan which would require a substantial expansion of the federal government's involvement in the private sector.

- **Capital Punishment and the Constitution**. This exercise focuses on the Supreme Court's interpretation of the Eighth Amendment. The issue raised in the exercise is whether the imposition of the death penalty is constitutional.

You may want to have all students work on each of the six exercises. If so, divide the class into small groups. Review the exercises and the questions with the class. At the conclusion have the students share their responses with the class.

You may want to divide the class into six groups and assign one exercise to each group. If so, have each group prepare a presentation for the other students in the class. All students in the group should participate in the presentation and respond to questions from other groups.

E. Concluding the Lesson

To conclude the lesson, have each group of students present and discuss the issues in one of the critical thinking exercises. All students should be encouraged to participate in debating the ideas related to each of the situations described in the exercises.

This lesson concludes the study of Unit Six and *We the People... The Citizen and the Constitution*. If you had students develop personal objectives or a list of questions during the introduction of the unit, students should now review those objectives or questions and determine to what degree they achieved their goals. In addition, you may want to use the questionnaire, "Reflecting on Your Experience," on p. 28 of this guide to engage students in an evaluation of their participation in the lessons. You may also want to conduct a concluding discussion in which students evaluate what they have learned during the study of this text.

Selected Bibliography

The books in this select annotated bibliography pertain to the origins, enactment, and development of the U.S. Constitution and Bill of Rights. Each entry includes ideas and information helpful to teachers in their curriculum planning and classroom instruction. The books and other materials on this list are merely a few of the many outstanding items available on various aspects of the Constitution.

Abraham, Henry J. *Freedom and the Court: Civil Rights and Liberties in the United States*. New York: Oxford University Press, 1988.
This is a penetrating analysis of the role of the federal judiciary in protecting and shaping constitutional rights and liberties. There is an excellent discussion of issues associated with the incorporation of the Bill of Rights through the "due processes" clause of the Fourteenth Amendment to the Constitution.

Alley, Robert S., ed., *James Madison on Religious Liberty*. Buffalo, NY: Prometheus Books, 1985.
Alley and other writers, including A. E. Dick Howard, Ralph Ketchum, and Robert Rutland, examine Madison's contributions to the constitutional right of religious liberty. There is an excellent chapter on the religious freedom debate in Virginia, 1784-1786, which led to the enactment of Jefferson's Statute of Religious Liberty. Madison's role in the passage of Jefferson's statute is discussed in detail in relationship with key primary documents.

American Bar Association *American Bar Association 1991 Law Day U.S.A. Planning Guide and Resource Manual*. Chicago, IL: American Bar Association, 1991.

American Bar Association. 319 Current Videos and Software for K-12 Law-Related Education. American Bar Association, Youth Education for Citizenship, National Law-Related Education Resource Center, 541 North Fairbanks Court, Chicago, IL 60611-3314, 1993.

American Bar Association. *The Bill of Rights Poster Series. A Teacher's Guide*. American Bar Association, Youth Education for Citizenship, National Law-Related Education Resource Center, 541 North Fairbanks Court, Chicago, IL 60611-3314, 1991.

Baer, Judith A. *Equality Under the Constitution: Reclaiming the Fourteenth Amendment*. Ithaca, NY: Cornell University Press, 1983.
This explanation of the roots of equality in America raises issues and alternative viewpoints. Key federal court decisions of the twentieth century are discussed.

Barnett, Randy E., ed. *The Rights Retained by the People: The History and Meaning of the Ninth Amendment*. Fairfax, VA: George Mason University Press, 1989.
This work includes several chapters by experts on the theories and issues associated with the ambiguous Ninth Amendment to the U.S. Constitution.

Barth, Alan. *Prophets with Honor: Great Dissents and Great Dissenters on the Supreme Court*. New York: Alfred A. Knopf, 1974.
There are case studies on six crucial Supreme Court decisions on constitutional rights, in which the dissenting opinions, years later, became the basis for reversals.

Bartlett, Larry, and Lynda Frost. "The Pledge of Allegiance in the Public Schools on the 200th Anniversary of the Bill of Rights." *West's Education Law Reporter*, v.67 n.3 p.867-80 July 19, 1991.

Berman, Daniel M. *It Is So Ordered: The Supreme Court Rules on School Segregation*. New York: W. W. Norton, 1966.
This case study is an excellent treatment of the judicial process in the landmark Supreme Court decision in *Brown v. Board of Education of Topeka*.

Berns, Walter. *The First Amendment and the Future of American Democracy*. New York: Basic Books, 1976.
This eminent scholar examines the origins and development in American history of First Amendment freedoms. He defines and comments on continuing issues about the meaning and application of these constitutional rights, especially the right to religious liberty.

Bonderman, Judith, et al. *Teaching the Bill of Rights: The Case of the Second Amendment. A Critique of Existing Educational Materials and Suggestions for Change*. Washington, DC: Center To Prevent Handgun Violence, 1991.

Brady, Sheila, et al. *It's Yours: The Bill of Rights. Lessons in the Bill of Rights for Students of English as a Second Language.* Constitutional Rights Foundation Chicago, 407 South Dearborn, Suite 1700, Chicago, IL 60605, 1991.

Brady, Shelia, et al. "Working Toward Justice in Diversity." *Update on Law-Related Education*; v.16 n.2 p.24-26 Spring-Summer 1992.

Calpin, Joseph L. "State v. Federal Rights*." Update on Law-Related Education*, v.15 n.1 p.18-91 Win 1991.

Cox, Archibald. *The Court and the Constitution.* Boston: Houghton Mifflin, 1987.
This is an excellent history of the federal Supreme Court and its part in constitutional development, especially the nationalization of the federal Bill of Rights in the twentieth century.

Charters of Freedom: The Bill of Rights. National Archives and Records Administration, Washington, DC: Office of Public Programs, 1993.

Crosby, Mary Neil. *"A Review of Innovative Approaches to LRE." Technical Assistance Bulletin No. 4.* American Bar Association, Special Committee on Youth Education for Citizenship, 750 N. Lake Shore Dr., Chicago, IL 60611, 1991.

Curry, Thomas J. *The First Freedoms: Church and State in America to the Passage of the First Amendment.* New York: Oxford University Press, 1986.
The roots of religious liberty in America are examined. Curry treats the issues and alternative views about religious liberty during the American colonial era and the founding period of the United States.

Farnbach, Beth Earley, ed. *The Bill of Rights—Alive!* Philadelphia, PA: Temple University, School of Law, 1992.

Foundations of Freedom Instructional Media. *Advisory List.* (Annotated-Bibliographies) North Carolina State Dept. of Public Instruction, Raleigh. Media Evaluation Services, 1992.

Friendly, Fred W. *Minnesota Rag: The Dramatic Story of the Landmark Supreme Court Case That Gave New Meaning to Freedom of the Press.* New York: Random House, 1981.
This is a detailed case study of the landmark Supreme Court decision of *Near v. Minnesota,* which expanded the freedom of the press through the "no prior restraint" rule.

Friendly, Fred W., and Martha J. H. Elliot. *The Constitution: That Delicate Balance.* New York: Random House, 1984.
There are 16 chapters about critical constitutional issues and landmark decisions of the Supreme Court about these issues. Bill of Rights cases and issues are highlighted.

Garrity, John A., ed. *Quarrels That Have Shaped the Constitution.* New York: Harper & Row, 1987.
Twenty case studies about landmark Supreme Court decisions are presented as dramatic stories in American constitutional history. Most of these cases are about constitutional rights.

Gottlieb, Stephen S. *A High School Student's Bill of Rights. Teaching Resources in the ERIC Database (TRIED) Series.* 132p.; EDINFO Press, 1991.

Hall, Kermit L., ed. *By and For the People: Constitutional Rights in American History.* Harlan Davidson, Inc., 3110 North Arlington Heights Road, Arlington Heights, IL 60004-1592, 1991.

Hall, Kermit L. *The Magic Mirror: Law in American History.* New York: Oxford University Press, 1989.
This work treats the history of the American legal culture and the law in the lives of citizens. It includes discussions of key constitutional rights cases and issues.

Henderson, Rodger C. "The Middle States and the Adoption of the Bill of Rights: 1787-1791." *Journal of the Middle States Council for the Social Studies*; v.13 p.38-50, 1991-92.

Hoge, John D., and Ann Blum, eds. *Georgia Elementary Law-Related Education Curriculum Supplements: Lessons for Fourth through Seventh Grade.* Athens, GA: Carl Vinson Institute of Government, University of Georgia, 1991.

Howard, A. E. Dick. *The Road from Runnymede: The Magna Carta and Constitutionalism in America.* Charlottesville: University of Virginia Press, 1963.
A distinguished constitutional lawyer and historian traces the development of limited government, the rule of law, and civil liberties from medieval England to the founding period of the United States and shows connections, similarities, and differences in the constitutional traditions of England and America.

Howard, Elizabeth. *Handbook for High School Teachers: Staff Development on the Topic of Constitutional Government*. Arc, 500 E. Border St., Suite 300, Arlington, TX 76010, 1992.

Hyneman, Charles S., and George W. Carey, eds., *A Second Federalist: Congress Creates a Government*. Columbia: University of South Carolina Press, 1967.
This volume includes primary documents on debates in the First Federal Congress, including debates that led to the enactment of the federal Bill of Rights.

Irons, Peter, ed. *Justice at War*. New York: Oxford University Press, 1983.
This is the story of the internment cases of Americans of Japanese descent. It includes interviews with people involved in these cases.

Irons, Peter, ed. *The Courage of Their Convictions: Sixteen Americans Who Fought Their Way to the Supreme Court*. New York: The Free Press, 1988.
There are sixteen case studies about Bill of Rights issues, the people who raised them, and the Supreme Court decisions that resolved them.

Kaltenheuser, Skip. *"The Bill of Rights: Celebrating Two Hundred Years."* *Humanities*, v.12 n.1 p.30-32 Jan-Feb 1991.

Kaminski, John P., and Richard Leffler, eds., *Federalists and Antifederalists: The Debate Over the Ratification of the Constitution*. Madison, WI: Madison House, 1989.
This collection of primary documents illuminates the basic issues and ideas about the nature of a free government, which divided Federalists and Antifederalists during the founding period. There is a section on the debate about a federal Bill of Rights.

Kammen, Michael. *A Machine That Would Go of Itself: The Constitution in American Culture*. New York: Alfred A. Knopf, 1986.
Kammen examines the cultural impact of the Constitution and Bill of Rights on the United States. There is a chapter on public opinion and knowledge about the Bill of Rights.

Kammen, Michael. *The Origins of the American Constitution: A Documentary History*. New York: Viking Penguin Books, 1986.
This collection of primary documents includes information about the origins and enactment of the federal Bill of Rights. Especially useful are reprints of letters exchanged between James Madison and Thomas Jefferson on the subject of constitutional rights.

Kammen, Michael. *Spheres of Liberty: Changing Perceptions of Liberty in American Culture*. Ithaca, NY: Cornell University Press, 1986.
Kammen analyzes the changing idea of liberty in American history, from the colonial period to the mid-twentieth century.

Kane, Peter E. *We Better Not Vote on It: Public Hostility Toward Freedom of Expression*. 18p.; Bill of Rights Bicentennial Lecture, Hochstein School of Music (Rochester, NY, November 19, 1991).

Kluger, Richard. *Simple Justice: The History of Brown v. Board of Education and Black America's Struggle for Equality*. New York: Alfred A. Knopf, 1976.
This book presents the story of the struggle against segregated schools, with emphasis on the landmark Supreme Court decision in the "Brown" case of 1954.

Kukla, Jon, ed. *The Bill of Rights: A Lively Heritage*. Richmond: Virginia State Library and Archives, 1987.
This volume is a collection of essays on the constitutional amendments that constitute the federal Bill of Rights. Issues about the meaning and application of these constitutional rights are highlighted. The essays are written for a general audience in terms that the nonspecialist can readily understand.

Laqueur, Walter, and Barry Rubin, eds, *The Human Rights Reader*. New York: New American Library, 1989.
This collection of primary documents, with commentaries by the editors and other experts, traces the global development of constitutional rights from origins in Western civilization to incorporation into documents of the United Nations.

Leming, Robert S. *Teaching about the Fourth Amendment's Protection against Unreasonable Searches and Seizures.* ERIC Digest. Bloomington, IN: ERIC Clearinghouse for Social Studies/Social Science Education, 1993.

Levy, Leonard W. *Origins of the Fifth Amendment: The Right Against Self-Incrimination.* New York: Macmillan, 1969.
This volume treats the events and issues that led to the constitutional right against self-incrimination.

Levy, Leonard W. *Emergence of a Free Press.* New York: Oxford University Press, 1985.
Levy details the origins of a basic constitutional right, freedom of the press, in political theory and practice. There is an emphasis on antecedents to the freedom of the press in England and during the American colonial experience. There is a chapter on freedom of the press issues associated with the Sedition Act of 1798.

Levy, Leonard W. *The Establishment Clause: Religion and the First Amendment.* New York: Macmillan, 1986.
Levy examines continuing constitutional issues, in historical perspective, having to do with the "Establishment Clause" of the First Amendment right to religious liberty.

Levy, Leonard W., Kenneth L. Karst, and Dennis J. Mahoney, eds. *Encyclopedia of the American Constitution,* 4 volumes. New York: Macmillan Publishing Company, 1986.
This is an excellent comprehensive work on the origins, creation, and development of the Constitution of the United States. Each of the constitutional amendments that constitute the federal Bill of Rights is discussed by a renowned expert. Each article is followed by a brief bibliography.

Levy, Leonard W., and Dennis J. Mahoney, eds. *The Framing and Ratification of the Constitution.* New York: Macmillan, 1987.
This volume includes chapters by different experts on ideas and events associated with the making of the U.S. Constitution. There is a chapter on the Bill of Rights by Robert A. Rutland.

Lewis, Anthony. *Gideon's Trumpet.* New York: Random House, 1964.
This is the story of the landmark Supreme Court decision of *Gideon v. Wainwright,* which expanded the rights of a person accused of a crime.

Lizotte, Leonne. "A Basic Right." *Update on Law-Related Education;* v.15 n.1 p.29-30 Winter 1991.

Lockard, Duane, and Walter E. Murphy. *Basic Cases in Constitutional Law.* Washington, DC: Congressional Quarterly, 1987.
This book includes basic facts, issues, and decisions in 31 landmark cases of the U.S. Supreme Court. Most of these cases pertain to constitutional rights.

Lutz, Donald S. *The Origins of American Constitutionalism.* Baton Rouge: Louisiana State University Press, 1988.
Lutz examines fundamental primary documents in the development of the American concept of constitutionalism, which is a key to understanding the related concept of constitutional rights.

Mann, Sheilah, and Cynthia Harrison, eds. *Bicentennial of the Bill of Rights.* American Political Science Association, 1527 New Hampshire Avenue, NW, Washington, DC 20036, 1991.

McClain, Janet, et al. *Celebrating the Bill of Rights and Constitutional Amendments: An Instructional Unit for Elementary Grades.* Unit III Products, Price Laboratory School, University of Northern Iowa, 19th & Campus Street, Cedar Falls, IA 50613, 1991.

McKee, Saundra J. "In Search of Our Bill of Rights." *Social Studies Journal;* v.20 p.19-21 Spring 1991.

Merrill, John. "Teaching Free Expression in Word and Example (Commentary)." *Journalism-Educator;* v.46 n.2 p.70-73 Summer 1991.

Miller, Barbara, and Lynn Parisi, *Individual Rights in International Perspective: Lessons on Canada, Mexico, Japan, and Nigeria.* Boulder, CO: Social Science Education Consortium, 1992.

Miller, Linda Karen. "Misfiring on the Second Amendment in America's Textbooks." *Journal of the Middle States Council for the Social Studies;* v.13 p.19-29, 1992.

Morgan, Robert J. *James Madison on the Constitution and the Bill of Rights*. New York: Greenwood Press, 1988.
This work examines the political thought of James Madison, which greatly influenced the framing of the Constitution and the federal Bill of Rights.

Murphy, Paul L. *The Constitution in Crises Times, 1918-1969*. New York: Harper & Row, 1972.
This book is a history of constitutional rights during times of social conflict and change during the early and middle parts of the twentieth century.

Patrick, John J., and Robert S. Leming, *How To Teach the Bill of Rights*. B'nai B'rith, New York, N.Y. Anti-Defamation League, Bloomington, IN: ERIC Clearinghouse for Social Studies/Social Science Education, 1991.

Patrick, John J., and Robert S. Leming, eds. *Resources for Teachers on the Bill of Rights*. Bloomington, IN: ERIC Clearinghouse for Social Studies/Social Science Education, 1991.

Pellow, Randall A. "Creating a Bill of Rights Activity Book." *Social Studies Journal*; v.20 p.12-15 Spring 1991.

Petitt, Elizabeth, and Anna S. Ochoa. "The 4th R: The Bill of Rights for Young Children." *Social Studies*, v.82 n.6 p.223-26 Nov-Dec 1991.

Powe, Lucus A., Jr. *American Broadcasting and the First Amendment*. Berkeley: University of California Press, 1987.
Powe discusses how the development of broadcasting in the twentieth century led to new First Amendment freedom of expression issues. The regulations of the Federal Communications Commission are analyzed and appraised.

Project '87 of the American Historical Association and American Political Science Association. *This Constitution: From Ratification to the Bill of Rights*. Washington, DC: Congressional Quarterly, Inc., 1988.
This collection of articles, reprinted from the Project '87 magazine, includes several excellent pieces on the making of the federal Bill of Rights and the nationalization of the federal Bill of Rights.

Rhodehamel, John H., et al. *Foundations of Freedom: A Living History of Our Bill of Rights*. Los Angeles: Constitutional Rights Foundation, 1991.

Rutland, Robert Allen. *The Birth of the Bill of Rights, 1776-1791*. Boston: Northeastern University Press, 1983.
This work is a masterful account of the key events, persons, and ideas in the creation of the federal Bill of Rights.

Rutland, Robert Allen, and Charles F. Hobson, eds. *The Papers of James Madison*, volumes 10, 11, and 12. Charlottesville: University of Virginia Press, 1977.
These three volumes cover the ratification debate, including arguments for and against a federal bill of rights. These documents, annotated by Rutland and Hobson, also cover Madison's successful campaign for a seat in the first U.S. House of Representatives and his role in the enactment of the federal Bill of Rights.

Schechter, Stephen L., and Richard B. Bernstein, eds. *Contexts of the Bill of Rights*. Albany: New York State Commission on the Bicentennial of the United States Constitution, 1990.
This work includes articles by Donald S. Lutz, John P. Kaminski, and Gaspare J. Saladino on the origins, enactment, and development of the federal Bill of Rights.

Schlene, Vickie J. "The Bill of Rights: An ERIC/ChESS Sample." *Social Studies Journal*; v.20 p.22-25 Spring 1991.

Schlene, Vickie J. "Using Teacher-Developed Materials in the Social Studies Classroom: An ERIC/ChESS Sample." *Social Studies and the Young Learner*; v.5 n.1 p.17-18 Sep-Oct 1992.

Schwartz, Bernard. *The Great Rights of Mankind: A History of the American Bill of Rights*. New York: Oxford University Press, 1977.
This work surveys the ideas, issues, and events that led to the American Bill of Rights, and it examines ideas and issues on the development of constitutional rights.

Schwartz, Bernard, ed. *The Roots of the Bill of Rights: An Illustrated Source Book of American Freedom*. New York: Chelsea House Publishers, 1980.
This five-volume set documents the development of the ideas of constitutional rights from the Magna Carta in 1215 to the federal Bill of Rights in 1791. This set includes a rich collection of important primary documents that contributed significantly to the contents and enactment of the federal Bill of Rights.

Sewall, Gilbert T., ed. *Social Studies Review,* Numbers 1-12, 1989-1992.

Sexton, John, and Nat Brandt. *How Free Are We? What the Constitution Says We Can and Cannot Do.* New York: M. Evans and Company, 1986.
This book raises and answers questions about the constitutional rights of citizens.

Starr, Isidore. "The Law in United States History: A Kaleidoscopic View." *Update on Law-Related Education*; v.17 n.2 p3-12 Spring-Summer 1993.

Thomas, Guy. "Freedom, but with Limits." *Update on Law-Related Education*; v.15 n.1 p.31-32 Winter 1991.

To Ourselves and Our Posterity: Recommendations from the Leon Jaworski Symposium on Teaching about the Constitution and Bill of Rights in the 21st Century (Washington, DC, September 11-13, 1991). American Bar Association, Chicago, Ill. Special Committee on Youth Education for Citizenship; Smithsonian Institution, Washington, DC. Office of Elementary and Secondary Education, 1991.

Urofsky, Melvin I. *A March of Liberty: A Constitutional History of the United States.* New York: Alfred A. Knopf, 1988.
This is a solid treatment of U.S. constitutional history. The author includes detailed discussions of important Bill of Rights issues.

West, Jean, and Wynell-Burroughs Schamel. "Rights in Times of Crisis: American Citizens and Internment." *Social Education*; v.55 n.5 p.311-13 Sep 1991.

Witt, Elder. *The Supreme Court and Individual Rights.* Washington, DC: Congressional Quarterly, 1988.
This volume provides a detailed treatment of principles and issues about constitutional rights. There is a discussion and comprehensive listing of Supreme Court cases on civil liberties and rights.

Zullo, Emil. "Back to the Future of the Bill of Rights." *Update on Law-Related Education*; v.17 n.2 p.13-18 Spring-Summer 1993.

Center Programs and Publications

■ *National Standards for Civics and Government*
These standards specify what students should know and be able to do in the field of civics and government. They will serve as a guideline to prepare informed, competent, and responsible citizens committed to the preservation and improvement of American constitutional democracy. Grades K–12.

■ *CIVITAS: A Framework for Civic Education*
An invaluable resource work that outlines the knowledge, skills, dispositions, and commitments necessary for effective citizenship. For curriculum specialists, teachers, librarians, local educational agencies, and writers.

■ **We the People... The Citizen and the Constitution**
A nationally acclaimed program on the Constitution and Bill of Rights. The instructional program uses cooperative learning activities. The culminating activity, a simulated congressional hearing, is an exemplary performance assessment model. High school classes may participate in a national competition. Curricula focus on the principles, values, and history of constitutional democracy. Grades 4–12.

❑ *With Liberty and Justice for All: The Story of the Bill of Rights* emphasizes the ideas and events influential in the development of the Bill of Rights and the importance of the document throughout our nation's history and today. Grades 9–12

■ **Law in a Free Society Series**
Interdisciplinary K–12 curricula based on four concepts fundamental to understanding our constitutional democracy.

❑ *Authority* ❑ *Privacy* ❑ *Responsibility* ❑ *Justice*
Separate texts on each concept for K–5.

❑ *Foundations of Democracy: Authority, Privacy, Responsibility, and Justice* text for middle grades and above.

❑ *Foundations of Democracy: Authority, Privacy, Responsibility, and Justice* senior high school text is forthcoming in 1995.

■ **Exercises in Participation Series**
Students develop plans to combat problems in hypothetical schools as a way of addressing similar problems in their own school. Grades 6–9.

❑ *Violence in the Schools: Developing Prevention Plans* Can be incorporated into a social studies or middle school core curriculum.

❑ *Drugs in the Schools: Preventing Substance Abuse* Fulfills state drug education program requisites and those of the Drug-Free Schools and Communities Act.

■ *The Morality of Democratic Citizenship*
by R. Freeman Butts. Shows teachers how to meet a national curricular commitment to civic education.

■ **Teacher Training/Summer Institutes**

To receive information on publications, programs, or services offered by the Center, fill out this form:

❑ *National Standards for Civics and Government*

❑ *CIVITAS: A Framework for Civic Education*

❑ **We the People... The Citizen and the Constitution**

❑ **Law in a Free Society Series**

❑ **Exercises in Participation Series**

❑ **Teacher Training/Summer Institutes**

❑ **Change of Address**

❑ **Add my name to your mailing list**

Name _____

Position _____

School/Institution _____

Address _____

City/State/Zip+4 _____

Telephone ( )_____ E-mail _____

Return this form to

Center for Civic Education
Dissemination Division
5146 Douglas Fir Road
Calabasas, CA 91302-1467

Toll Free: (800) 350-4223
Fax: (818) 591-9330
E-mail: center4civ@aol.com